A Lamp
in the
Window

A Lamp
in the
Window

LILLIAN M. WHITLOW

ARPress
ILLUMINATING IDEAS,
EMPOWERING VOICES

ARPress LLC
45 Dan Road Suite 5
Canton MA 02021
Hotline: 1(888) 821-0229
Fax: 1(508) 545-7580

Ordering Information:
Quantity sales. Special discounts are available on quantity purchases by corporations, associations, and others. For details, contact the publisher at the address above.

Printed in the United States of America.

ISBN-13:   Softcover   979-8-89356-694-9
            eBook   979-8-89356-695-6

Library of Congress Control Number: 2024904035

ACKNOWLEDGEMENT

PHOTOS: Take from BIBLE READINGS
FROM THE HOME CIRCLE

2nd Edition 1920

By The Review & Herald Publishing Association

Legacy Genealogist

Also

Reference contributed by

WIKIPEDIA FREE ENCYLOPEDIA

FOREWORD

My mama was the best storyteller, ever!

My constant request as a young child was, **"MAMA, TELL ME A STORY."**

She would begin with the fairy tales; such as **"Little Red Riding Hood"**.

As the years passed, she began telling me about her childhood in Minden, Louisiana with her father, Houston, her mother, Ollie and her siblings. Like most families during that era, everyone had gardens and farm animals; such as cows, chickens and goats. Each child would have a pet among the animals. Clemmie, my mother's pet was a young calf, named **Bossy**. Their young brother, Dee's favorite pet was a goat that he called **The Kid**, and Quincy, her younger sister's pet was a rooster, she called **Charlie**. Neither pet liked the other. The neighbors weren't too happy about them, either.

Bossy didn't worry about anything. All she wanted to do was find her mother, Anna, for breakfast, lunch, dinner and all in between meals. **The Kid** liked gnawing all of the tender vegetables from other neighbor's gardens, and **Charlie** always got his time off. Instead of crowing at 6 o'clock in the mornings to get the farmers up, he would crow at five.

Once they realized what Charlie was doing, Mitch, a next-door farmer called Houston one morning to complain about Charlie's timing.

"Houston, when are you going to put Charlie in the pot? He got me up this morning at 5:00 o'clock, and he got me up yesterday morning at the same time. He needs to know how to tell time. He stands at the corner of my house, near the front door and crow every morning, and we farmers hit the floor every time."

"I'll work with him **Charlie**, Mitch. You know, **Charlie** is Quincy's pet, and you know how she loves that rooster." Houston" yelled. "But Mitch, look at it this way. You got an early start. That should mean something."

"Just the same, Houston, teach Charlie how to tell time. I didn't need an early start. He stands at the corner of my house every morning and crows at 5"00 o'clock."

"I'll do what I can but get as much done as you can during that extra hour, Mitch."

"Well, do what you can, Houston, but do it soon, and let me know when you are going to put Charlie in the pot. I want the first bite."

"I'll do that, Mitch. You've got my word on that." He said calmly.

"Sure," Mitch answered in a sarcastic manner.

There were many childhood experiences she shared with me, but as I grew older, and became a mature adult, she wanted me to know about the family's history, so I could pass them on to my children.

In order to pass them on, the stories must be recorded and written down.

My mama lived in Lawton, Oklahoma, a place I called home, because my grade school and high school years were done there. On February 1996, my mother called me to see if I could come home to visit. I was curious. Valentine Day had passed, and President Day was Monday, February 19th. We didn't celebrate these holidays so much, that I needed to come home in the winter. Since I could sense a bit of urgency in her voice, I said I could. At 6:15 PM, I arrived in Lawton, at the Fort Sill Airport. The weather was cold and wet from a week of rain. There was no one there to meet me at the airport, so I took a taxi home, where she greeted me at the door.

"Come on in out of the cold. It's warm inside."

It was warm and toasty from the bitter cold outside. I could smell my favorite dish from the kitchen; beef stew with plenty of onions, celery and garlic. The aroma was all over the house. "I know what you cooked for supper. I can smell it. It's my favorite." I went to the kitchen, and she followed me.

"Yes, it's beef stew. I thought you would like that. I also have a pan of hot water corn bread on the stove. Sit down and rest your feet for a while."

I sat down at the small kitchen table. Hot water corn bread was another one of my favorites. "What's the occasion?"

"Well, I thought I need to tell you all about our family history. I want my grandchildren to know their heritage."

"You have told me enough about it through the years. I can pass it on."

"It needs to be written down where they can read it for themselves." She said.

"Alright. How do we start, and when?" I asked.

"I have a tape recorder. And we can begin tomorrow, Friday 16th."

"Why the 16?'

"No special reason," she said.

"I would like to sample the stew and corn bread, if you don't mind. There will be enough left for tomorrow, I promise."

"Sure, there will be some left for tomorrow, because I will give you a sample." We both laughed while she dished up a small bowl of stew and a small piece of hot water corn bread. After a good night of rest, we had a light breakfast, and listened to the morning news on the black and white television set. I was anxious to get started on the taping. Surely, there must be something else she hadn't told me through all the years of oral history of the family. We sat in the dining room at the table. She inserted a cassette tape in the recorder, and then, turned the volume up and began.

"I'm talking about my great grandfather, my father's father. John Frazier"

"He was a slave boy, and very nice looking, very clean, so they kept him in the house with the Frazier family as a house boy. John was also Master Benjamin Frazier's son. His name was John Frazier. The Fraziers had two daughters. When the Fraziers had to leave at night for some kind of business or entertainment, John was told to stay with the girls, while they read their readers for school. When they finished a book, he did, too, because he read silently along with them. He knew that slaves weren't allowed to learn to read, so he kept it to himself.

John was seven or eight years old at the time. He and other slave children had a favorite place they liked to gather and play in the evenings. John's favorite friend was Benjamin. He and Benjamin liked the same little girl, Charlotte. Charlotte was free, because her mother was an Indian and was free. Children took the same status of their mother. Her father was probably African. Charlotte was pretty, with long braids hanging down her back. Their favorite game was playing "tag". John would chase Charlotte and Benjamin would follow behind him, but Charlotte would only let John catch her. They would laugh and giggle and play tag again. Soon Benjamin gave up and began chasing another little girl. Benjamin was a slave boy and treated as such, but John was also a slave boy, but he wasn't treated as a slave. He could stay and play a little longer.

"Where was this?" I asked.

"Somewhere in Texas, I think. Oh yes, it was Nacogdoches, Texas."

"One evening, while the children were out playing, they saw falling stars. The sky was filled with falling stars. They tried to catch them. Since they couldn't catch them, they went inside to tell their families that something was falling, and they tried to catch them, but they couldn't. When they got inside, it was quiet and the older people were on their knees, praying, so they fell to their knees and began to say their prayers, too."

"What was falling?"

"Go to my bedroom, and get a book off of my trunk," she gestured.

I always regarded my mother's trunk and bed as scared and holy places. No one was allowed to sit on either. If you arched your body toward her trunk or bed, you would hear a loud voice coming from a tiny body, "Don't you sit on my trunk" or "Don't sit on my bed."

Everyone knew that you don't sit on Clemmie's bed and trunk.

I approached the trunk slowly and picked up a book, titled: **BIBLE READINGS for the HOME CIRCLE**. I brought the book to the table and gave it to her. The pages were pale yellow from age, but the book was almost in perfect condition. I gave the book to her, and she held it closely to her chest. "This is the same book that my father read to the family when we were growing up. Some of us were old enough to read it ourselves, and at night while we sat around the wood stove, we read some parts of it to the family." She reached for the book, and I gave it to her.

Mama turned to the pages with the subject: **SIGNS OF THE TIMES**: There was a vivid photo of **Falling Stars at Niagara Falls**. Another photo was a full page of a village filled with falling stars, which happened November 13, 1833, Frederick Douglas wrote something about the falling stars. It's here in this book. She turned to the first photo.

Mama brought the book slowly up to her chest. "This is the book we read together as children."

Bible Readings For The Home Circle 1920

She turned to the page with the subject: **SIGNS OF THE TIMES**: There was a vivid photo of **Falling Stars at Niagara Falls**. Another photo was a full page of a village filled with falling stars which happened November 13, 1833. Frederick Douglas wrote something about the falling stars. It's here in this book. She turned to the first photo.

Falling Stars at Niagara Falls

This picture shows star falling in the village, where the people lived.

Photo of falling stars in the village

"'No one knew what to do, because they said this was a sign sent from God. The adults assured the children, that the stars weren't falling, and they were safe."

"Let me read what **Frederick Douglass** said in his book, **My Bondage and My Freedom**."

Frederick Douglass

She read:

My Bondage and My Freedom

"I witnessed this gorgeous spectacle, and was struck with awe. The air seemed filled with bright descending messengers from the sky. It was about daybreak when I saw this sublime scene. It was not without the suggestion at that moment, that it might be the harbinger of the coming of the "**Son of Man**"; and in my state of mind, I was prepared to hail **Him** as my friend and deliverer.

I had read that the stars shall fall from heaven, and they were now falling."

Frederick Douglas

1

As the years passed, John and Charlotte became teenagers, and courted for a while. They were still in their teens, when Charlotte's mother, Elena, gave John permission to marry Charlotte. Master Frazier gave John permission, also to marry. He could do the chores at the house during the day, but he could stay with his family at night and return in the mornings. Over the years John and Charlotte had five children; two daughters, Mary, and Dorothy, and three sons; John Jr., Paul and the baby, Houston.

Years after the scene of the falling stars, no one knew what to do, because they said this was sent from God. About that time, the slaves knew that it was time for them to be free. It had been whispered around the living quarters. John knew they were free, but he believed the slave masters planned to tell the slaves later, because when they would be told, all the crops would be gathered. John knew the official date would be December 6, 1865. He had read it in the morning paper.

Master Frazier wasn't careful about leaving the papers around in the house. He knew his daughters weren't interested in news. Although John was twenty-four, he couldn't read anyway, because slaves were forbidden to learn to read. Farmers thought if they learned to read, they would, someday. know that they were free, and crops would be left unattended, because the slaves would drop their hoes, rakes, spades and other farm tools, and just walk off. However, the slaves knew that it was time for them to be free. It had been whispered around in the village.

It was believed that the slaves masters planned to tell the slaves on June 19th, but they were free before then. John wanted his friend, Benjamin to know the good news, but he knew that Benjamin had to keep the news a secret. He and Benjamin, both had young families, and the idea of their children being free was more than he could keep to himself.

When John saw Benjamin the next day while they were in the field together, John said to him, "Benjamin I have some really, really good news to tell you, but you got to promise not to tell anybody. This is so good you will want to jump and holler, but you can't do that either. It is so good."

"Alright, John. What is it?" Benjamin said impatiently.

"We're free. Now Benjamin, you can't tell a soul, because they will know that I can read."

"You can't read John." Benjamin said in a jealous rage.

"Yes, I can, Benjamin, but you can't tell a soul."

"Yes, I can. Now, don't tell a soul," John told Benjamin again. Although Benjamin didn't seem to believe John, he nodded his head. Benjamin couldn't believe that freedom was near.

"Benjamin, do you remember when we were little boys, we'd say, "I cross my heart and hope to die?'

"Yeah, I remember, John, but I don't hope to die. I have too much to live for."

"Well, don't tell anyone, because it will get me into big trouble. You know what I mean?"

"Yeah, John, I do."

An hour later, Benjamin's master scolded him for not doing his evening chores; such as cutting wood for the cook stove and airing out the blankets for their beds. "What have you been doing all day, Benjamin? Why haven't you done you jobs?" He scolded.

"I don't have to do any more jobs. Do you think we slaves don't know that we were set free December 6, 1865 this year? We were and still are free. That's why I haven't chopped the wood and aired out blankets."

"What do you mean, you are free?" His master scolded.

"John said that we are free, and he should know, because he can read, and he read it in the newspaper." He replied meekly.

"When?"

"This morning."

The masters would know that they had to do something about that, because slaves wouldn't do anything they were told to do anymore. The news got back to John and his young family. His mother-in-law, Elena had to make plans to get John away from the masters, because they would kill him. She went to the post office and sent a wire to her sister and brother-in-law in Orange County, Texas. She wanted Gloria and Joe to accept John, until everything was cleared.

"Send John on," They replied. "He will be safe here with us. Don't forget to describe our house to him. We will burn a lamp in the window, day and night until he gets here."

Elena talked to Master Frazier, and asked if he would take John as far as he could to the border. John will have to wade in shallow water for a while until he is on safe territory. Charlotte prepared food and water for John to take with him. "Eat sparingly," she said. The food and water were secured on each end of a rope that he could hang around his neck. Master Frazier had already had a talk with John about telling the slaves that they were free. He prepared his wagon with loads of potatoes, to take to the market. John would hide by lying on the floor, covered with the potatoes. Master Frazier would cover John with a large woolen blanket. With the master's wife sitting in the front with him, and his two daughters sitting in the back with John, no one would dare search them. John was to bathe in the lye soap that was freshly made, and put on some pants, long sleeve shirt and a heavy coat that belonged to Master Frazier. If dogs were looking for John, they wouldn't find him.

"The house is white with a white picket fence," Charlotte told John. "It's not a tall fence. It won't come up to your knees, John. There is a small front porch with four or five steps to the porch. You will recognize it because there will be a lamp in the window. It will have a red flame that will burn day and night, until you get there. When you cross the river, you will have a few miles to walk into Orange County, Texas to the house. It is on a narrow street, so walk straight ahead north until you get to the house with a lamp in the window. You will see some pine trees and some birch trees along the way." She hid her tears from the children until she could go inside the house. My aunt's name is Gloria and my uncle's name is Joe. They're your aunt and uncle, too. Aunt Gloria is Mama's sister."

Her baby, Houston, was two years old and unaware of the troubles. He was happy playing on his stick horse. That was his main toy, day or night. The older children: John Jr., Dorothy and Mary knew that their father was going away, and that they may never see him again, but Houston was having a good time with his stick horse.

2

By midnight, Master Frazier, his wife and two daughters came for John. John leaned down, and hugged Charlotte, his children and his mother-in-law, Elena. He called his baby, Houston to come to him. He picked him up and kissed him on the cheek. Charlotte promised John that they will be there soon to see him. When he and Master Frazier walked toward the wagon, he continued to look back at Charlotte and his children, until he was inside and safely hidden in the wagon. Master Frazier had John to lie down deep into the potatoes, and he covered him with an old blanket that he used for covering the produce for the markets. The two girls sat on opposite benches across from John.

"I will get him to the river safely," Master Frazier promised. Master Frazier was kind and soft spoken and was respected by other slave masters.

"Thank you so much," Charlotte said to Master Frazier, as she waved goodbye.

"I know John is going to be just fine. He's smart enough to read and tell the slaves that they are free. He can read and that's something that no one other slave can do. He had the smarts to know how to learn to read."

"I know, Mama, but see what it is doing to him. He has to leave his family and friends in order to live, just because he can read."

"If you are calling Benjamin his friend," Elena said "I don't think he was much of a friend to tell his master that John could read. He knew that John would probably get killed for telling their slaves, that they were free and didn't have to work anymore."

"Well, he will be free soon, Mama. Auntie Gloria and Uncle Joe will take good care of him. We can visit him soon."

When Master Frazier got near the river, he heard a loud galloping of horses behind him. He glanced back and saw five horses in a cloud of dust carrying men with whips. "Haw!" Master Frazier heard galloping hoofs coming toward them. He slowed his wagon to a near stop. He didn't want to give the impression that he was fleeing with John, so he let them catch up with them. The horses slowed down with a yell of 'Whoa.' "Don't say anything," he warned his wife and daughters. "I will do the talking. John, you be very still and quiet." His wife sat in the front seat with him. Her wide skirt nearly filled the seat. The two girls sat in the back across each other. Their wide full skirts covered most of the back of the wagon. John lay on the floor between the girls among one or two bushels of potatoes. He and the potatoes were covered by a brown woolen blanket.

The leader of the group got off of his horse and steered his horse near Master Frazier's wagon. The other four horsemen stayed behind. When he peered inside the wagon and saw Mrs. Frazier and his daughters, he took his hat off. bowed, and moved backward. "I guess you know we are looking for John?" he said.

"Why do you need John?"

"He's your boy, and we thought you would know where he is."

"If he's my boy, why do you need to know where he is? When we leave, he keeps the house. Sometimes he goes to visit his family. You sound like he's in some kind of trouble."

"Your boy can read. Did you know that?" He said sternly, as he starred at Master Frazier.

"What are you talking about?" Master Frazier appeared flustered and surprised. "John can't read. Why do you think he can read?"

"He told one of his friends that he read that the slaves were free, and you know if they know that they are free, they won't do anything we say. We got crops to finish, just like you."

"You all go on back and take care of your land. John can't read. Try to find out why his friend told you that he could."

John's long legs began to cramp, and one foot slipped out from the blanket. Master Frazier and the horseman saw John's foot at the same time. Master Frazier trembled slightly. He was afraid that they were caught, and John would be taken back to be killed by the other masters. The lone horseman and Master Frazier's eyes met. The horseman stared briefly at Master Frazier. No words were spoken. With a blink of an eye, the horseman tapped his horse and rode away to reach the other horsemen.

"We are caught," Master Frazier told his wife. He saw John's foot. He rode away real fast, and he's going to tell the others. I won't try to outrun them. They will know for sure that we're taking John away where he can be safe from them."

"Maybe not." Mrs. Frazier said.

He caught up with the other four men, tapped his horse on the rear, and yelled **HEE HAW**, and they continued toward their village.

"Are they out of sight yet," one of the girls asked. She covered her eyes with her hand. She was too afraid to look.

"They are gone." He breathed loudly. "I'm thankful for that. By the time we get back they will know that John is gone." He turned and looked toward the girls. "How did John learn to read?"

"He learned with us, Papa. He watched us read, and then he would ask questions, and we helped him."

"Papa, what do we do when we get back to the village?" The younger daughter asked.

"I'll figure something out. John, how are you doing back there?"

"I'm doing alright, Master Frazier, but I don't ever want see, nor eat another potato."

"I'm sure you don't, John, but. I will get you as close to your journey as I can. It's a long trip, but we will make it perhaps early tomorrow morning."

"Is that far, Master Frazier?"

"You're almost there. You will have a long walk over into Orange County, Texas. You will have perhaps gotten to the river by mid night,

7

or early in the morning to wade across the river. I have a long rod with a spear at the end to use if you see anything in the water that might harm you. After you cross the river, you just might see someone with a wagon going your way to Orange County, Texas, and if they look friendly, ask for a ride. You can sit at the back with your long legs, dangling." He laughed.

Forty-five minutes later, Master Frazier reached the shallow part of the river. He got out of the wagon, uncovered John and reached his hand to John to help him out of the wagon. John was stiff and sore from the long bumpy ride. He stretched his long legs and raised his arms into the air. The stretching didn't help his stiffness, but he felt safe and that was enough for him.

Master Frazier patted John on a shoulder and gave him a rod, about five feet long. "This rod has a spear at the end. It might be helpful crossing the river. If you see an unfriendly creature coming toward you, you can stab it." He chuckled.

"I hope I don't see anything coming toward me, Master Frazier. That's why we're leaving."

'You're right, John. Lean down."

John bent his six feet and six inches body down to Master Frazier five ten body, so Master Frazier could drape the rope around his neck, with food that Elena had prepared for him for his journey across the river. On one end of the rope was a syrup bucket of food, and on the other end, was a smaller syrup bucket with water. He looked John in the eye, and said slowly, "Let us know as soon as you get there, John. Send a wire to Charlotte, and she will let me know." He patted John on the arm. "Remember," he said. "Let us know as soon as you get there."

"Yes sir." John stepped into the river cautiously. He looked back and saw Master Frazier still standing on the edge of the river. He waved at them and turned around to begin his long journey. This wasn't a pleasant journey for John. He knew he would never see the Frazier family again. Although he, was Master Frazier's son, he was their slave, too, but he was always treated as a member of the family. Leaving was hard on him. He hadn't had any fear of death before, but now he has to run from his loved ones to save his life.

John looked across the river, and as far as he could see, was water. Land wasn't in view. He knew that this was not an easy task, but it was a safe one. Crossing the river wasn't his only concern. There was a possibility of snakes, alligators and unknown bugs that he might encounter along the way, but he must go on, and one day when he is safe, he'll send for his family. He adjusted the food and water containers around his neck, clutched the pole he held in his right hand and began his journey.

Master Frazier didn't move the wagon until John was far into the river. He climbed into the wagon beside his wife, steered his horses to the left toward their village. "He's going to be alright," He promised his family. Master Frazier probably had the same sad feeling that John had. He knew that was the last time that he would see his only son, John. They turned the wagon toward home. The trip home was a long quiet journey.

John proceeded on his journey to the lamp in the window. He took his rod and poked the bottom of the lake to see its depth as he was wading across. He stopped every hour and took a bite of food and a swallow of water from the buckets. Since he was going to an unknown area, he didn't know the exact distance, but he knew the food and water wouldn't last long, so he only took bites and sips of water when he was hungry.

The wind that had blown gently, began to blow aggressively. His steps toward his journey were shortened. Every three steps he took, it seemed that the wind blew him one step back. He used his rod to keep his balance.

John had high hopes. When his journey across the river was over, he might get help along the way to find the lamp in the window. Finding the lamp in the window meant that he was free at last. His biggest fear in the water was snakes and alligators. He didn't see snakes and alligators, but he got several bites from bugs. He saw a small knoll to his right, which was a few feet from the river. At the end of his river journey, he finally put his feet on land, but it wasn't as easy as he had thought. When he reached land, his feet felt heavy, his strength had drained, and he was barely able to make it to the knoll, but he stumbled to the base of the knoll and fell on it. The sun was slowly sinking in the West, and daylight was fading away. The knoll was a good place to rest for a while, he thought.

He didn't remember anything else, until the sun warmed his body. He knew he might have slept there overnight, and it was morning, because the sun was slowly rising over the horizon in the East. He realized that this was an overnight trip. He ate the remaining food in the bucket and drank all the water he had in the other bucket. He took the rope with the buckets at each end from his neck and dropped the rope and buckets on the side of the knoll. He then raked them with his rod into a neat pile. He didn't need the rod anymore, so he placed it across the pile. He must then begin his journey.

John. had an idea to write a note saying, "**John slept here**," and placed it on top of his belongs, but he didn't have paper nor a pencil. Oh well, he must travel on. He was in Orange County, Texas now.

John set his feet on dry land for the first time in two days. His legs were aching from wading through rough areas of the lake. His knees were stiff and sore. His flesh was itching from bug bites, and his eyes were burning from the early sun light, but he had a journey to make, no matter how long it would take.

He was told to find road and go north until he could see a white picket fence in front of a house with a lamp in the window. The lamp would be lit, until he got there. This second trip was going to be another long trip, because he didn't see any houses, so far. About thirty minutes into his journey, he heard a wagon clanking along. When the wagon drew near, he looked around and saw a couple who looked friendly. The man steering the wagon had a red scarf around his neck, and he wore a wide brim black hat. His wife clothing was close around her neck, and she wore a bonnet. He believed the couple were Quakers, and he felt safe.

"Going somewhere?" the male voice called and stopped the wagon.

"Yes sir. I'm looking for a house with a lamp in the window."

"Well, most houses have lamps in their windows. What special about this one?"

"The lamp is lit. It will burn day and night until I get there."

"Well, get in the back of the wagon, you must be very special to them. I think you can jump that high to get in the wagon. I don't know where the house with the burning lamp, but I can take you as far as we're going," the gentleman said.

"Thank you so much, sir. I'll find it." John put both hands on the end of the wagon, and swung his body around to a sitting position, with his legs dangling toward the ground.

"Here you are."

"Are you all right back there?"

"Yes, sir. I'm just fine. Thank you."

"Well, we're on our way to the house with the lamp in the window."

"Yes, sir." John answered.

They rode in silence for more than an hour. "Have you seen the house, yet?"

"No sir."

"We have another five or ten minutes on the road before we turn off, but your trip should be shorter."

"This is a big help, Sir. I can find it. Thank you so much for your help."

"You are so welcome. Be sure you take care of yourself.

"Yes, Sir, I will."

3

"**W**hoa!" The couple stopped their wagon a few minutes later, to let John off. "Be sure you take care of yourself," the man called to John.

"I will do my best, sir," John called back. "Thank you, Sir."

John jumped from the wagon before thinking about his sore legs. "Oh, he cried. He bent down and rubbed his knees. The wagon had made its turn toward their destination, but he had to continue on his journey. He composed himself and began walking toward the lamp in the window. As far as he could see, he only could see unlit houses on both sides of the road. He was willing to enter a white picket fence house, whether it had a lamp or not, but he didn't see one of those either.

He continued his journey until he saw the house with the white picket fence and a lamp glowing brightly. He stopped in disbelief; how could I be so lucky. He hobbled as fast as he could on his sore legs until he got to the gate. He opened the gate and began walking toward the steps. There were only five steps to the porch, but John stumbled and collapsed on the second step. Gloria came to the door and saw John. "Joe, come here. He's here!" She shouted.

"Who's here?"

"John. John Frazier". He stumbled and he fell on the steps."

Joe ran to the door. His neighbor, Jim, who lived across the street ran across to help. "Thank you." He said to Jim. "Let's get John inside. He has had a long walk getting to Orange County, Texas."

Jim locked his arm around one of John's long arms, and Joe had the other arm. John was tall and hadn't lost much weight on the journey. Although he was thin, he wasn't able to give any help on entering the house. The two men had to drag John inside and propped him in a chair. Gloria put a kettle of water on the wood stove and went outside and took the oak tub hanging on a nail on the wall of the house. She took the tub to the kitchen, because that was enough space for Joe to give John a good, hot bath.

In the meantime, Joe got a towel from the kitchen drawer and dipped in in a bucket of cold water. When he went back to the living room where John was seated, he washed John's face to revise him.

"I think he's coming around," Jim said.

"Jim, can you stay awhile longer, and help me bathe John?"

"Sure. That's why I'm here. To help."

"I have some clean trousers and a shirt that he can wear. We're about the same size and height."

"I think you both are," Jim said, but I can't help you there. I'm just about half your size."

Joe laughed. "You are small, but not that small."

"Bring him in the kitchen." Gloria called to the men. "I have his bath water ready." She left the kitchen.

John was alert and could walk alone. "I'll follow you." He said. When he saw the tub, he took his trousers and long sleeve shirt off, and dropped them to the floor. Joe and Jim helped John in the tub. Joe washed John's head and gave the wet rag to him to do the rest.

Let me know when you are through." Gloria called from the living room.

Joe and Jim sat at the table, while John bathed himself.

"Ah, this feels so good." John said. He was thoroughly revived.

When he was done with his bath, he reached for a towel to dry himself.

"Here you are." Joe said as he reached a towel to him.

"Thank you."

"You're much obliged." Joe said.

"I have a little fat back, corn bread and a little stew left from dinner". Gloria said. "Let me fix y'all a plate."

"I will have to pass on that, Gloria." Jim said. "Fat back is salt pork, and I can't eat too much salt, but I will take another offer sometime. I think I'd better get back to the house, before my wife calls me for something."

"All right, Jim. You're welcome at any time." Joe said, and he followed him to the door.

"I can take some of your dinner Aunt Gloria," John said.

"Sure, and you can call me Gloria, John. Everyone calls me Gloria."

"Thank you, Gloria."

John sat at the table and ate and talked. He told about his long journey across the lake and the knoll, which was the end of his journey across the lake.

"What happened to your baggage?" Joe asked.

"I left everything at the knoll. I didn't realize how heavy those things were until I shed them."

Joe peered out the front window and noticed that the sun was sinking slowly toward the West, and John's eyes were blinking to a slow stop. Joe noticed that John was ready for bed, so he got up from the table and got a pair of his pajamas and gave them to John. He tapped John on his arm. "John, you look like you need these. I will help you to bed if you need me."

"Thank you, Uncle Joe, but I can make it." John got up and walked to the front bedroom and dressed for bed. The bed was warm and cozy. It was a treat that John hadn't had in a few days. He fell asleep right away.

"How long did it take you to cross the river?" Gloria asked.

"Oh, about three or four days."

"I guess John was tired. Let's let him sleep for a while."

"I think that's a good idea." Gloria replied.

4

After Gloria and Joe had done their evening chores, such as cleaning the kitchen, gathering eggs from the hen house and milking their one cow, it was time for them to prepare for bed, too.

"I'd better check on John before we go to bed Joe." Gloria said.

"That might be a good idea. I'll go with you."

When they went to John's bedroom, his face was covered with perspiration. Although the evening had been warm, it wasn't warm enough for John to be sweating that much.

"Let me feel his head." Joe said. He touched his forehead and was shocked to know that he had fever. "Gloria, he is burning up with fever. He was happy and well at the dinner table. How could he get sick that soon? I know it wasn't something he ate, or we would be sick too."

Dr. Anthony will be home soon. I will go to his house and get him to come and check on John. He gets off from the hospital soon, and he won't mind coming here to check on John. He's just up the street."

"In the meantime, I will try to keep his fever down with cold water. I'll keep washing his face with this rag until Dr. Anthony gets here."

"John, can you hear me?" Joe asked.

Although John was breathing, he didn't respond. Gloria saw and heard Dr. Anthony steering his wagon in front of his house. His home was three or four block up from their home, but Gloria ran all the way to the doctor and told him about John.

The gray-haired Indian doctor brushed his straight hair from his face and got down from his wagon. "What happened to him?" He asked.

Gloria told Dr. Anthony about John's escape by wading across a lake to get to Texas. "He was jovial and talking until it was time for him to go to bed."

"When did he get sick?'

"I don't know." Gloria said. "When we checked on him before going to bed ourselves, we found him sweating."

"Get in the wagon, Gloria. John might have been bitten by some kind of insect that is giving him fever."

Gloria got in the back of the wagon. "Gloria, you can sit in the front with me. We will check on your friend and see what we can do."

Gloria got out of the back and sat in the front with Dr. Anthony.

When they arrived at their home, Dr. Anthony got down from the wagon with his little black bag and walked toward the house with Gloria behind him. "We'll see what we can do, Gloria."

"Yes, Dr. Anthony. Thank you so much."

Joe met them at the door, and held it open for Dr. Anthony and Gloria to enter. "Hope you can help him, Dr. Anthony.'

Dr. Anthony set his bag in a nearby chair. "We'll see what we can do. Joe." He raised John's pajama top to check his heart, but he noticed several red spots on his abdomen.

What's that," Gloria asked. She lifted his pajama top higher and shook her head slowly in amazement.

"I don't know right now," Dr. Anthony said. "But I will soon find out." He connected his stethoscope to his ears and John's chest. "His heart is racing. Did he eat anything when he got here?"

"Yes, he did, and he ate well," Joe said.

"When did you notice that he wasn't doing well?"

"Dr. Anthony, he was lively and sounded well. He told us about his trip here and encountered 0 several bug bites, but he didn't see alligators, snakes or any such things that would harm him.

"Well, Gloria. It might have been the small things that harmed him. I don't know what kind of bugs that bit him, but they have done a lot of damage. He has red spots all over his back and chest. They were able to bite through his clothing, so they must have been large bugs. I will write a prescription for him. Take it to the nearest drugstore soon and start on the medication as soon as possible." He scribbles out something on a piece of paper and gave it to Joe.

"I'm on my way now, Dr. Anthony. He doesn't look any better." Joe left the house in his wagon, and

Dr. Anthony followed behind him to his wagon. "Call me, Gloria, if you need me again."

"Yes. Sir." Gloria Answered.

She was back from the drug store in thirty minutes. He carried the small bottle of medicine inside and gave it to Gloria.

I hope this works." He said.

Gloria read the instruction on the bottle with green liquid inside. "Ugh," she said. "This looks like it will help anything. Joe raised John's head, while Gloria gave him a teaspoon of the green liquid. John frowned, indicating that the medicine wasn't pleasant.

"It doesn't taste good, John, but it will help you to feel better."

John didn't respond. He closed his eyes. Gloria blew the light out in the window, and she and Joe went to bed. The next morning, Gloria woke up around 6:00 AM and checked on John. He was breathing heavily and gasping for air. She ran to the bedroom and woke Joe. "He's worse. What do we do, now?' "I'll call Dr. Anthony." "I don't think that's necessary, Gloria. Ask him what he wants. He might be able to tell you."

Gloria went to John and knelt to the floor to get closer to him. "John, what do you want us to for you."

"Please reach my wife and tell her to come here, and bring my baby, Houston." He panted. I want to tell her how to take care of the children."

"I will do that as soon as possible. The post office doesn't open until 9:00 o'clock. I'll be there when it opens."

John didn't respond. He seemed to go in and out of consciousness. In the meantime, Gloria dressed for the short trip to the post office. The walk would only take about fifteen minutes.

When she arrived, she was the first customer in the post office. She said a few hellos to familiar clerks and gave a note to the clerk with information to place a wire to Charlotte. It stated:

"Your trip is urgent. John is very ill. Come as soon as you can, and bring your baby, Houston."

After sending the wire, Gloria rushed home, but the trip seemed longer than before. When she got to the gate, she paused, and took a deep breath, opened the gate and rushed in. "It's done," she said.

5

Charlotte arrived the next morning at 9:30, with her two-year-old son, Houston. Gloria met them at the train station as they got off. After a big embrace for Charlotte and Houston, she rushed them to the wagon, and unhitched it from a post. When they were settled inside the wagon, they proceeded home.

"I hope you are in time, Charlotte. John had a rough night, and he's not doing better this morning. We had a doctor to see him yesterday evening."

"What did the doctor say?"

"He noticed a lot of red marks on his body. It looked as if he had been bitten by some dangerous bugs. He didn't know what kind of bug that could have left those marks, but they made him very ill with a very high fever. I hope the medicine that the doctor prescribed will help."

"Did it help?" Charlotte asked.

"Not yet. "Whoa," she said to the two mules pulling the wagon. "This is our home. Do you recognize it?"

"Yes, but it's been a long time."

"Can you get out? I'll help you with Houston." Gloria got down from the wagon, and lifted Houston down. "He's a big boy, now."

"He turned two three weeks ago. Let's hurry. I want to see John."

"Follow me, Charlotte. I'll carry Houston."

Charlotte followed Gloria inside the house. John's bed was in the front room, left side of the front entrance. Charlotte rushed to his side and sat in a chair by the bed. She held him hand and said, "John, I'm here and I brought Houston with me. He wants to see you, too."

Houston rushed to a corner where he saw a broom stick. He straddled it and began to play hobby horse with it. Gloria began to sob audibly. Houston got off his hobby horse and went to Charlotte. He saw that she was crying, and he lay his head on her lap, and began to cry, too. "He's gone, Gloria."

"I know," Gloria said, and began to cry. "We tried to save him."

Joe rushed in from the kitchen. "I checked on him while you were gone, Gloria, and he didn't recognize me. I knew then that he wasn't any better."

"It seems as if I got here just in time to make funeral arrangements." Charlotte sobbed.

"We can help. We have a family plot as you know. John can be buried by Grandma and Grandpa. There's plenty of space out there, and it's not far from here." Gloria hugged Charlotte. "We will get through this."

"When do you think we can bury him, Gloria?"

"Charlotte, how long can you stay?"

"Not long. Mama is looking after the other children. One of my sons is ill, and I need to be with him."

"Which son is he, and how old is he?"

"His name is Paul and he's eleven."

"He is so young" Joe said. They need to get back as soon as possible. How soon can we get ready for John 's burial?" Charlotte added.

"Two days from now." He answered.

"I'll talk to our pastor, and we can take care of everything within two days, and you and Houston can get an early start home. Charlotte, please say hello my sister, Elena. It's been a long time since I saw her. I know you want to get back to Paul. I hope he's better."

"Yes, I feel like I need to be there, now." Charlotte said.

"As soon as you get home, please let us know about Paul."

"I certainly will, Gloria."

Their pastor, Rev. Luke scheduled John's burial for the Friday of the week at 11:00 AM. On that day, Gloria, Joe, Charlotte and the baby,

Houston were at the grave site on time. Rev. Luke said a brief prayer and began the obituary. When the service was over, Joe took Charlotte and Houston to the train station for the trip to their home.

"Let's keep in touch," Gloria called to Charlotte.

"We will," She responded. "I hope we can have pleasant meetings. John's death is more than I can bear."

"We're here to help," Charlotte.

"And I appreciate that." Charlotte responded.

Charlotte and Houston had a quiet trip home on the train. Houston slept all the way there when Charlotte and Houston walked inside the house, Elena met them as they entered. She hugged them both. "I know you are coming from a sad occasion, but Paul is getting worse. His fever is higher than usual, and I can't get him to eat anything."

Charlotte rushed to his room. "Let me see him."

Paul raised his arms from the bed and hugged Charlotte.

"How are you feeling, Baby?"

"I feel better, Mama. I just had a bad cold, and Grand Ma took care of that."

I knew she would take care of things. Do you feel like getting up?"

"Yes, Ma'am. Paul pushed himself forward, and sat on the edge of the bed, and then he slowly put his feet on the floor and stood up. "See, Mama, I'm better." Paul is more like himself. He just was sad to know that his father, John Sr. had died. He'll get over his mood. He was his father's little buddy." Elena said.

"I know." Charlotte said. "But we've got to make plans on leaving this place. I don't want to stay here any longer without John."

"When do you want to leave, Charlotte?"

"I don't know Mama, but soon as we can."

"It's easy talking about it, but we have to give ourselves some time. We're looking forward to some cold weather. After all, it's approaching winter." Elena said.

"What about in the spring?"

"That will be a good time, Mama."

"That's fine with me, but with all this stuff we have; children and all, we will have to take our wagon. "Mac said that he and Anna will go with us and bring their wagon." Elena said.

"Mama, how did they know that we wanted to leave?"

"I told them that I thought it would be a good idea. That is what I did when your father died. I just couldn't stay in the same place any longer."

"I like that idea, because you have a smoke house filled with more food than some of the corner markets. If they can take everything in the smoke house, we won't have to worry about food along the way."

"That's true." Elena said. "But how are we going to take all of our clothing and beddings?"

"We'll find a way, Mama."

"Charlotte, we can't wait until the time to leave, to find a way."

"I know, but I believe that Mac is going to see if Deacon Thomas will help us. He has a large, covered wagon, too. It's larger than our wagon." Charlotte said.

"Well, who is going to steer his wagon, if he lets us use it, and who is going to bring it back to him?"

"Mac will have that all mapped out, Mama. He's going with us."

"What about Anna? Is she going too? I've never seen them that far apart."

"Mama, they'll figure that out."

6

Mac knew that he couldn't let Elena and her family take this trip alone. It was too much for him to do alone, too. After a few days of pondering, and worrying about the spring trip, Mac decided to ask for help.

"Anna, do you think Deacon Thomas will go with us? His big wagon will take all of the food and stuff that Elena got in her smoke house."

"That's a good idea, but what about his wife?"

"I think she will like it. She will get to go on a trip. She hasn't been on one in a long time, I bet."

"When are you going to ask him, Mac?"

"Today."

"Well, hurry and let me know."

"I'm on my way out the door. I don't know what I'm going to say to him, but I will have it in my mouth when I get there." Mac walked and ran the block and a half to Deacon Thomas' house. He was nearly out of breath when he got there.

Deacon Thomas was in the back yard when he saw Mac rushing toward his house. He rushed to the front to meet Mac. "What's wrong Mac?"

"I need help, Deacon Thomas." Mac was panting, and almost out of breath.

"Why don't you sit down, and take your breath?" Deacon Thomas, balding, slight of built and dark complexion, pulled up a seat and sat down. "What kind of help do you need, Mac. You know I hurt my back, and I can't do much, such as lifting heavy things."

Mac sat down in a straight back chair by the door and crossed his legs. "There's no lifting to this, Deacon Thomas. Well just a little, but you do it all the time. I need help in getting Elena and her family to Orange County and to her final destination. You have a large wagon. You know that Elena got a shack in the back of their house, that we call her grocery." He laughed.

"Yes, I know about her grocery store, because my wife, bought stuff from her."

"That is why we need you. Your wagon is big enough to carry her entire store. My wagon and their wagon will carry household things, such as clothing and bedding. We will have plenty to eat along the way, cause we will have Elena's grocery store with us."

"I like the idea. Agnes wants to go somewhere anyway."

"Where did she want to go? When we leave Nacogdoches tomorrow, we will have less than one hundred miles to Marion County.

"Mac, she just wants to get away for a bit. Let me talk to her about this trip, and I will let you know later today."

"When do you want me to come back?"

"You don't need to come back. I will come to you later today."

"Thank you, Deacon Thomas," and he started toward the door.

"Mac?" Deacon Thomas called to Mac. "You don't need to call me Deacon Thomas. Just call me Joe."

"I'll see you then, Joe." Mac rushed home. When he reached the porch, the door open. Anna ran to him and grabbed him by the arm. "What did he say? What did he say?" She repeated.

"Give me a little time to catch my breath, Anna."

"Is he going with us? Tell me" She shouted jumping up and down.

"Be still, and be calm, Anna. He will ask his wife, Agnes, and get back to us this evening."

"What time this evening, Mac?"

24

"I didn't ask Anna, but he'll keep his promise." He said calmly. I believe his wife will agree, because she wants to get away to any place."

"Should we tell, Elena the good news?"

Mac sat down on their sofa. "Let's wait until he comes over and tells us the good news. I believe it will be good news, but to be sure let's wait, Anna."

"I'll do my best," she teased. She walked back to the kitchen.

"What are you cooking for supper?" Mac called to Anna.

"You will have to wait until supper time." She called.

"So you're trying to pay me back about the times?" He laughed.

"No, but it will be good and worth your waiting."

"I hear someone on the porch." Mac said.

Anna ran to the door, opened it and looked at Deacon Thomas. "He's here, Mac."

"Who's here, Anna?"

She opened the door. "Deacon Thomas, come on in. We were just talking about you."

He laughed. "I hope it was something good."

"It is," Mac said as he approached the door. "I thought you were coming later. I haven't told Elena yet, but we can go over there together and tell her. She can have a good night sleep."

"I want to go over there, too," Anna said.

"I would never leave you behind, Anna." Mac said tenderly. "How is your wife, Deacon?"

"She's packing a few things for the trip."

"I see. She's just like my wife, Anna. She is already packing things. She's already ready to go." Mac said.

"Does she know where we're going?" Elena asked.

"No. She's not worried about where we're going. She just wants to go anywhere."

Charlotte came out of her bedroom. "She is welcome to go, Deacon Thomas."

I'll tell her, but you and Mac can call me Joe. I am Joe to everyone else, except the children. Let's go to your smokehouse and see how much you've got in there, Elena."

"Charlotte can take you and Mac out there. I'm baking tea cakes for the children. That's something I do just about every week."

Charlotte was standing near Paul's bed. "Sure, I can take ya'll out there. Be prepared because it's nearly full."

"We're okay with that, Charlotte." Mac said.

"Let's go." She reached behind the stove, and got a braided colorful, ribbon necklace with a key dangling from the end. She coiled it around her wrist. "Follow me."

"I'm behind you Charlotte," Mac said.

"And I'm behind you," Deacon Thomas said. He noticed several keys on a braided cloth- like rope. "Elena, what else is in that smokehouse?" He laughed. You don't mean for anyone to get inside without noise, do you?" The keys jangled while Charlotte walked toward the smokehouse.

"Y'all come on," she said.

Deacon Thomas looked at the wooden smokehouse before entering. This smokehouse hasn't ever seen any paint. It's so dry, it would drink several gallons of paint."

"It's not what's on the outside, Deacon Thomas. Charlotte said. "It's what's on the inside. Come on in." She beckoned to them.

"You betcha!" Deacon Thomas said. "Elena got everything, but what about meat hanging from the ceiling, like ham?"

"Elena, doesn't hang anything in the smokehouse that she can put in a can or jar." Mac said. "If she can't put it in a jar, she will leave it alone."

"Why is it called a smokehouse, if she won't smoke anything?"

"It's just an old-fashioned name, Deacon."

"Well I like the way she's got it arranged in here. The shelves are filled with pint and quart jars. All pints on one side, and the quarts on the other side. That makes it easier to pack. I have enough boxes and crates to take it all."

"Do you think so, Deacon?"

"Yes, and if you don't want to call me Joe, just call me Deacon. That's fine with me. When do we leave for Marion County, Texas?"

"May 15." Charlotte said. "We have two more weeks to get ready. You have two sons, don't you, Deacon?"

"Yes. Joe, Jr. and Ken. Joe Jr. is seventeen and Ken is fifteen."

"Are they going with us?'

"No, Charlotte. They're going to help us pack our wagon with Elena's smoke house goods but they're going to stay and keep our home safe."

"Will they be safe alone, Deacon?" Mac asked.

"My mother, their Grandma, lives next door. She lives there with my sister and brother-in-law. She will probably move in with the boys until we get back. They're her only grandchildren, and she'll do anything for them. We won't worry. Furthermore, our house is small, and there's not much to clean.

7

On May 13, late in the evening, Mac heard loud noises coming from Elena's smokehouse. "Hon, do you hear that noise?'

"Yes, and I see where it's coming from, too."

"Where?"

"Elena's smokehouse. I see Deacon Thomas's boys getting out of their wagon."

"Wow!" Elena said. "The last time I saw those boys, they were little boys, and Now, they're handsome young men." She stood by the door, looking out at her smokehouse.

"They must have the dates wrong. We have two more days before we leave. I'll go out and talk to them." Mac rushed out to the smokehouse.

"Good evening," he said. "You're a bit early. We leave Friday."

"We know that, but we thought it would be easy to bring the wagon today and leave it. We will take the mules home and bring them back when everything is loaded. That will be easy on them and us, too." Joe Jr. said.

"That makes a whole lot of sense." Mac said.

"Uncle Mac, do you know their names?' One of the boys asked.

"Whose names?

"Our mules."

"No. I didn't know they had names."

"Yes, sir. One on your left is Coco, and the one on your right is Dapper."

"Why did you name a mule Dapper?" Mac asked.

"Dapper is particular where he eats, and Coco, doesn't care, just as long as he eats."

"Since I know that, we don't have to worry." Mac said.

"No, Sir." Joe, Jr. replied. "We will take Coco and Dapper home and come back later today and begin packing. Dad said it was easy, because she has pint jars on one side and quart jars on the other side. We can put all the pints in boxes and the quarts in crates."

"Why separates the jars?' Mac asked.

"It's easy that way. Also, as long as 'y'all know where the sizes are, you'll know how much you'll need for your meals." Joe. Jr. said.

"That makes a lot of sense." Mac said.

"Yes, Sir. Thank you."

Ken unhitched the mules against their protest. There was a lot of – "HEE HAWS" from the mules., and soon they settled down. Joe Jr. took Dapper, and Ken took Coco, and they led them home".

Elena heard the confusion and went to the back door. "What's going on out there?"

Mac walked towards Elena. "Deacon Thomas and his boys brought the wagon over, so we can begin packing it soon. We have two more days before we leave, but we don't want to wait for the last minute."

"Are their mules friendly, Mac?"

"They appear to be Elena, but the Deacon will be able to handle anything that might go wrong with them. Their names are Coco and Dapper."

"I've never heard of such name for mules." Elena said.

"I think you will find out why they got such names, when we begin to travel." Mac said.

"How did they get their names?" Charlotte asked.

"Coco is a dark brown, with a white belly, legs and a white band across his nose.

Dapper is gray, with a white belly, white legs and has a white band across his nose, too. But Dapper is careful where he walks. He will avoid mud puddles and anything that will disfigure him in any way." Deacon said.

"Now, Deacon" Mac said. "That's going to be impossible."

"What do you mean?" Deacon Thomas asked.

"We are leaving in the rainy season, so Dapper will see a lot of mud puddles."

"Just give a yank, and yell, **HEE HAW**"

"Will that work?' Elena asked.

"It has never failed." Deacon Thomas said.

"It has always worked for us." Agnes said.

"I have baked six dozen of cookies. "Elena said. I will give Coco and Dapper's wagons one and a half dozen each. If that won't last the entire trip. Our wagon will have more, but we will have plenty of food to eat, too."

"I think the food from the jars will be plenty for me," Deacon said. "I'm not much of a cookie eater. Now, if you have some cake, such as a lemon cake, I'm all for that."

"They all laughed and agreed with Deacon Thomas. "I would like to have some lemon cake, too, Elena said.

"I was just thinking about that, Elena." Deacon Thomas's wife, Agnes said. "I have time tonight to bake a lemon cake and bring it with us in the morning. What time are we leaving anyway?"

"Now, that we're fully packed, we will leave 7:30 sharp in the morning. This is our line-up" Mac said. Elena and Paul will ride in my wagon. We will lead. I will make a soft and thick bedding on the floor for Paul. Elena will sit on one of the benches on the side, where she can help Paul with medicine when needed. My wife, Anna will sit in the front with me.

Charlotte and John Jr. will follow me, with her girls, and some bedding and clothing.

John will steer the mules."

"How old is John," Deacon asked.

"He's fifteen," Mac said. "And he's good with the wagons."

John looks just like his Pa, Deacon said. He is going to be as tall as his papa. I think his papa was six feet and 6 inches. He will get there in a few more years. He looks able to steer these mules, too."

8

On Friday morning at 7:15, everyone stood by their wagons and waited for Mac's instructions. "Good morning," he said. "This is a wonderful morning to leave." Mac noticed that no one responded to his greetings. "Well, how is everyone?"

One of Charlotte's girls Mary yawned and said, "We're okay, Uncle Mac. When do we get started?"

"As soon as we are in line and the mules are happy," Mac replied. "I see that the wagons are loaded with food and goods, so please get your wagons behind me, in the order that's planned." Mac got inside his wagon, and pulled his wagon ahead so that the other two wagons would have enough space to enter and follow, then he got out..

"I believe I would like for everyone to gather in a circle and be quiet for a few minutes. We have had this family with us at church every Sunday for many years, and in the community for so many years, we just can't get loaded and go. So let's gather and bow in silence."

Without saying a word, everyone gathered as ordered. John lifted Paul from the wagon and brought him to the circle. Charlotte held Houston's right hand and joined his left hand with one of Paul's hand. They all held each other's hands, while they bowed their heads in a few moments of silence.

When the silent moment was over, Deacon reached inside of his pocket on the right, and pulled out a small black pouch. "Wednesday night at prayer service, our pastor asked the members to give a donation for y'all. I didn't count it, but every cent of it is in this pouch. It is a gift from hearts." He reached it to Elena, and she accepted with tears flowing down her face.

"It is so hard to leave y'all. It's like leaving my family behind. Charlotte cried and held Elena. "This is one of the hardest things I have ever done, Deacon. Please let them know how much we appreciate this offering."

"Now, I think it's time to get in our wagons and head south. We will follow you, Mac."

"I need to go back for something," Elena said.

"What for?" Mac asked.

"You'll see."

He followed her to their house. She pulled a string from her neck. Mac noticed that a key was dangling from the end. "What is that?"

She locked the pad lock on the door. "It's a key. I forgot to lock the door." She put the key around her neck and drop it inside her bosom. "Now, let's go." She said.

When they reached the group, Mac continued with his instructions.

"One or two or three things I want you to remember," Mac said. When you hear me yell **HEE HAW**, we're going straight ahead. When I yell **HEE**, we're turning right, and when I yell **HAW**, we're turning left."

"Did everyone get that?" If so, get inside the wagons in the order that I have already quoted, and we will steer the mules South."

"Do you think Dapper is ready?' Elena teased.

"I believe so. We'll soon know, though." Deacon said.

"I still think horses would have been a little faster,' Elena said.

"Of course, they would be faster in a way, but much slower, because they need more care than mules. They need to eat often, where mules can go without food for a while. So, instead of eating, they are traveling and getting us to our destination sooner than horses."

"I guess you're right, Deacon."

"I know I am, Elena. I've tried them both on traveling, and I will use the mules every time."

"Grandma?"

"Yes, Paul?" She knelt and touched his brow. "You're not as hot as you were. Are you feeling better?"

"Some better, Grandma, but I want to pee."

"I have a little bucket here near me, just so you can pee, Paul. Here it is." She gave it to him. Paul turned his back from Elena and began to pee in the bucket. When he was through, he gave the bucket to Elena.

"I will take care of this on our next stop. I don't think we have many more stops before we reach Orange County. "These mules have really brought us along the way. I will always trust them from now on."

"I told you, Elena, that mules are the best transportation we have. I like horses for riding when I'm in a hurry. Now, if I want to get some place safely, I will use the mules every time."

After two or three hours along the way, Elena asked, "Do you think we should pull over and give the mules some rest? I know I can take some rest. My rear is tired of riding on these bumpy roads, and it isn't doing Paul any good either."

"I see a good spot over there by the lake, we'll pull in there and give the mules a break. The girls and boys might like to rest their legs, too. How is Paul?"

"Mac, I think he is better. I keep checking on him, and his fever seems to be gone. I don't have a way of measuring it, but it feels like he's getting better." Elena said.

Mac signaled to the other wagons to follow him to the lake. There was plenty of water for the mules, and a playground for the children. When the wagon stopped at the lake, everyone got out, except Paul.

"I'll stay in," Grandma.

"Don't you want to get out and stretch your legs, Paul for a little while?"

"Not now, Grandma. I'll sit on the edge of the wagon and look out. If I think I want to get out, I'll call John.

"Alright, Paul, but I will be near you when you call."

Yes, Ma'ma, Grandma.

John jumped down from the wagon, holding a red, round ball in both hands. "I got it," he called to the other children.

"What kind of ball is that?" Charlotte asked.

"That's a dodge ball," Deacon said.

"How do you know?" Elena asked.

"My boys and some of their friends play it on our vacant lot a lot of times. When they don't have enough for a team, they will drag me off the porch to fill in. It's a lot of fun."

The girls jumped down from the wagon and ran into the open field. John followed with a large red ball.

"What are they going to do with that ball?" Elena asked.

"I think they are going to play a game, called dodge ball. Charlotte said.

"I believe I will play with them, since they don't have an even team." Deacon said.

"Well, help yourself," Elena said. "I don't want to dodge anything." She watched them throw the ball at one another. As they threw the ball at one on the other team, that person batted the ball away with both hands.

"How did they learn this game?" Charlotte asked Mac.

"They heard their grandfather on their dad's side tell them about dodge ball. It started in Africa more than two hundred years ago, but it didn't seem like fun to me. The tribes threw stones and petrified matters at each other with the intention to harm the other side. When they were hurt, both teams would help each other, immediately.

One day as the tribes were pelting each other with rocks and small pellets, a missionary saw the activity. He saw how they showed pity toward one another. With the attitudes of the tribes, he thought something good could come from this sport without hurting one another. He was able to get the teams to change the rock and petrified matter for a leather ball. The leather ball was hard but wouldn't hurt anyone. Soon, this ball game became a harmless sport."

"Deacon, you can have that sport. I don't want to dodge anything." Elena repeated.

"I will see to it, Elena,"

"Thank you, Deacon."

"We have made several stops along the way," Deacon said "I think we're getting close to Orange County. I will ask when we get to a train station. There, we can freshen up before we pull into Orange County."

"That's a good idea," Charlotte said. "Why don't we get back into the wagons and pull out."

"I was just about to say that, too," Mac said. "How's Paul?" "I believe he's better, Mac." Elena said.

9

"Let's go. **HEE HAW**," Mac yelled, and they followed straight ahead.

"Whoa," Mac yelled.

Elena jumped. "What's wrong, Mac?"

"Nothing, Elena. You were asleep. We're here. You should know Orange County, because you were here just a few months ago."

"You're right Mac, I was nodding, but how do you know this is the right way?"

"We have been traveling long enough to be here, and I see the train station over there." He pointed to the right. "We can go there and freshen up a bit. What do you think?"

"Let's go." Elena nodded.

"I'll let the others know that we're going to turn."

"Okay, but will they know where we're going?"

"Do you see those large red letters that say, **UNION PACIFIC TRAIN STATION**?"

"Yes, I do. It's the same station that I came here on, but I was riding inside the train, and not mules."

"**Haw**," Mac called out to the mules, and he steered his mules to the left toward the train station, and the others followed. "We won't be in there long, but just enough to freshen up a bit and used the toilets." He said. "Oh, I see plenty of grassland in the back of the station. Let's go there and the mules can eat, while we're inside cleaning up."

"That's okay with me," Charlotte said.

Mac steered his team of mules toward the rear of the station, and the other teams followed. "They will be fine here until we get back."

"Mack, are you sure?"

"Yes, Elena. They will be okay."

I'm ready," Elena said. "Let me see if Paul is ready, too." She knelt down and touched Paul's face. He was cooler than before. "Paul, how do you feel?"

"I'm okay, Grandma."

"Do you feel like getting up and walking a bit?"

"Not now, Grandma."

"We're here and we want to look our best, when we see your Aunt Gloria and Uncle Joe.'

"You go ahead, Grandma. I'll see them later."

"Okay, Paul, but if you don't feel well, let me know. I have some more medicine in those bottles down there with you."

"No, thanks, Grandma. I don't need them. Y'all go on in the station. I'll be just fine."

Elena got out of the wagon and stood to the right side. She wanted to talk quietly to Charlotte.

Charlotte got out of her wagon, holding Houston by the hand, and rushed to Elena. "You can steer the mules near Mac. I will stay with Paul. John you can go in."

"No, Mama, I'll stay with him until you get back, and then I'll go in." John said.

"No," Charlotte demanded. "I want to stay behind with Mama. We'll be on later. Now, you run on with Mary and Dorothy and the others, and we'll be on later."

"Yes, 'am, but I won't be gone long. You and Grandma can go to the station when I get back."

"That's fine, John" Elena said.

When Mac jumped out of the wagon, he began to bend his legs backward and forward and flexing his arms.

"What are you doing?" Elena called to him.

"Just limbering up," he said.

Deacon and John began stretching and flexing their arms and legs, too. "Ah, that feels great," John said.

"We need this," Mac said. "We have less than a hundred mile left on this journey, and we will be at Joe and Gloria's house. We are not stopping again until we see that lamp glowing in the window, and I hope that is going to be very soon. I hope that lamp is still burning."

"It will," Elena said.

"Elena, do you think they're up this time of morning?" He pulled his watch change and turned the watch face over. It's about 9:30. "We might be a bit early."

"Of course, they're up, and have done a half day's work. I know Gloria," Elena said. She's my sister, and we were raised to be early risers.

"Then, we'll get there just in time," Mac said. "Let's go to the station. Standing here and just looking at the rear of it won't help us at all."

"How is Paul resting at night, Mama?"

"Charlotte, he just sleeps until I wake him for some more medicine. He will open his mouth for the medicine, but not so much for the water."

Charlotte looked toward the train station, when she saw John running with a cup in his hand. What is that he's holding, Mama? When did he leave the wagon? I didn't see him go."

"He's holding something," Charlotte said "I believe it's for Paul. He probably saw something that he thought Paul would like."

John stopped when he reached the wagon. "I bought Paul a little Nehi soda pop. It's sweet, and he might like it."

Paul was sitting on the edge of the wagon, with his legs hanging down. John held the cup to Paul's mouth and Paul took a sip of the Nehi soda pop. "I like this, John. What kind is it?"

"Orange. Do you like it?"

"Yeah."

"I thought you would, but I want to see you drink some water, too. Can you do that?"

"Later, John. I will."

"I will give you some water when we get back on our trip. Will that be alright with you?"

"Yeah." Paul said and he pulled himself up further in the wagon and lay down on his pallet.

Charlotte walked a distance from the wagon where Paul was resting. Elena followed her, because she felt something in Charlotte's voice that concerned her. "What is it, Charlotte?"

"Mama," she rubbed her hands. "I am really worried about Paul. I don't think he is doing as well as he pretends."

"I am worried too, Charlotte, and I think we need to prepare ourselves for the worse. He doesn't appear to have any fever, but something else is going on, because he doesn't want to sit up."

"We'd better get back in the wagon, Mama."

"Sure. It's just a short distance. "Let's walk over there and wait around in the front, until they are all out of the wagon. That's not too far for Houston to walk. If he gets tired, I will pick him up."

"Sounds good to me," Charlotte said. "So let's go'

Charlotte and Elena met the other as they pulled up in the rear.

Mac and the other teams followed their plans, while Mac steered Coco and Dapper to the rear of the station. John and the Deacon followed. There was plenty of apace for the three wagons. Also, the field behind the station had tender limbs from the trees and tender growths from the ground. The mules were well fed while everyone was inside the train station.

The freshen-up period was brief. Elena and Charlotte wanted to get back to the wagon to check on Paul, and to let John go in the station to freshen up, too.

After a while, Mac clapped his hands. "Let's get going," He helped Anna inside the wagon, and walked to the other side to get in. "Is everybody in and ready to go?"

"Yeah," they shouted.

"Hee Haw," He shouted.

10

Thirty minutes after leaving the train station, Mac yelled, "**HEE**", and made a right turn.

"Why are you turning, Mac?"

"I got a hunch, Elena."

"What kind of Hunch?"

"I see something burning brighter than a flame. I believe it's the lamp in the window. That street crosses this one, so you can see it clearly."

"Mac, you're right." Elena said. "You're right." She repeated.

"We'll be there in five or ten minus. Our mules are tired and need the rest that they'll get when we get settled. I hope Joe can help us with settling the mules."

"Don't worry, Mac. He can take care of everything."

Just as Mac had said, they were at the lamp in the window in five minutes. Gloria was standing in the door, with the screen ajar. She shaded her eyes and began jumping up and down. "They're here." She called to Joe.

Joe ran to the door and saw three wagons pulling up near their road. He ran out to meet and greet them. "Follow me around the corner." He beckoned. He ran around the corner to the back of their home, and the three wagons followed him. Mac and Deacon got out of the wagons and went to meet Joe.

There was a barn, a small creek and plenty grass for the mules to eat from the land, drink water from the creek and rest comfortably in the barn.

Mac viewed everything carefully. "Joe, I believe everything was designed for our arrival years ago. This is perfect."

"Who are all of those folks still in the wagons? Get them out so we can meet them." Joe said.

Mac went to the wagons and helped Anna out, and motioned for the others to get out, too. He tapped on the other two wagons. "Joe wants to meet everyone, so y'all get out."

John got out first from his wagon and lifted the back flap up and pulled Paul to him, so he could lift him out."

Joe looked at John and Paul. "Who is the little one?" Joe asked.

"That's Paul. He is sick and needs help to walk." Mac said. "He won't be any trouble. We'll take care of him."

When everyone was on the ground, Deacon Thomas led them to Joe and Mac. "This looks like the garden of Eden," he said. These mules will enjoy this land."

"Are the mules friendly?" Joe asked.

"My two mules are Coco and Dapper" He pointed toward them. "Now Coco is quiet and carefree, but Dapper is particular. He's careful about where he sleeps, eats, and walks."

"Well, how did y'all get here with Dapper?" Joe asked.

"With lots of care, but we made it." Elena added.

"Introduce me to the others here," Joe said.

"Joe, when we get inside the house, we will introduce everybody. Gloria is at the back door waving her hands for us to come in. When we settle inside, then we can meet everybody. You have already met Coco and Dapper, so everybody follows me to the house, and let Joe and Mac take care of everything out here." Elena said softly.

"I can take care of Paul, Mama. Y'all go on to the house, and we'll follow." John said.

Everyone went inside, and left Joe and Mac to take care of things outside. "We will be in a little later", Joe assured them.

41

Gloria met them at the door. "Come on in and have a seat in the kitchen. I'll bring up a few chairs from the living room so everyone can sit at this table. How was your long trip in this hot June weather?"

"We don't have any complaints," Elena said. "The mules did a good job getting us here."

"We're a little sore back here," Mary motioned to her rear end.

"And mine, too," Dorothy added.

"You will get over it in a little while." Gloria assured them.

"Aunt Gloria, what did you cook?" Charlotte asked. "It smells so good."

"It's a surprise. You'll like it. What are the men doing outside?"

"Aunt Gloria, they're putting the mules away somewhere in the barns, and putting the wagons in safe places. I think."

"Charlotte, every place around here is safe. We neighbors tend to each other. If they can't find enough space out there, they can go next door to the missionaries' yard and find plenty of space."

"I'm not worried a bit," Elena said. "I know they will take care of everything."

Gloria noticed that John was holding Paul. "What's wrong with him?" She asked.

"He's been ailing for days," Elena said.

"Come with me, John, and we'll put him in the same bed where John, his father, was. He'll get more rest there, and so will you."

"Yes, Ma'am." John followed Gloria to the front bedroom and gently lay Paul on the clean, white sheets. "How do you feel now, Paul?" He asked.

"I'm better." He answered.

"Okay, I will check on you later. Hear?"

"Alright." Paul answered weakly.

Gloria set the kitchen table with ten plates. "I don't know if we have ten of you, but just in case, we'll have enough space. This old round table has served many people and can serve more, so y'all can wash up in this sink."

"When did you get water in the house?" Elena asked. The missionaries helped us dig our well so water could reach the house just like the water reaches them. It's also cool enough to drink."

"Let's get washed up and call the men in. I know the men are tired and can use a little rest. I'll call them in, too."

Charlotte went to Paul to check on him. She felt his forehead. It was warmer than before. "How do you feel, Paul?"

He didn't answer. She went back to the kitchen. "Mama, I just checked on Paul, and he is a little warmer than before. He's asleep and didn't answer me when I asked how he felt."

"Let me see him." Elena went to Paul and felt his forehead and noticed that he was warmer than earlier during the day. "Paul? Paul?" she called.

When he didn't answer, she said, "I guess he's getting the sleep that he needs, Elena said.

Gloria called the men in to wash up and they all sat at the table and ate pot roast with all its trimmings and side dishes. Charlotte held Houston in her lap.

"You can give him a seat all by himself. I'll put a cushion in the chair by you, and he can eat all by himself. I understand that he had a birthday along the way."

"Yes. Houston is three years old, now. Elena said.

"Y'all help yourselves, and when y'all are through, I will go over next door with you and help y'all settle in. They have a bathroom to take care of your needs, so enjoy the food, and then go next door to rest. I'll take care of everything here. I am used to doing that, but Joe helps a lot. You will be well rested tomorrow, and we can sit and visit."

"I'll stay and sleep in the bed with Paul." Elena said. "I won't get much sleep, because I'll be checking on him every so often."

"I'll take Houston on over with me, but I'll be back early in the morning. I know I won't get much sleep, though."

Houston tugged at Charlotte's arm. "Let's go Mama."

"Alright, Houston." They were the last out of the door.

"Elena, go and rest some. We'll have time tomorrow to visit."

"Alright, Gloria. I'm on my way."

43

After Charlotte and her family and others had gone next door, Joe followed Gloria to the kitchen. "I'm worried about Charlotte's little boy, so I'm going to get Dr. Anthony to come and look him over. He's home now."

"I think that's a good idea." She said.

"He rushed out the front door near Paul's bed. Elena rushed to the kitchen. "Where is Joe going, Gloria? He left here in such a hurry."

"He's going to get our doctor to look at Paul. He wants y'all to rest without any worries."

"I hope he can help us, Gloria. I don't know what we'd do if we lost him too." Elena said.

Dr. Anthony will take care of Paul. Don't worry. Ten minutes later, Joe and Dr. Anthony were on the porch. Before Joe could open the door, Charlotte rushed over.

"I noticed the black bag that's in his hand." She pointed to Dr. Anthony. She rushed in and Joe and Dr. Anthony followed her. She patted his face. "Baby, are you feeling better?" Paul didn't answer. "Let me see him. He turned Paul over and checked his skin for rashes or unusual markings. "I see a few spots on John's back. They might have contacted the same ailment. This is what I want to do, and that is give all of you shots for smallpox. So get your family together. It won't take long. Gloria, I need some boiling water for the needles."

"I have boiling water on the stove for the dishes. You can use what's on the stove, Dr. Anthony."

Dr. Anthony walked to the kitchen, while everyone stood around Paul's bed. When he returned, he had twelve prepared needles on a basket. "Who's going to be the first brave one?"

"Me." John said. "After I get my shot, Houston can get his, and we'll go back to the house."

After the parade of shots were over. They went next door for bed. There was only one protester, and that was three-year-old Houston. He cried all the way to the other house.

"Now, I think it's time for everyone to get some rest. It's after nine o'clock. If you need me tomorrow, don't hesitate to come and get me."

"Thank you, Dr. Anthony," Joe said. Others agreed and expressed their appreciations.

Joe sat up until 11:30. He wanted to make sure that all were in bed and resting comfortably. He went to the front door and opened it quietly. All lights in the houses on his street were out. The neighbors' dogs ceased to bark. Everything and everyone seemed to be at peace, so he went to the lamp in the window and cupped the globe with both hands and blew the flame out. The flame in the lamp had burned for twelve days, and now it is silent, too. After a few seconds he went to the back bedroom and retired beside Gloria.

11

The next morning, about 7:30, piercing screams came from Gloria and Joe's house. The screams were heard throughout the neighborhood. Neighbors stood on their porches and looked toward Gloria and Joe's house. Charlotte heard the scream. She recognized that it was Elena. She had heard it before when her father died. She ran to the house and saw Joe and Gloria consoling Elena, while she held Paul's frail body in her arms.

"Oh, it's my baby." Charlotte cried and ran out the door, with her two daughters following her. John picked up Houston and followed them to Gloria and Joe's house. Mac, Anna; Deacon Thomas and Anna followed behind them.

"He's gone, Charlotte," Elena said. "We tried so hard to save him, but we just couldn't." Charlotte took Paul from Elena, and held him tightly in her arms, as she wept over him. She couldn't stop screaming. He's not gone", she cried.

Dr. Anthony heard the screams, too, and he knew where they were. He rushed to the house and walked in and saw everyone in a huddle. "Let me see Paul, Gloria."

Gloria lay Paul on the bed. Dr. Anthony felt Paul's forehead, his arms and legs. They were cold. His body had cooled below normal temperature. "He went away peacefully," Dr. Anthony said. "I am so sorry for your loss. I know it's not the right time to talk about funeral plans, but if you need help in burial arrangements, please let me know."

He looked back at Charlotte. "Charlotte, let me help you with some medication."

"Nothing can help me. I just want to die, too."

"Charlotte, you have other children who need you. Dying now isn't a good idea. Let me help you." He noticed that Charlotte was sinking to the floor. Joe caught her and lifted her in a chair that was near the door. "You have to hold on, Charlotte. You gotta to hold on."

"I don't know how to do that, Joe."

"The same way you held on when John died."

"I am still reeling over John death, but the loss of a child is more than I can bear. How do I do that?"

Elena went to Charlotte and pulled Charlotte's head to her side. "I will help you get through this, Charlotte. We just got to make it. We can't give up. I believe Paul wouldn't want us to mourn over him. He put up a good fight, and he pretended to be doing well, when he wasn't feeling well at all. He tried, Charlotte. Let's try to. I know it's hard. I know we can pull through."

Gloria and Joe were comfortable with Dr. Anthony's decisions about burial arrangements. Dr. Anthony and his wife were middle aged, without children, so she and Joe had always filled in as family. "Thank you so much, Dr. Anthony."

"I will contact the same funeral home, and ya'll can contact your pastor. We can have the same arrangement that we had for John. We can have grave side services for Paul."

"I will talk to Charlotte and Elena and see what they say," Gloria said.

They agreed and the ceremony was planned and carried out within three days. Paul was buried beside his father, John Frazier. After two or three days of mourning with Joe and Gloria, Elena had Mac and John. prepare the wagons for leaving.

Elena gathered everyone together in Gloria and Joe's front room. "Let's gathered everything together and pack the wagons tonight. In the meantime, we will clean the home we were able to use and leave it neat and clean as we found it."

"What time of morning do you want to leave?" Mac asked.

"We will leave in the morning at sunrise. Gloria and Joe, we'll see each other again soon, when there is no sadness or sorrow. We are so grateful that y'all helped us during these sad times."

"We're family, Elena. You would have done the same thing for me and Joe. When you get to your destination, please let us know. I will pray for y'all's safety."

"It's about time for bed. It's after 5 o'clock, so we can get up and leave early."

"Alright, Elena. Let me know if I can help. Gloria looked up towards the sky. It looks like it's going to rain. If it rains, are y'all going to leave?"

"We traveled through some rain to get here, Gloria, so we can travel through some to leave. This is the rainy season, so if we wait until it stops, we'll be here several more months. Y'all have been kind enough. We don't want to wear out welcome. After all, this is our second visit in a few months. I'll talk to Mac and see what he thinks about the rain. I know he will still want to leave."

"Whatever you say, Elena. Joe and I have enjoyed everyone, although the occasion was a sad one."

"When we get to Marion County, Texas, we'll be closer, and we can visit each other often. We can travel by train and get from one place to the other in three or four hours. The train is faster than the mules."

Gloria laughed, "I hope that's a promise, Elena. Joe and I will get up early to see y'all off."

"No, please don't. I don't like good-byes, so, "Until we meet again.""

"Well, "Until we meet again," Gloria said.

"We will leave the house clean, and please let the missionaries know that we appreciated their home."

"They will be happy, Elena, that they were of some service."

Elena left Gloria and went next door to her family. They were getting ready for bed, because Mac had told them about the early departure. "I notice that ya'll have cleaned up."

"Yes, we did, Mama," Charlotte said. "So let's get to bed early, so we can get up early for the long journey. Did you thank Joe and Gloria for us, Mama?"

"Absolutely."

Charlotte heard a soft knock at the door. "Who's that?" She went to the door and saw Gloria standing there.

"As soon as y'all get to Marion County, send us a telegram and let us know that you made it there safely."

"Now, Gloria, go back home, and don't worry. When we reach Marion County and get settled in somewhere, y'all will hear from us."

"Joe and I will be waiting," Gloria said, and she went home.

Elena walked over the rooms and noticed that the children were asleep, so all she had to do was prepare for bed herself. Charlotte sat up in the bed, when she noticed Elena was in the room with her. "We went in early," she said. "But I can't sleep."

"I know, Charlotte, but try to get some sleep. You need it. Where is Houston?"

"He went to sleep early. He had a busy day," she said and laughed.

"I know. He plays so hard, and his day is busy every day. I must get some sleep myself."

"Good night," Charlotte said. "I just wanted to make sure that you were alright."

"I'm alright. Good night everybody."

Although the house was quiet, no one slept that night. John and his sisters, cried softly during the night. They didn't want Charlotte and Elena to hear them. It might cause them to break down, again, so they cried softly, while Houston slept.

12

Early, the next morning, Mac ran next door, and panted as if he was out of breath. "Get up. Rise and shine, Elena."

Elena sat up in bed on her elbows, looked at the clock straight ahead on the dresser, rubbed her eyes, and yelled. "Mac, are you crazy? It's only 5:30."

"Just joking, Elena. Joe and I prepared the mules and wagons for the trip this morning. After we got everything settled, we sat down and had our coffee for the morning, so I'm wide awake. I just wanted to see you smile again."

"Mac, I haven't had a cup of coffee, and I won't have a cup until we're on our way. How long will it take us to get to Marion County?"

"Elena, we're about two hundred miles away. If the mules travel without any problems as they did come here, we should get there in seven or eight days; ten at the most. I think the weather is going to be good for traveling. It did look like rain for a spell, but the sun is just peeping through, and I think it's going to be a great day for traveling."

"Mac, you need to get some rest before we leave. You haven't been still, since you've been here." Elena said.

The children were still asleep. Charlotte was awake all during the night, but Elena couldn't sleep, either. She was also in mourning and worried about getting to Marion County and finding a place to stay. Getting there was easy. Mac would see to that, but there were more important things than getting to a location.

Mac had noticed Elena's sad expression and knew that she was worried about something. "What are you worried about, Elena?"

"Mac, getting to Marion County is easy, but what do we do when we get there?"

"What do you mean?"

"Mac, we need a place to stay, and when we get a place to stay, we need food, daily. These jars of food that we brought are almost gone, and I am so tired of canned food. I want something fresh sometimes."

"I know what you mean Elena, but let's take one thing at a time. When we get there, we'll find all the things that we need. It might take a little time, but I believe it will happen."

"I hope so, Mac."

"Just trust me, Elena."

"Where will we stay, and how do we make a living. We prepared for this trip without thinking about what to do when we get there."

"We will work that out soon after we get there, Elena. Don't worry. Anna and I will stay with ya'll as long as it takes. If things don't work out alright, you can go back with us. Everything there is just as we left it. Let's try to work thing out, before we make any decisions."

"You're right, Mac. That makes sense."

Mac saw John standing out by the wagons. He thought something was wrong, so he rushed to him. "Are you okay, John?"

John jumped in surprise. "Yes sir. I had to pee, and I didn't want to wake anybody."

"You won't wake anybody up, John. This is a good time for us to have a little talk. You're the man of the house, now. Your Grandma is worried about where y'all will they stay when y'all get to Marion County. You can't live in the wagons forever."

"I know, Uncle Mac. I will take care of the family." He adjusted his pants.

"I believe you will, John. When we get there, I will find the train station, like I always do. I can get information about where to go for the mules to graze. If I can get information about the mules, I might be able to get information about the best place to go with them."

"I like that idea, Uncle Mac."

"Well, John, we'll do that, and with your help, we'll find something descent for everybody."

"We can do that, Uncle Mac."

"I am glad that they're sleeping. I know they didn't sleep very much last night. I will let them sleep as long as they want to."

"What about the deacon and his wife? Are they still sleeping?"

"I believe so, otherwise, he'd be outside with us trying to get some fresh air, too".

"I like them, Uncle Mac. They didn't have to help us, but they did, and I don't know how to thank them."

"Just tell them just what you told me. They'll understand. Deacon wouldn't have it any other way. He'd want to help."

"When we find a place to finally settle in for our home, will you and Aunt Anna come and live beside us?"

"John, I don't know how that can happen. However, we have lived beside each other for years there in Nacogdoches, Texas. We witnessed all the birth of y'all, and it's has been like family. When people ask about us, they turn and ask about y'all, too. It's been like that all along. The separation is going to take time to get used to. We're comfortable with being Aunt and Uncle. We will do our best, but I don't know if we can do it or not, but we might have to."

John looked at Mac with tears in his eyes, he said, "Uncle Mac, I don't want y'all to get used to being away from us, because we will never get used to being away from y'all."

"The best thing to do, John, is to let things work themselves out. We might move, too. I have given that some thought, but I didn't want to say anything. I believe you need to dry your face, and let's get back and see what they're doing. We need to eat breakfast and get on our way."

13

The next morning, Mac rushed next door to Elena. "It's for real now, Elena. Rise and shine."

"I'm already up and waiting." She said. "It's 7:30 and still early, but I'm ready."

"What are you waiting on, Elena?"

"No particular thing. I was just sitting here by the window, thinking."

"I told you, Elena, not to worry. Anna and I will stay as long as it takes to make sure that y'all are safe."

"That is such a burden on y'all, Mac, but we sure appreciate it. How are we going to get everybody up and ready to leave?"

"It will take a little time, Elena, because they have to have something for breakfast, and then, they'll be ready to leave."

"How many more days do we have to travel, Mac?"

"Not many, Elena, but just as I told John. When we get to Marion County, I will go to the train station, and get information about locating a desirable place for our mules and a proper place for us to stay at the same time. If we can do that, we can find a place to stay until y'all get settled in."

"That's going to take a long time. You and Anna have already been away from your home for days."

"Elena, we don't have anyone there waiting for us. Our two responsibilities are our mules, and they're here with us. They helped to bring us here and they'll take us back. I told you, we will be with y'all as long as it takes so quit worrying. I will find a little job while we're waiting for something."

"What is the something?" Elena asked and laughed.

"Whatever it takes, Elena. You might need to check on Charlotte and the others. I had a little talk with John. I believe he's going to be a big help to y'all.

"I know that. He's just like his dad. That's why we can't stay there in Nacogdoches any longer; too many memories."

"His dad, John Sr. was one of my best friends, Elena, and I know how hard it's going to be for me to make it without him, but that's something I will figure out. Do you think everybody is ready to go, now?"

"I'll check with Charlotte and see. You know, she's got to get Houston ready, and he's not easy to wake up."

"We have a little time, but I would like to get on the way before it gets too hot. It's about 7:30, now. By the time it's too warm, we will be able to stop by some lake or creek and let the mule eat and drink, and about Houston, y'all can't let him boss all the time."

"I know, Mac. But he's the baby."

"He'll grow up some day, Elena, but go check on them anyway."

"I'll be back soon." Elena called back to Mac.

"Alright." He replied.

When Elena reached her family, she found them dressed, fed and ready to go. "We've been waiting, Mama, for a long time." Charlotte said.

"I had a little talk with Mac about something."

"What was it about?"

"Charlotte, when we get to Marion County, we have to have a place to stay. We can't live in wagons forever."

"Mama, Mac will have that all mapped out."

"Of course, he will, Elena." Anna said. "Mac is good at things like that. I don't ever worry about what we're going to do, or not do. I trust Mac."

"Of course, you trust Mac." Elena said. "He's your husband."

"Just wait and see." Anna said.

54

Mac went to Deacon's wagon. "Hey, in there. Are y'all ready to leave?"

"Yes, we've been waiting for you to tell us what to do. Joe and I have already had our second cup of coffee."

"I believe everybody is ready, so let's get out of the wagons and get together for some instructions."

"What instructions, Mac?" Deacon asked.

"I'll tell everybody what they are when we get together, Deacon."

Everybody got out of their wagons. Mac motioned his arm around, indicating that he wanted everybody to get in the circle. Once everybody was properly positioned, he began; "Now, we're going to head north from here, so remember my instructions. When I say **Hee Haw** we're going straight ahead. When I say **Hee**, we're turning right and when I say Haw, we're turning left. Now once we get on the road, it's going to be straight ahead for a long time, so you will hear **Hee Haw**, and it will be like that for a long time. Now, when we're getting ready to stop, I will say "**Whoa.**"

"I believe everybody."

"Uncle Mac, what do you call when we have to pee?"

"Well, John hasn't figured that one out yet, but no one will have to wet on themselves."

"When do we get our next meal?" Dorothy asked.

"I want to know that answer, too," Mary said.

"We've got this far well fed, and we will continue." Elena said. "Let's get started.

"Have the mules been fed?" Charlotte asked.

"Charlotte, everybody had food this morning, and there is more left in that basket over there if anybody wants more." Mac said. "Deacon and John, y'all can get in line behind me, and let's get on the road."

After everyone was settled in their wagons, Mac yelled, "**Heeee!**"

Deacon and John. followed Mac with a right turn. A few moments later, he yelled "**Haw** and **Hee Haw**." They turned left and kept straight ahead.

"Will we get there today, Mac?"

"I am sure, Elena, we will pull into Marion County before sunset today."

"Are you very sure, Mac?"

"I'm very sure." Mac stressed.

"Are you alright back there, Elena?" Anna asked.

"As alright as I can be, Anna. How are you this morning?"

"I'm fine, but I am anxious to get there."

"Me, too."

"I believe I see something over there. Anna."

"Where?"

"I see some buildings over to my right. Look."

"Elena, have you been in Marion County before?"

"A long time ago, Mac, but things do change. I believe we're near. Let's keep moving."

There was a crude sign on the side of the road, with large block letters that read: MARION COUNTY. "We're here," Mac yelled.

"I'll find the railroad station from here and I'll go in," Mac said. "And when I come out, I 'll have some information about where we are going to stay tonight."

"What about the other nights?" Elena asked.

"We'll take one step at a time, Elena."

"We've trusted you this far, we will trust you all the way, Mac."

"That's the right spirit, Elena." Mac said.

Mac led the two wagons to the rear of the station, as he had done many times. When he got out of his wagon, he instructed the others to stay in the wagons, unless they had to go to the restroom. "When I come back, I will have all the information we need, so don't worry. We will have a safe place for the night. Tomorrow, we will find a permanent place for a while.

"That sounds good, Mac," Charlotte said. "We can live with that."

"In the meantime," Mac said. "Why don't y'all get out of the wagons and stretch your legs. If you need to go inside to the restroom, you can follow me."

"Deacon and Anna got out first, because Anna wanted to go inside to the rest room. "Wait up, Mac. We'll follow you." Deacon said.

Mac stopped. "Anybody else want to go in. Don't be bashful, now."

No one responded. "I guess that's it. Let's go.' He said.

When he reached the train station, he waited for Anna and Deacon to go in first. Anna and Deacon went to the restrooms, and he went to a window for information. It appeared that the man behind the desk had lots and lots of information, because he waved his arms back and forth as if giving Mac some directions. "Thank you, sir. You have been a lot of help."

Anna and Deacon came out from the rear. "Did you get information that's useful?" Deacon asked Mac.

"Yes, and everything he told me is useful. Let's hurry back to the wagons and get started. We don't have far to go before we find a suitable place."

"Uncle Mac, all I see is grass all over. How are we going to find a suitable place in all of this grass?"

"Just trust me, John. When we get to the sign that led us here, I will say **HAW** that means…"

"I know what that means, Uncle Mac. We're turning left, but to where?"

"You will soon find out."

"I'm ready," Elena said.

"I am, too, Charlotte said.

"Then, let's get on the road."

"Uncle Mac, all I see is green grass. I don't see any buildings of any kind."

"You will, John. You will." Mac assured him, "so just get back in your wagon."

After twenty minutes later on the road, Mac saw what the clerk at the railroad station told him. He saw fields of green forgotten pastures, three or four abandoned shacks and a creek running over with rainwater. He could also see buildings ahead in that area. The mules seemed satisfied. They began to nibble the grass and pulled the wagons over near the creek where they could drink water. Their passengers didn't seem to mind the move. It was fun to the children.

"Is this where we're going to stay, Mac?'

"No, Elena, but it's a good start. Y'all get out and bend your knees" he yelled to the others.

"I can do that," John called back.

Deacon called Mac back to his wagon. "What is it Deacon?"

"Mac, as soon as we get settled in a place, we will have to head back home."

"I hear you, Deacon. We appreciate all the service y'all have given us. Please thank your wife for us. We couldn't have done this by ourselves."

"Mac, y'all are welcome. Please let us know when you get back home, but we're going to stay until you get them settled in."

14

"**H**AW!" Mac yelled. When he reached the sign where they entered, he made a left turn, and the other wagons followed.

"Do you know where we're going, Mac?"

"Not, really, Elena, but I'm trying to follow that man's instructions." He continued to steer his wagon forward for twenty more minutes. "I believe I see something, Elena."

"I do, too. I see some houses and lots of green pastures. It seems like an ideal place just for us."

"We'll go there. If y'all found a place here to stay, how long do you think you'll stay here?"

"Huston will be six years old in three more years, so he can go to school. Charlotte won't need me anymore to be a babysitter for her. I might go back to Nacogdoches, Louisiana."

"I thought you left Nacogdoches, because of bad memories. Your husband had just died, and you couldn't stay there anymore."

"Mac, I found out that you don't leave bad memories behind, they follow you wherever you go. You have to face them and learn to live with them until they fade away."

"I hope you can do that, Elena."

"I have already, Mac."

"Do you know anybody who's still there?"

"Yes, my cousin. You remember her. She came to visit me a few years ago. She's still in our family home, where we grew up together as sisters. She wants me to come back and stay, and I am thinking about it."

"I remember her, Elena, and I think y'all will get along just fine. What will happen with Charlotte and her children, when you leave?"

"She's smart, and she'll find a way."

"I think John wants to teach school. He will finish school this next year, and he can begin teaching. The money from his teaching will help the family. Mary and Dorothy will soon be able to teach, and they will be able to take care of themselves and help the family, too."

"That sounds good, but you know, these days, girls want to marry and start their own families, and the money they make will take care of their families."

"That's true, Elena, but Charlotte can find something to do, too. Don't give up on her, Elena."

"If she won't meet some man, and continue to have more babies, I think she will find something to do to help the family. I saw a man just starring at her when we went inside that last train station. There will be some here to stare at her, too."

"Elena, when they find out that she has a brood of children, they will soon look away." Mac said with a chuckle. "Haw." Mac yelled.

He turned left and saw exactly what the man had described. "This is it."

Mac steered his wagon into the opened field where the mules could eat, drink and rest. The other wagons followed him. He saw the perfect spot. "I'll pull right in here by this lake. I don't think they can drink this lake dry before we go." He laughed.

"Let's see if they can, Mac." Elena replied.

John got out of his wagon and went to Mac. "Uncle Mac, do you think we can stay here for a while?"

"It looks like a good place to me, John. We can try it for a spell."

"I see a market over there on the corner. I can just see the sign that reads, MARKET. They will have cookies and candy."

"If it's a market, they will certainly have cookies and candy. Let's go up a little further, and it will be in walking distance from the wagons."

John went to his wagon and Mac got into his wagon, and they moved forward toward the village. Although they were near a small community, they weren't too far from the pond and grass for the mules. Mac got out of his wagon and approached John.

"We don't want to go in too far where the mules can't get to the grass and lake." Mac said.

"As long as we are near a market," John said.

"Do you have a sweet tooth, John?"

"I believe I do, Uncle Mac. As long as I can hop and skip to a market, I will be just fine."

"Do you have any money?"

"A little, Uncle Mac, and it will get enough candy for me, Houston and the others."

"Just as long as you have enough to share, I think you will do alright." He went to his wagon and got in. "What were you and John talking about?" Anna asked.

"We're trying to find a place where the mules can thrive, and everyone can be satisfied. John wants to be near a market, where he can go and get candies and goods for them to munch on."

"You don't have to go too far; I can see a market from here." She pointed over to her left.

"Let me steer everyone in the direction. **Haw**," he said.

Deacon and John followed him to a better pasture, where the mules could rest under the shade of trees, eat and drink from a small creek.

John got out of his wagon and ran to Mac. "Uncle Mac, this is it. I can skip and run over to the market there on the corner. Do you see it?"

"Yes, but are you sure you want to go over there?"

"Yes, sir."

"Then, you go and come back and tell me what you saw. We can park right here in the spot. In the meantime, I think I'll take a little nap."

"Yes, Sir. You go ahead and take your nap." John walked and ran to the market. He had never seen a market like this before. Here were jars of candies, baskets of wrapped cookies and groceries. John didn't know what to buy, because he wanted some of everything he saw. He saw a man approaching him. He stood with his hands down by his sides.

"Howdy, young man. Do you see something you want?"

"Not yet, Sir, but I'm looking."

"Where are you from?"

"Nacogdoches, Texas."

"That's a long way from here. When did you get here?"

"We just got here?"

"Do you have a place to stay?'

"No sir, not yet."

"What's your name?"

"John. John Frazier."

Well, John, I have some empty houses and shacks, but they were my slaves' quarters. How many are with you?"

"My Grandma, my mother, two sisters and a three-year-old brother. The other grown people came to help us with their mules and wagons."

"Y'all really need some place to stay?"

"Yes, Sir. The other two men and their wives will be going home with their mules as

soon as we can find a place to stay."

"Where are you staying, now?"

"In our wagons.

"If y'all can be slaves for four or five months, you can live in my slaves' quarters. There's plenty rooms, but you have to be slaves, to live in those quarters."

"Yes, sir. I will get my candy and go back to the wagons. I will have to let you know a little later.'

"Take your time."

"Yes, sir. But where do we live when we are through with the crops?'

"The houses will be yours. When you get through with the crops, y'all will have paid for them."

John laughed. "You really mean that?"

"Yes, the house and shack will belong to y'all."

"Thank you. Thank you." His attention turned to something else. To the left of the counter was a side room with men making beautiful, colorful jars. "What is that?"

"That's pottery."

"Can anybody make pottery, Sir?"

"Yes. Come by some time, and I'll show you how to make pottery."

"Yes, Sir." John said happily. He gave the clerk behind the counter a hand full of hard candy. The clerk put his candy in a small bag.

"Thank you," John said, and he rushed out the door with some exciting news. They will have a home, because they will be slaves for a few months. He just knew that they will be so happy.

Back at the wagons, Charlotte missed John. "Mac, where did John go? He's been gone a long time."

"He went to that market over there." He pointed in the direction. "Do you see it? It's not far. I'll go over to the market and see if he's ready. He just went after some candy for them." He pointed toward the children.

"You don't have to go, Mac. He will probably be back soon."

"I'll go anyway, Charlotte. I can use the exercise." He rushed toward the market. Before he reached the market, he saw John coming towards him.

"I know it took a long time, Uncle Mac, but I have some good news, and some that might not be so good."

"What's the good news, John?"

"I saw how pottery is made, and I think that's what I want to do."

"Now, John Jr" John's full name when someone is vexing. "What is the bad news?"

John shifted his feet back and forth. He rubbed his forehead in hesitation. It's like this. We will have to do somethings."

"John, Jr., what is the bad news?" Mac said, stressing each word.

"Uncle Mac, it's like this." He shifted his feet back and forth again. "We need a place to stay real soon. We can't stay in trailers forever. Y'all will be going back home, and Deacon and his wife have already gone."

"John Jr., what is the bad news?"

63

"Well." He stammered. "I met a man who needs a few hands to do some garden work."

"What kind of garden work, John?"

"Uncle Mac, it's like slaves work. You work for nothing, but he gives you a place to stay."

"What is this man's name, John?" Mac asked sternly.

"Jefferson Nash."

"What is the deal with Mr. Nash, John?"

"We can become his slaves..." He stammered.

"Slaves?" Mac shouted. "What did you say to him?" Mac skipped backward. "Slaves. Did you say slaves?"

John stammered and twisted his hands. "I told him that my mother and sisters and I would be his slaves until we completed the work on this one crop."

"Oh, boy," Mac shuffled about. "Oh boy, you've put your folks into slavery. They've never been slaves before."

"Well, they are now." John said.

"Did you tell them yet?"

"Not yet, Uncle Mac. I want you to be with me when I tell them."

"John?' Mac shouted. "Are you out of your mind. They will kill me., if Anna won't kill me first. She will think I had something to do with this."

"Uncle Mac, you said I was the man of the house, and it's up to me to take care of the family."

"By putting them into slavery? I didn't have that in mind, John."

"Uncle Mac?"

"What is it now, John?" Mac said calmly.

"It's too late. I have already told Mr. Nash that we would do his crops for a place to stay." John said calmly.

"John, how long will it take, and how many crops will he have y'all do after you do this one?"

"This will be the last one, and it will take about one year and a half, or maybe only a few months or less."

"That's about a half year. Where will y'all live after you do the crops?"

"We will have paid for the house that we will be living in. It will be ours."

"Make sure, John, that I am in my wagon, safe and sound, and on our way back to Nacogdoches, when you tell them that they are slaves. Just kidding, John. I will stand by you when you tell them, so they can kill us both."

"I feel better, now, Uncle Mac, when do y'all plan to leave for Nacogdoches?"

"I will have to tell Anna about this. I know she won't want to leave until y'all are okay. I don't know how she's going to take slavery and all. John, go back to the wagon and help out with whatever is needed, and I will quietly tell Anna, so if you hear someone screaming over toward our wagon, you will know that she knows."

John laughed "I will listen for the scream, Uncle Mac."

"I will, too, John." He turned and walked to his wagon.

"But Uncle Mac?"

"Yes, John. What is it now?" Mac turned and faced John.

Mama will have to sign the petition. I am sixteen, now, but the petition to volunteer to enter into slavery got to be done by an adult. Do you think she will sign the petition?"

"After living in the wagon for days, I think she will. After a while, the train station is going to get tired of us coming in to clean up ourselves. They have been good to us so far, but we can't wear out welcome."

"I hope you're right Uncle Mac. I will quietly tell Mama, as soon as I get back to the wagon. When are you and Aunt Anna leaving for home."

"John, we won't leave until y'all are settled and doing okay. I talked to some men yesterday. I didn't tell you, but they are woodsmen. They travel with a company where they help build the towns by cutting down trees. They will cut down enough trees around here to build y'all a house. I saw one looking at your Mama, and I think he might like Charlotte. They will help y'all. I don't think Anna and I will have to worry about how y'all are going to make it."

"Uncle Mac, we need all the help we can get. When we get our house, will y'all come back to see us?"

"Yes, we will, John. Y'all will soon get tired of me and Anna. You see, we won't have to come in a wagon anymore. We can take the train."

John walked to his wagon, while Mac stood still pondering about slavery.

Petitioning to become a slave was extremely unusual, but not unheard of. Such petitions became more numerous as civil war loomed the southern states, fearing that free blacks might persuade slaves to rebel, so they enacted laws that would suppress their influence. For instance, in Georgia, non-resident blacks were prohibited from entering the state. If they violated that ruling, they would be sold into slavery. New taxes were imposed on free blacks. If they couldn't pay, they would be sold into slavery. If a city ordinance was violated by a free black, he would be sold into slavery. Some free people of African descent may have believed forced enslavement was inevitable, so they opted to voluntarily become slaves.

When John told the family that their only hope for a little while, is to volunteer to be slaves, Mary and Dorothy yell at him. "Why do you think we want to be slaves?'

"For a place to stay." John yelled back. "Do ya'll have anything better? At least, I'm trying. What are y'all doing? We're stepping on toes and all over each other in this wagon. I can't take it anymore."

"How long is this slavery?" Charlotte asked.

"It's only for the time it takes to complete his crop that's already planted. His vegetables are already planted, but they need care, such as hoeing out the weeds, and keep them watered. There is a well in the middle of the field where we can get water, and we won't have to tote it too far."

"I need to think about that, John. What did Mama say?"

"Nothing. She's going to keep Houston out of trouble, while we tend to the crops. She will have her hands full with that chore." John said.

Mary and Dorothy began to cry out loudly. "We don't want to be slaves. Can't we do something else?"

"I don't know, but if you don't have something figured out by 7:30 in the morning, you come to the field in your dungarees on and hoes in your hands ready to work."

"What are you going to do" Just be our boss?" Mary asked.

"No, Mary. I will probably be out there before y'all get up. The sooner we are through with this crop, we will be through being slaves."

"What about next year," Dorothy asked.

"We only agreed for this crop." John said.

"We will do what we have to do, so let's don't think about it until tomorrow." Charlotte said.

"What?" How could you!" Anna screamed.

"What's going on over there?" Elena asked.

"Uncle Mac just told Aunt Anna, that we would have to be slaves for a while. He thinks she will think he helped plan this, but he didn't have anything to do with this. This is all my idea."

"Why didn't you let Uncle Mac have something to say about this?" Mary shouted to John.

"Uncle Mac got enough to do already. He has to drive those mules for several days to get home. That's enough for one person."

15

Charlotte had four children and she knew that they couldn't stay in a wagon. Volunteering for slavery was her best option, so she met with Mr. Nash and signed the petition with a mark. John C. Perry and Bryant Taylor were the subscribing witnesses. Mr. Nash was wealthy. He was in the iron and steel business, so he could well afford as many slaves as he wanted. Charlotte and her family moved into their slave home.

John not only did farm chores, he began to learn how to make potteries. Mr. Nash had a pottery mill in a room at his market. John noticed the pottery and the men making them. He told Charlotte that he wanted to make pottery, too.

"I don't know how you can do that John. You know, we signed up to do farm work."

"I know, Mama, but I will do both."

"Do you know when Mac and Anna are leaving, John?"

"Not exactly, but I know it's soon."

"I don't know what we're going to do without them" Charlotte said. "We couldn't have gotten this far without them. I'll stop by their wagon and see."

"I'll be with Grandma. I haven't talked to her lately. I want to see what she plans to do while we wait for our own house.

"You go ahead, John. I'm on my way to Mac and Anna." When she reached their wagon, she wiggled the door flap. "How are y'all doin' in there?" Charlotte called.

"We're cleaning up and packing our things. We think y'all have everything settled for a little while."

Anna pulled the flap back. "Yes, we have, but we're goin' to miss y'all.

"You will see us again, Charlotte."

"Thanks, Anna. That makes me feel better."

I'm going over to see Elena, while y'all stand here and talk."

"Tell Mama I'll be over there in a little while." Charlotte said.

Mac trotted the few feet to Elena, who was standing out by her wagon with her arms folded across her waist.

Mac noticed that Elena seems to be in deep thought. "Elena, are you going to be alright staying here? You can go back with me and Anna if you like."

"Mac, Houston is three and a half years old. When he is six, he can go to school, and I will go to Natshetoshe, Louisiana."

"Who do you know there?"

"My cousin. You remember she used to come and visit. She is living in our old family home, and I will join her."

"We will miss you, Elena."

"I will miss you and Anna, too." She reached around her neck and pulled out a green braided chord with keys hanging from the bottom. She rolled the braid in a ball. "Put out your hands, Mac."

Mac held his hands out and cupped them in front of him. Elena placed the keys in Mac's hands and closed them. "I want you to have these."

Mac opened his hands. "Elena, these are keys to y'all's house. We 're going to take care of everything, just like it's ours. You know that."

"That's what I want to hear Mac, because that house and farm belong to you and Anna, now. We will never come back to stay. The family agrees that y'all should have our home."

"Elena, I don't know what to say. You know we will take care of everything, just in case y'all decide to come back. We're leaving tomorrow."

"What time?"

"I don't know what Anna is planning, but it's going to be early."

"I want to know, so I can say my goodbyes. Mac" Elena rubbed her hands together.

"No, Elena." He placed his hands on her shoulders." Remember, it's 'Til we meet again'."

"I know, but I'm not ready to say, 'Til' we meet again. It's getting late. Why don't you and Anna come into our new home and sleep in a real bed for comfort before y'all leave.?"

"We'll nap a little while in the wagon, Elena, but may God bless y'all."

"And may God bless you and Anna, too. I will get up early and watch y'all leave. You won't see me, but I will be up."

"I believe you, Elena." Mac slowly walked away.

The night was silent. Dogs weren't barking, and all were silent and in bed. Elena closed her eyes, but in a few moments, she was asleep, too. Around three o'clock in the morning, Elena heard rattling of the reins and sounds of wagon wheels. She lay quietly, thinking that it must be a dream. Minutes later, she heard, **"Haw"**. She knew that voice well. It was Mac, but Mac said they would leave in the morning. Again, she heard **"HEE"**.

"Where is he turning right?" She said to herself.

Approximately five minutes later, she heard, **"Heeee Haw."** They're on their way. He didn't wait for morning. She got up and looked out to see for sure if they were still there. If so, she would see their wagon, because she had to be dreaming about them leaving. She looked out of the window, and she wasn't dreaming. Mac and Anna were gone. She heard the last sound of Mac's and Anna's wagon about 3:30 AM. She knew that she wasn't dreaming, and they were gone. It would be her sad duty to tell the family and especially John Jr., that Mac and Anna were gone.

Elena tried to sleep, but she had to make plans for days to come. Slavery wasn't in their plans, when they made the plans to come to Marion County. They were escaping bad memories, but they have to face worse memories, such as being slaves. She knew all about slavery, because many of her friends were slaves, and her son-in-law John, Sr. was a slave, but there wasn't anything pleasant about being a slave, but whatever it took to get a place to stay and live comfortably, she would tolerate it for a while.

Elena felt the sunshine in her face. She knew that she had overslept, so she dressed quickly, went to the kitchen to prepare breakfast. This was Sunday and they had to go to church around eleven o'clock. After church they would eat and prepare for their new job, slavery.

"Mama, I've been thinking about slavery. I don't like the idea, but it's just for a little while. I hope John got that right."

"He wouldn't lie to us, Charlotte. You know him better than that."

"Yes'am I do. I was hoping that he was just joking."

"No Charlotte, John Jr. wasn't joking. We had better clean up everything in the kitchen and get ready for bed, 'cause we have a long day tomorrow.

John joined Elena and Charlotte in the kitchen. "Are y'all ready for tomorrow morning?"

"As ready as we can get, John," Charlotte said.

John walked into the kitchen and joined Elena and Charlotte. "I think Uncle Mac and Aunt Anna will be here and see us in the field as slaves. I want him to see us before they leave."

"Why?" Charlotte asked.

"Just because." John said. "They will be here tomorrow morning."

"John, Mac and Anna have already gone." Elena said.

"They can't be gone, Grandma. Uncle Mac said he would be here until we go to the field. He promised that he would be with me through it all. John cried. He said he wouldn't leave us alone without seeing that we are okay. He promised, Grandma." He cried again.

"Come to me John." She hugged him, as he bent down to her. "Mac didn't want to say any goodbyes, John. It was too sad for him. He knows that we are going to be alright. He and Anna can take the train and come and visit any time. Mac won't be satisfied until things get better, and they will get better. I promise."

"You always have a solution, Grandma."

"I do my best, John."

71

16

Elena rose early and dressed for church. She put a large housecoat over her church wear and began making breakfast. "Rise and shine." She yelled.

John ran to the kitchen, where Elena was putting tin plates on the table. "Oh, it's you, Grandma." He said slowly.

"Yes, it's me. Don't sound so disappointed. I'm making breakfast."

John went to the back door and looked out. "When did they leave, Grandma?"

"I heard them pull out around three this morning. I thought I was dreaming, because they said they were leaving in the morning, but three o'clock was morning. They are well on their way by now."

John looked at the clock on the table. "It's just a little after eight o'clock, Grandma. He sat down at the table. "They can't be too far. I bet if I had a horse, I could catch them."

"I'm glad we don't have a horse, John", she laughed. "If you caught them, what would you do with them?"

"I don't know, Grandma. What are we going to do without them?"

"John Jr?" She often called him. We'll find away. We'll find away. I promise."

"I know, Grandma. You always have the right answers. Tomorrow is Monday. We will get up and begin our chores. You don't have to go with us, Grandma. If you stay here and watch Huston and make the meals, we can and will do the rest."

"Sounds like you have it all planned out, John."

"I think so Grandma, but I don't know how Mary and Dorothy are going to take being slaves."

"They will have to learn, John. Your sisters will learn." She assured him.

"I wonder what Uncle Mac and Aunt Anna are doing now, Grandma. Maybe they have stopped at two or three train stations by now."

"They are probably just taking their time. They don't have to rush home for anything. As long as they have each other, they are just about complete."

"They're still lonely, Grandma. I plan to visit them sometimes. I can always take the train and get there in a day or two."

"Sure, you can, John. I plan to do the same, but it won't be soon."

"We still have our house there. I can stay there for a few days."

"No John, I gave the house to Mac and Anna, because we will never go back to stay."

John jumped for joy. "Really, Grandma? Really? I am so glad you did that." He wiped away his tears. "We will always be in their lives."

"We will. Now I need you to get everyone up and ready for church." She noticed that John had on his best suit and bow tie, and ready to go. "You are already dressed, I notice. Now, don't get your clothes greasy when you eat breakfast, John."

"I won't get my clothes greasy, Grandma, 'cause I'm not going to eat breakfast until we get back."

"Well, see how your Mama and sisters are doing. They should be already dressed. I don't want to be later on our first day of service."

John ran to the back where Mary and Dorothy were dressing. How are y'all doing in there? Grandma wants y'all to come to breakfast so we can get to church on time."

"Mama? Are you ready?" He called to the middle room. "And what about Huston?"

"I'm ready to walk out the door with Huston." She called to John.

When Charlotte walked out of her room, holding Huston's hand, the girls were behind her. John looked at them all, and said, "I have the best-looking Mama and sisters and Lil' brother in the whole world. Y'all look really, really good."

Mary and Dorothy turned around, brushing back their long, straight, black hair to the back of their shoulders. I hope we look this good to everybody else." Mary said.

"Y'all will, but tomorrow morning, y'all will have to braid your hair and put on hats to shade your faces from the sun when we go to the field. Tomorrow is our first day of slavery." He said.

"We were having such a good time, why did you bring it up?"

"I don't want y'all to forget it. Let's go to the kitchen and if you want to eat now, hurry and eat, so we can go to church. I have the wagon ready."

"I hope Mama won't be disappointed, but I don't want to eat now. I'll wait after church."

"I don't want to get my dress dirty and greasy, so I will eat after church, too." Dorothy said.

"Me. Too," Mary said.

"Unless Grandma is going to wait until we come home, we can leave now." John said.

"Who's going to tell her?"

"I will," Charlotte said.

They walked to the kitchen dressed and ready for church. "I see everybody is ready to go. What about breakfast?"

"We decided to eat when we come home." Charlotte said.

Charlotte wrapped a piece of meat in a biscuit and gave it to Houston. He took a bite and put the rest on the table. "I don't want to eat now," He said.

"Grandma, I hear the men working on our new home. It might be ready before we're free. Can we stop by our new home after church, and see what they have done?"

"Yeah, I want to see it, too." Dorothy said.

"Me, too" Mary said.

"Well. We'll stop by and look as long as y'all like." Elena promised.

"Let's go." John said. He looked at Houston. "Little brother, you look really good this morning, and when you get inside church, I want you to be really good, too. If you need to go to the toilet, let me know, and I will take you. Okay?"

"Okay," Houston said slowly.

Charlotte and her daughters gathered their long skirts around their legs and followed John and Elena out of the door. When they reached their wagon, John helped them in, and he seated Houston in the front of the wagon with him. "I don't want to mess up your clothes, so let's be careful when you sit down. I did dust the benches in here, but I don't know how well."

"John, we are going to be just fine. I can hardly wait until we get to the little church." Elena said.

"HEE." John yelled and the mules made a right turn to the dirt road. "We're on our way." John said. When they reached the corner, John yelled HAW" and the mules made a left turn, and the church was in view.

"Look, Grandma," John said. I believe this is where you want to go. It's the First Baptist Church."

"Where are you going to hitch the mules while we're in church?" Dorothy asked.

"There is a hitching post back of the church. I came by and checked things out yesterday. All ya'll have to do is go inside and sit down. I will find you. I'll get y'all near the door and let ya'll out." They got out of the wagon with John's help.

"You think of everything, John." Mary said. "I don't know what we'd do without you. You are the best brother, ever."

"Thanks, but I have a great family to help out. It's not such a big chore." John said. "Y'all just go on in, and I'll be there as soon as I get the mule hitched.

Charlotte led the family inside the church. There were about twenty people already seated. Some turned around and looked at them as they entered the door. There were many happy faces, because they had visitors. Charlotte led the family toward the front, and they sat in the middle aisle. Everything seemed so quiet, until an usher went to them with pencil and paid.

"Good morning, the usher said. "We're so happy to have you as our guests this morning, and we wish you would consider worshiping with us every Sunday, but first I need your names and a little information."

John walked inside the church and saw his family. He rushed to them, when he saw the usher. "Do y'all need me to give the usher some information?"

"You came in just in time." Elena said. "I was just about to."

"I'm John Frazier," he told the usher, and this is my mother, Charlotte," he pointed toward her. John introduced the others with whatever information the usher needed.

"Thank you," she said, and she led them to a row in the middle of the church.

"John. Did you get the mules hitched?" Charlotte asked when they sat down.

"Everything is alright. I just want to make sure that ya'll are alright, too.

"John, you can take care of the mules, but let us help with something. You're just running yourself to death. We could have helped the usher about us, but you rushed in and did everything yourself. You will soon be too tired to do anything. Let us help."

"I promised Uncle Mac that I would take care of the family, Dorothy, and that's what I'm doing."

"He didn't mean everything, John. We will help, too." Mary said.

At eleven o'clock, the pastor, Rev. Ross, walked in and sat down behind the pulpit. His wife walked in after him and sat at the piano and began playing the piano for the choir to march in. and stood in the choir stand behind the pastor. Everyone stood and sang along with the choir as they marched in. After the first verse of the song, Rev. Ross asked everyone to be seated. He noticed unfamiliar faces and asked the usher to acknowledge their guests.

The only usher was taken by surprise. She usually introduced guests after the sermon, but she went to the front of the room and proceeded by asking the visitors to stand. Everyone turned and looked at the Frazier family, because they were the only visitors. Charlotte stood, holding Houston by the hand, and the others stood with her. The usher read their names and it was obvious who they were, because they each raised their hand when their name was called.

Rev. Ross asked if they would like to speak. There was silence for a few seconds, and then Elena answered the invitation. She motioned for the rest of the family to sit down. She addressed the pastor and members and told of the family traveling for miles by mules and wagon to escape sad memories. Instead of escaping the sad memories, the memories followed them. "We become slaves tomorrow just for a place to stay, but we don't mind. It will be just for a little while."

She looked toward the deacon section and recognized three men who are building their new home. When they have completed the requirements of Mr. Nash, who needs his farm weeded out so his crops can grow, they will be free. "This is a surprise to us to see the men who are helping us here in the church. I know we came to the right place, when we entered Friendship Baptist Church." When she finished her statements, she thanked the congregation for listening, and she sat down.

The congregation clapped and said a lot of amen's. "You are truly at the right place," Rev. Ross said. "With your statements, I believe we have already had a sermon, so we can open the doors of the church." Meaning inviting them to join Friendship Baptist Church.

Elena stood and began walking toward the pastor, who had walked to the edge of the altar. John Jr. and the others followed her, and they stood in front in a straight line to receive fellowship from the church. The members of the church formed lines according to the usher's instructions and marched around to shake the new members' hands. Mrs. Ross played the piano as the members gave fellowship to the new members. When the last members of the audience were finished, Mrs. Ross stopped playing and walked down to the new members and gave fellowship to them, by shaking their hands. "You are so welcomed." She said to them.

Rev. Ross motioned all to be seated. "When do you begin your first day of slavery?"

Tomorrow morning at 7:30." Elena said.

17

Elena was in the kitchen at 6:o'clock on Monday morning. She prepared a big breakfast for the family, because she knew the work would require all the strength that they had. John Jr. heard Elena quietly humming a hymn, and he got up to greet her. After he was fully dressed, he went to the kitchen, and kissed Elena on the cheek. "Good morning, Grandma."

"Good morning, John. I hope this will be a good and blessed morning for y'all"

"I have a feeling, Grandma, that this will be the most important day of our lives. Mary and Dorothy have softened to the idea of becoming slaves, so I don't have to worry about them complaining anymore."

"Why do you think they are softening to the idea of becoming slaves?"

"After we left church, yesterday, Grandma, they said that they were ashamed of acting like they had acted. They said that they had a choice, but the slaves for many years didn't have a choice, and they were often beaten, and sometimes their children were taken and sold into slavery."

"I'm glad they're agreeing to become slaves for a little while." Elena said.

Moments later, Charlotte and her family joined John Jr. and Elena in the kitchen. She held Houston by the hand, and said to Elena, "Mama, he is yours until we finish for the day.

I'm looking forward to my assignment." She looked down at Houston, and said, "Houston are you ready for Grandma to take care of you today?"

Houston said honestly, "No, Grandma. I want to go with Mama."

"They're going out there to work in the hot sun all day, Houston. You don't want to do that do you?"

"I want to go, too. I want to go, too." He cried.

"Houston, you can go, but if you get tired, you have to stay until we get through. We'll come back for lunch. If you want to stay with Grandma, you can."

"I don't want to stay with Grandma. I can go back with you."

"We'll see, little brother." John said.

Dorothy knew that Houston was trying to escape Grandma's spankings. She showered her children and grandchildren with love, but she didn't spare the rod, so she volunteered the task of taking care of Houston while working in the fields. "Houston can bring his stick horse and stay along with me and Mary. We'll see after him."

"Do y'all think you can handle Houston and do your chores in the field?'

"Of course, we can Mama." Mary said.

"If you think so, we' better eat, get our hoes and rakes and rush to Mr. Nash's field." Charlotte said.

"I am ready," John Jr. said. "I'll meet y'all out there."

"What do we do when we get there?" Mary asked.

"Just get a row and begin chopping the weeds from the plants." John said. "We need to clear the field and prepare it for the fall planting."

"Then, I'll follow you out the door."

"I'm right behind you." Dorothy said.

Charlotte and Houston followed. She tried to get Houston to stay with his Grandma, but he kicked and yelled, so she made him promise to come back when he got tired. They were the last to go to the field.

When Elaine had drunk her third cup of coffee, she went to the kitchen door and looked across the fields and saw four heads bobbing up and down in a huge field. Sadness came to her suddenly. She realized that her family was in slavery for a lifetime. The four of them would never be able to complete Mr. Nash's field before the next planting.

Tears streamed down her face at the thought of a lifetime of slavery. They had never been slaves, and slavery had ended. Her sobs became audible. She was alone and everything became apparent. Mac and Anna were gone, and perhaps near home by now, and her entire family will be away daily trying to do the impossible. She walked to the front door, because she heard drums and loud singing. The drums got louder, and she opened the screen and walked to the edge of the porch, and recognized Rev. Ross leading a band of people carrying wooden handles across their shoulders.

Rev. Ross was beating the larger drum accompanied by three smaller drums carried by three other members. Elaine opened the door wider and walked to the edge of the porch. There was a large crowd. It appeared to have been more than a hundred worshipers and perhaps neighbors and friends. She shaded her face from the morning sun with both hands. Her tears dried on her face and a broad smile appeared. "They're coming this way", she cried. As they got closer, she stood outside by the door to greet them, but she didn't want to stop their rhythm, so she began to clap to their beat. She waved her hands for them to come closer, and she joined in the march to the rear of their house, where Charlotte and her children were working in the field.

Houston won the argument about staying with Elena. Dorothy told him to get his stick horse and follow them to the field. About an hour after they had begun working, Dorothy looked around and didn't see Houston.

She screamed out his name, and she still didn't hear him. Finally, she looked toward the sandy road and saw Houston jumping over and over a log. The log didn't look like any ordinary log that she had seen, "Houston, she yelled. What are you doing? Come here."

"I'm just playing with my friend." Houston said. He began to walk toward Dorothy.

When Houston walked away from his friend, the log-like figure raised up on short stubby legs. Dorothy ran and picked Houston up and ran back to the crowd, that stood in silence.

"That's my friend."

"Houston, that is not your friend. That's an alligator, and he will eat you. I'm taking you back to Grandma."

When Dorothy and Houston reached home, Elena was standing at the front door. "What's wrong?" She asked Dorothy.

Dorothy told her about Houston and the alligator, so she thought she had to bring him home."

"I hear drums. Don't you?"

"Yes, Grandma. I got to get back." And she trotted back to the field.

Elena held Houston's hand as Rev. Ross approached her.

Rev. Ross silenced his drum, and the other drummers did likewise. "Sister Elaine, we came to help your family. They will never complete that field by themselves." He waved his hand over the vast land. We've got to get these children in school when school starts, and that will be after Thanksgiving, Mrs. Elena."

"Rev. Ross, I was just praying for a miracle. That's a lifetime of slavery for them."

Charlotte and her children stopped and wondered what the commotion was all about. She couldn't wait any longer, so she rushed to the crowd. "Good morning," she yelled to the crowd. "I'm so happy to see you this morning, Rev. Ross. We have begun our first day of slavery. I don't know how we will ever complete it, but we made a promise, and we will keep it."

"You won't have to keep it by yourselves, we came to help, and we will be here every day until the job is done."

Charlotte began to cry and so did Elena. "Thank you so much, Rev. Ross. We appreciate y'all's help."

"I will get that big water barrel and keep it filled with water, so y'all can drink when you get thirsty. We have a lot of tin cups, and I will bring them out and put them and put them by the barrel."

"We appreciate that, Sister Elena. We brought our own food, and some water, but the extra water will help, too. So let's get started." Rev. Ross yelled.

The crowd seemed to have filled the field. They scattered far apart and chose rows to work on. Some were able to work on two rows at a time. The end of slavery was going to be brief. It was clear that this crowd came to end slavery.

Each day, the crowd met at their church to work in the field. The crowd grew larger. As the news got around through the community, all who were able, got hoes and rakes and joined the crowd. Many children joined in, too. It was like having a picnic to them. They were happy to join the crowd, because their mothers packed buckets of food for a full day. At the end of each day, which was five o'clock, they would lay their tools at the end of their row, to be picked up the following days.

Each day, Elena would fill the water container and push it in a wheelbarrow toward the field, where the workers could get water when needed. She took it on her own to keep the water container fully supplied with water from her deep well.

Each day after the volunteers had completed work for the day and left the field, Elena had a large dinner for her family. On the first day of slavery, Elena said, "I wonder if Mac and Anna have made it to Natchitoshes, yet."

"Grandma, they left eight or nine days ago. They have to be there now, or close to home by now," John Jr. said. "By the time they get there and settled into their new home, we will probably be out of slavery. The crowd gets bigger each day, and I can see an ending in sight. Can't you, Grandma?"

"Yes, I can John Jr. I expect the end will come Friday of this week."

"Today is Tuesday, Grandma, so that means that we have only three days left of slavery. I learned a lot these days of slavery. Grandma."

"What did you learn, John Jr."

"How good people are to each other in times of needs. I have met a lot of friends during our slavery days. I will miss them, when everything is over, Grandma."

"You can still keep in touch with each other, John. You will see them at church and gatherings in our neighborhood. You can't forget them."

"Tomorrow is the beginning to the ending of slavery, and I will be glad to tell Mr. Nash that we are through."

"I will be standing beside you, when you do." Elena said.

18

Thursday morning at 6:30 AM, John was up and dressed. He rushed to the kitchen where Elena was making breakfast. Good morning, Grandma."

"Good morning, John. Why are you up so early? Everything is closed now. Mr. Nash won't be in his store before nine o'clock." She began to stir the porridge in the pot.

"I just couldn't sleep any longer, Grandma. I wonder what he will say when I tell him that we will be through with his field, and we're ready to end slavery. Do you think he'll agree with us, Grandma?"

"He seems like a reasonable man, John Jr. When he sees how cleans his field is, he'll be ready to plant his fall crops."

"I hope so, Grandma."

"When everything is over, what do you want to do, John? In other words, what do you want to be in life?"

"I want to be a teacher, Grandma. I am on my last year in school, and when I get through with school, I can take a test to see if I qualify to be a grade schoolteacher. Also, I want to make some of those bowls and jars I saw in Mr. Nash's shop."

"That sounds good, John, but won't you need more education?"

"Yes ma'am, but I can go to school in the summer and finish the courses I need to be a teacher. I can also study how to make those bowls and jars. One day I can be famous with my bowls and jars."

"I believe you will be famous someday, but if you really want it, you will have to work hard to get it. Now, it's ten o'clock. You can go over to Mr. Nash's market and talk to him about y'all freedom." Elena sat down to the kitchen table to drink her cup of coffee.

"That sounds good to me, Grandma. I can wait another hour or two. In the meantime, I will have some of that breakfast you're fixing. It smells too good to wait any longer."

"It's your favorite. I have some ham, eggs and toast that I toasted on top of the stove."

John Jr. got a plate from the cupboard, and reached beside the sink, opened a drawer, and got his knife and fork. "Now, I'm ready, Grandma. I will try to leave something for the others. I know it's going to be hard, but I'll try." He laughed.

Elena laughed. "I think you can leave enough for the others. She laughed. He began to eat hurriedly, so he could go to the market to speak to Mr. Nash. "I hope Mr. Nash is at the market when I get there. I don't know exactly what time he gets there, but he's always there when I'm there. Grandma, I'm going to start using my full name, John Milligan Frazier."

"Why?" Elena asked.

'Cause, John Milligan Frazier sounds important. I guess I'd better get on my way. I hope he's there."

"He'll be there. Do you really need me to go with you, John?"

"No, Grandma, you don't need to go with me." He finished his breakfast and walked to the back door to look over the field. It was crowded with new and old workers. Every day, a few more came to work. They were near the end of all of the rows, and it appears that they would be through with Mr. Nash's field before Friday. "Grandma. We'll be through before Friday. I will ask Mr. Nash to walk over with me to the field. I want to see how he likes it."

"I already know how he likes it. He couldn't have gotten this done better than this with his slaves. We owe a debt of gratitude to the church. The members have been wonderful, and the pastor, too."

"I know they have been wonderful Grandma, and we have to let them know that." He rushed to the front door. "See ya, Grandma."

"I know you will have good luck." Elena said.

"I can't wait, Grandma. I'll be back soon and tell you what he said. When Mama, Mary and Dorothy get back from the field, they'll have some good news. I guess Houston is going to have a short nap today. He's still asleep."

"Well, don't wake him. But I should because he won't take his nap this afternoon. Do what you think is best, Grandma. I'm on my way to see Mr. Nash. When I leave there. I'll trot to the western Union at the train station, to see if we have anything from Mac and Anna."

"They're probably just settling in, and haven't had time to write us, but I hope so. You just go ahead, and see what Mr. Nash is going to say about his field. It looks pretty good to me."

John rushed out the front door. "See ya Grandma."

When John got to Mr. Nash's market, he saw Mr. Nash standing by his ceramic shop. He rushed in and went to Mr. Nash.

"What is the hurry about, John?"

"Good morning, Mr. Nash. I came to talk to you about your field." John tried to act calm and not breathless. "As you know, we have plenty of help and we're just about through. I wanted to know if we can end slavery by Friday."

John, I have noticed the workers, too, and it seems that you're right. Ya'll can have your freedom by Friday. That's tomorrow."

John jumped for joy. "Mr. Nash, that's the best news I've heard in a long time. My family will be so proud, and I know the other neighbors will be happy, too, but they enjoyed every day of the work."

"Well, you tell them, John, that they are free on this day. I walked over the field yesterday, and I didn't see anything else that they needed to do. They have completed the job, and all are free. Tomorrow morning, y'all can sign the release papers. Ya'll can still keep the house. I don't need it for anything, now. John, you can also come by sometimes and look inside the ceramic shop. This might be something you might want to do someday."

"I would like that Mr. Nash. As far as the house, we enjoyed every day living there, but as you know some men of our church built our house. They completed it last week."

85

"That's good news, John. Tell me, what do you plan to do for yourself? Do you want to go to school? What do you want to do?'

"I have one more year of high school, and then I will take a test to see if I can teach grade school. I can go to college in the summers. I'll have to find one, first."

"Your plans sound good, John. You will make a good citizen, and I will help you to attain your goals. You just keep of the good works, and good things will happen for you."

"Thank you, Mr. Nash. Now, I'm going to the train station and to see if we have a telegram from Mac and Anna, and I will tell everyone of our freedom when I get back."

Mr. Nash laughed. "You're going to make them wait?"

"A few more minutes won't hurt Mr. Nash. Thank you. I'm on my way." John rushed out the front door and trotted to the train station. When he reached the train station, he was greeted by a friendly clerk at the door. "What's the rush?"

"I believe we have a telegram." John said.

"Come on in, and we'll see."

John followed the clerk inside the station. "Business seems to be a little slow today" John looked around the large area. Where's everybody?"

"Today is running slow. That's why I was standing out by the door. If you receive a telegram today, it will be the first for the day. and it's after four o'clock." He went behind the desk and rambled through some mail. "What name am I looking for?"

"I believe it would be in my Grandma's name. Her name is Elena, Elena Scott."

"What is your name?"

"It's John M. Frazier, but it would be more likely be in her name."

"You're right. Here is a telegram from Orange County. It must be for your Grandma. Her name is on it."

John reached for it. "Thank you so much." He reached for the telegram, as the clerk handed it to me. "I know who it's from, and my Grandma is going to jump for joy."

"John, you need to take it to her."

"Do I owe for this?"

"No. Just take it to your Grandma. I bet she's been expecting that letter for a long, long time."

"Thank you. I want to see her face and hear her screams when she sees this."

John said, and he rushed out the door and ran toward home. When he opened the front door, he rushed in and fell on the floor, with exhaustion.

"What did he say? What did he say?" Elena urged John to respond.

"I have some good news, Grandma." John puffed and with the back of his hands, he wiped the sweat from his brow.

"I can't wait any longer, John. Now tell me, what did Mr. Nash say?"

"Grandma? Do you want to hear the good news from home?" John wanted to prolong news from Mac and Anna. He had read their message, and he knew that Elena would shout and cry.

"No, John. I want to hear what Mr. Nash said.

"Alright, Grandma. Mr. Nash said that we could sign the release papers from slavery on Friday afternoon. After we sign those papers, we will be free. He likes the work that we have done to his field."

"That's good news. Now, what are the news from home?"

"Mac and Anna are going to have a baby."

Elena, dropped to a chair. "What did you say?"

"Grandma, I said that Anna is going to have a baby."

Elena jumped for joy. "Why did they wait until we left to let us know. I would still be there."

"They probably didn't know themselves, Grandma. Anyway, what could you do.?"

"I could deliver the baby myself. I have waited for years for them to have a baby, so I just gave up."

"They probably gave up, too, Grandma. I know Mama is going to be surprised, too, but first, I will tell them that we're free Friday evening, so she can sign the release papers. She will get two pieces of good news. She'll hear about the baby and about our freedom."

John waited toward the end of the day to go to the field, where the group was still working. He ran to the back row, waving his hand and yelling, "We have completed the job, and now, we' re free. We're free."

Rev. Ross yelled, "Are you sure, John? I don't see anything else to do, but we want to be sure that we've done everything that's necessary."

The crowd stopped digging and raking in awe. They weren't sure of John's message. Some dropped their rakes and hoes, as if it would help them to understand what John was saying.

"Yes, Sir. Rev. Ross, I talked to Mr. Nash this morning, and he is satisfied with our work, and declared us free, and the work in the field is over."

Everyone raised their rakes and hoes above their heads and began to shout and give thanks for their journey along the way. This was good news and sad news. The good news was the family was free from slavery, but the sad new was missing the new friends they had met. They may never see them again.

Rev. Ross beckon the group to come near him. He waved his hands around, indicating for the crowd to form a close circle. When they gathered with their tools by their sides, he informed them that the task was over. We have completed the job. Our friends are free."

The crowd looked away from Rev. Ross in a different direction. He joined their glances. Mr. Nash was walking toward them with a roll of paper in his hands. They began to mumble to each other, "Why is he coming out here? I thought we were through. Why is he holding papers in his hands? What else does he need these poor people to do?"

Rev. Ross saw him coming toward them, and he began to walk toward him. "Good afternoon, Mr. Nash. I hope you're satisfied with the work we've done." He waved his arms about the field.

"I'm more than satisfied, Rev. Ross. I understand that ya'll have picnics every summer at your church, and I want y'all to know that you don't have to buy a thing. My market will furnish all the bread, meat, soda pops, and whatever else y'all need, just let me know a few days ahead, so I can get everything ready."

Everyone in hearing distance began to jump and shout for joy. "Y'all are just too welcome. You can have as much as you need. If I don't have all you need, I have friends who can help, also."

Rev. Ross reached for Mr. Nash's hand. As they grasp each other's hand, Rev. Ross said, "I want you to know, Mr. Nash, that it was a privilege to help this family or anyone else in need. We will certainly accept your offer about the picnic." Both men began to laugh, and the crowd joined them in their laughter.

The crowd mingled with each other. There were handshakes hugs and promises to meet again.

It was towards evening, and just about time to sit down at the table and eat. With all of the commotion, Elena hadn't begun the evening meal. "Grandma, do you think we need to get ready for dinner?"

"Yes, John. I caught the hint. I know I'm late on the job." They both laughed.

"If you need any help, Grandma, I'm available."

"I don't think I'll need help, John, but if I do, I'll remember your offer."

19

After Elena had prepared the evening meal, she had everyone to sit at the table for a little talk. Charlotte held Houston's hand and seated him at the table beside her, and the others joined them. "What do you want to talk about, Grandma?" John asked.

"It's about Mac's and Anna. Anna and Mac stopped along the road and bought some fresh fruit. It made her sick, but it didn't bother Mac at all. They are home now, but the doctor and his wife are on vacation, and won't be home for two more days."

"How do they know that Grandma?"

"John, the doctor put a notice on his front door."

"I hope it's nothing that they ate here with us," Charlotte said.

"They will know in a few days, when the doctor gets home." Elena said.

"How do you know, Grandma?" Dorothy asked.

"John, show them the telegram that we got today from Anna. She has all the information in that telegram."

"What do you think it is, Grandma?"

"John, if Mac is well and not hurting, it can only be one thing."

"What's that Grandma?"

"John, Anna might be pregnant."

John jumped for joy. "I'm going to be an uncle."

"How can you be an uncle, John?"

"Before they left, Mary, we declared to be kin. He would be my uncle and I would call him Uncle Mac."

"Then what are we to him, John?"

"Dorothy, y'all can be his nieces. They don't have a family. We're the only family they know, and they are like family to us."

"I like that idea, John." Elena said. "When they come to visit us with their baby, we'll have plenty room for them."

"That sounds good to me. "Charlotte said. "But when do we move to our new house?"

"Those men, who built it will move us. They were waiting for the field to be cleared, and we're declared free. Charlotte, you will have to go to Mr. Nash tomorrow morning and sign those papers that will free us."

"I will certainly, and gladly do that, Mama."

"I will gladly go with you, Mama," John said. "But those men who built our new home have done enough. Let's don't ask them to help us move, too."

"We can do our best and have everything in and ready by the time we have the church picnic."

"If the church's picnic is in August, we only have three more weeks to prepare for it."

"Grandma, we don't have that much to do. Mr. Nash said that he would give all of the food that is needed. I will help with games for the children, and I'm sure they have some of last year plans that they can use. It seems like we came to Marion County just in time to meet such wonderful people."

"That's what I think, too, John." Charlotte said.

"In the meantime, we'll start gathering our things together, so we can help with the moving to our new home." Elena said.

"I walked over there yesterday and walked around our new home. It is just what we need and what we want. It is so pretty, Grandma. You're going to like the kitchen. I peeped in they even put a stove with an oven in the kitchen. There is a pot belly stove in the living room. They thought of everything."

"Mr. Nash is giving us all the furniture here, so we have enough beds and other furniture to make our new home a real home. How do you like that?"

"I don't have any complaints, Mama." Charlotte said.

Mary, Dorothy, and John all agreed. "I hope the bedrooms are as large as these here."

"Mary, they're larger. You and Mary can primp all you want to."

Thanks, John. We knew you would take care of things."

"Y'all are welcome, but we have other things to think about."

"What's that, John?" Charlotte asked.

"School."

"What about school?" Mary asked.

"Everybody of school age will go to school this fall. Mama and Grandma, we will teach ya'll how to read, too. Y'all will be our first pupils." He laughed and they joined in.

"John, who's going to teach us?"

"I am. When I graduate this year, I will began teaching. Mr. Nash said that he would help me get prepared for a teaching job. I can start now, before I graduate."

"Your Grandma and I are too old to go to school, John."

"But you're never too old to learn. I can teach you here at home."

"What about Houston?"

"They will have retired teachers working with children under school age. Houston will fit in very well. I can take him with me, and turn him over to the retired teacher and go to my duties as a teacher. He can go to school before I graduate. We can take him and turn him over to the teacher.

"You're going to make the best teacher that Marion County ever had. You've got everything worked out already. I'm so proud of you, John."

"Thanks, Mama."

"I plan to visit Mac and Anna soon."

"How soon, Grandma?"

"As soon as y'all get in school."

"Who's going to take care of Houston. I work at Mr. Nash's market."

"Charlotte, Houston is your child. I have taken care of him all of his life. It is my time to enjoy what life I have left. When school starts, he can go with John. With John, Mary and Dorothy at the same school, he should be in good hands"

"I thought you would help me with him, Mama, until he could go to school." Charlotte said tearfully.

"Charlotte, where do you think Houston will be going, when he leaves with John, Mary and Dorothy?"

"I don't know, Mama."

"You can go on to work. Prepare Houston for school before you leave. John, Mary and Dorothy will take him with them to their school. I will leave in the fall to visit Mac and Anna."

"I guess that's what I'll have to do, Mama."

"I know that's what you have to do, Charlotte." Elena said sternly. "I need a break from tending children. The retired schoolteacher can see to him with the other little children, until Mary and Dorothy are ready to come home."

"I know, Mama, but what are you going to do when you go to see Anna and Mac? Won't you be seeing after their baby? If not, why would they need you?"

"They don't need me, Charlotte, but I've known them since they were youngsters, and they have no one else, who cares enough to see after them. That's what I've always done. Anyway, little Mac can't talk nor walk Little Mac only needs to be held, fed and loved. I can do all of that. If Anna is going to breast feet him, I'll take care of the rest."

"How do you know that the baby is going to be a little Mac, Grandma?"

"Mary, it's alright if it is, and it's alright if it's not."

"I guess that's what you'll be doing for the rest of your life, Mama, because they're going to let you do just that."

"I will gladly do that, Charlotte but it won't be forever. Little Mac will grow up." Now, I think we need to talk about the church picnic. I know Mr. Nash said that he would furnish everything, but shouldn't we take something, too?'

John, who was listening at Charlotte and Elena's confrontation, chimed in, "Grandma, you can bake some of your teacakes."

"You're right, John. I can bake two or three batches of my famous teacakes. I know the children will enjoy them."

"The grown-ups will, too, Grandma."

"I will have a chance to bake them in our new home, too."

"Speaking of our new home, y'all need to start getting things together to take to our new home. It's nice for the men to build our home, but I think it's too much to ask them to help us move, too."

"We can start moving the lightweight things tomorrow, Mama. We have about three more weeks before the picnic, and I believe we can have everything moved by that time."

"I have all of my things together," Mary said.

"Me, too." Dorothy added.

"Whoopi! Ya'll mean that y'all are already packed. All of those dresses are ready to go?" John teased. "Then, we can get everything out in about two or three days. I kept all of my things together in a box. I can move everything I own in one trip."

20

Elena, Charlotte, and her family had most of their belongings packed and ready to load the wagon. They crammed their belongings in their wagon with only one trip. "It's good that we don't have to walk from one house to another." Elena said.

"Our mules have served us well, Mama. The men also built them a barn, and I know they'll like their new home, too."

"We need to get on the move," John said. "Just standing around talking about moving won't get us anywhere."

"I agree with you, John." Elena said. "Ya'll know we have to sleep here tonight, because we can't take the beds with us. Anyway, we'll take what we can and come back for the night."

"We're ready to move, Mama. The wagon is packed with the things that we can carry on our wagon."

"How are we going to thank the men for building our new home, Grandma?"

"Dorothy, that is something we can do Sunday at church."

"Who's going to do the talking, Grandma?"

"It's not going to be a long speech. Would you like to do the thanking?"

"No, Grandma. I'm not a speaker. I believe John can speak for us. Can't you, John?"

"If I have to, I will, Dorothy. Let's get moving to our new home. The mules are ready."

"Let's go." John demanded. "Let's get this first load in our new home. They rushed to the wagon and climbed in.

When everyone was seated in the wagon, John yelled, **"Haw."** The mules obeyed and turned left. When they reached the road, John yelled, **"Hee,"** and they obeyed again, and turned right. He steered them to their new home. **"Haw"**, John yelled, and the mules turned left toward their barn.

"We're here, Grandma. I will stake the mules here near the house, until we unload the wagon. When everything is out, I will see if they're going to like their new home. I think the barn will keep them dry and safe."

"Since they're not staying here tonight, why not do that tomorrow. Don't confuse them."

"I was just thinking about that," Mary said. "They don't seem to be hard to please but that might confuse them."

"Hurry, and let's move in, Charlotte said.

"Do you know if the doors are unlocked?"

"I have the keys, Grandma."

"I knew you would have everything we need, John. You're just like your daddy."

"And I want to be like him, Grandma."

After John had staked the mules, He helped Elena out of the wagon. The others, including Charlotte, got out, too."

John stood at the door, holding the keys in his hands. Elena and Charlotte stood motionless behind him. Mary and Dorothy sat on the front of the porch with their legs hanging down to the ground.

"Well, what do we do?" John asked. No one answered. He inserted the key into the keyhole, and turned it. The door opened immediately. "Grandma, why don't you be the first to go inside our new home? I have seen it."

"I want Charlotte to be the first to enter our new home." Elena said.

"If y'all don't know whose going in first, I'll go in." Dorothy said, and she jumped up from the side of the porch."

"Me. Too." Mary said, and she joined Dorothy.

John opened the door wider and went into the living room. "Y'all come on in. We don't have all day. What are you waiting on?"

Elena went inside and was followed by Charlotte, Houston, Dorothy and Mary.

"Whoopi," they all yelled.

"I knew the house would be wonderful, but not this wonderful," Charlotte said.

"They put a lot of love in building this home for us, Charlotte." Elena said.

"We'll, have a lot of thanks to give them, when we go to church Sunday." Charlotte turned around and around, spreading her arms as she spoke. "They gave our freedom back to us and built this wonderful home. We will forever be in their debt."

"I don't think they want us to call it a debt, Charlotte." Elena said. "They will know, however, that we're truly grateful. Let's unload."

"We only brought clothing and soft things in the wagon. We will have to figure out how to bring the furniture and the cook stove and the potbellied stove in the living room. We can't lift those things ourselves." John said.

"I hadn't thought of that," Charlotte said. "It will take a whole lot of men to lift those things on the wagon. Our wagon might not be strong enough to bring those things, anyway."

"Mama, let me go and talk to Mr. Nash. He said we could have everything in that house. He just might know how we can carry them."

"Let's unload the wagon, now, and then we can think about the heavy things," Mary said.

"I will talk to Mr. Nash about those things tomorrow or this evening, when we go back." John said.

"John, you do what you think is best. So far, you haven't made a mistake, so we trust you."

"Thanks, Grandma. Now, that we have everything is our new home, Let's get back into the wagon, and head home."

When they reached, home, John staked the mules and ran to Mr. Nash's market. Mr. Nash was outside near the front door. "Good evening, Mr. Nash, I was just coming to talk to you."

"It looks like you have just about taken care of everything, John. What do you want to talk about?"

"Mr. Nash, you once said that we could have all of the furniture in this house. We appreciate that, but we're trying to figure out how to get these big things; like the stoves and beds out and onto our wagon. They might be too heavy for our wagon, too, but we sure do need them."

"John, your wagon can't carry those heavy things, like the stoves. Y'all can take some of the furniture, but I have a crew that works for me. I can get them to use their flatbed wagon and load those things tomorrow morning. They work early, so y'all will have to be up early and ready to go about eight o'clock. It will also take several loads, so be patient with them.""

"Don't worry, Mr. Nash we can do that. Mr. Nash, how big is your crew?"

"It varies, John. It depends on how big the load is. I think six or ten strong men can do the lifting. With your wagon carrying the lighter things, y'all can be moved before Sunday."

"Why before Sunday, Mr. Nash."

"My men don't work on Sunday, so everything you plan to have moved, you have to do it tomorrow."

"We will be up and ready by eight o'clock, Mr. Nash. I will run home and let them know."

"Walk, John. Stop running everywhere."

"Yes sir." John walked a few steps, and then, he began to run. Mr. Nash looked at him and smiled, shook his head and walked toward his market.

When John reached their new home, he began to shout, "We got help!"

The family opened the door and walked toward John. "What did you say?" Charlotte asked.

"Mr. Nash has a crew of men who can lift the heavy stuff, like the stoves. He said it would take six or eight men to lift those stoves. One of his crew members has a flatbed truck, and it's strong enough to take heavy things. We can start packing our clothing and bedding and pack our wagon this evening. His men will be ready to begin loading tomorrow morning at 8 o'clock, so we have to be up and ready to move by that time."

"You did a good job, John." Charlotte said. "Let's see if the mules are ready to go again. We can load up everything tonight."

"Keep out a few pillowcases, so we can stuff some belongings in them. I think the pillowcases will hold a lot."

"That's a good idea, Grandma," Mary said.

"Let's go to the mules and get them ready for another heavy trip. After we move this time, they can have a long rest. They have a wonderful field where they can eat, and a stream nearby to drink all the water they want."

"You're right Mama," Charlotte said. The men who built this home couldn't have found a better place for us and our mules. It seems as if they thought of everything."

"They did, but all that they didn't think of, we can do the rest," John said. "Let's go, but Dorothy and Mary, don't use all of the pillowcases." He teased.

"How can we use all of the cases?" Dorothy asked.

"Y'all have lots and lots of dresses. I doubt if we have enough cases for everyone."

"We got them here, John." Mary said.

"Barely." John teased. "Let's go to the mules."

Dorothy and Mary began to run to the barn. "We'll beat y'all there." Dorothy said.

"Y'all just run on," Elena said. "I'll get there later."

"One more thing," John said. When we bring our clothing and other belongings, we can come back and get bedding, such as quilts and mattresses. The men can load our three beds, slats and dresser on their flatbed truck. When we get all of the heavy stuff loaded in our new house, we can come back and clean up."

"It seems like you've got everything planned just right, John. We can do that."

"Let's go and get on our way." John said.

"Hee Haw", John commanded the mules.

John guided the family through all of the moving. He knew what to take and what to leave for Mr. Nash's crew to bring. By eight o'clock all of their things were loaded. They went into the rooms and looked around. "I'm going to miss this old house," Elena said.

"Me, too, Mama, but it served us well. Now, maybe it will give the same help to someone else."

"I hope they won't have to be slaves to get that service." Dorothy said.

"They won't," Elena said. "John, we must send a telegram to Mac and Anna. I know they think we've forgotten them."

"Grandma, I will do that Monday morning. We will have at least one night of sleep in our new home, and I know they'll want to know how everything worked out."

"We can wait until Monday, John."

"Thanks, Grandma."

Saturday morning, at eight o'clock, Mr. Nash's crew was on in front of their home. Two of the eight men rode inside the wagon with the driver, and the other sat on the flatbed truck with their legs hanging towards the ground.

Elena went to the front door, and she called John. "They're here, John."

"I see them, Grandma. I will go to them.

John looked out the door and saw several large men sitting on the truck. "Come, look, Grandma."

"I see them, John. They seem to be big enough to do the job."

John went to the wagon to greet the men. "Good morning, y'all right on time. Get out and go inside with me." He said pleasantly.

They got out of the cab section and the men stepped down from the flatbed and followed John. John was average size, about five feet nine, but these men made him look like a little kid. They were over six feet, stout, and Elena called them burly.

When the eight men entered the house, they looked around as to size up everything. It seems as if they knew exactly what to load. John, and his family stood in awe at their strength. Within forty minutes. Their flatbed truck was loaded with the stoves, beds and heavy pieces and ready to go. The men who rode on the flatbed to the house, also rode among the heavy load, going to their new home.

"Haw", the leader of the crew yelled to the mules. The mules turned left from the house. When they reached the dirt road, he yelled, "Hee" and they turned right. His last command was, "Hee Haw" and they went straight ahead. John and his family got into their wagon and followed them.

It was clear to the Frazier family, that this was a crew with few or no words. When they reached the new home, the crew staked their wagon and unloaded the beds and stoves. Elena was inside to show them where the things were to be placed. When everything was properly placed, the crew went toward the door to leave.

Elena stopped them. "We want y'all to know that we appreciate everything you did for us this morning. Our church picnic will be in three more weeks, so please attend, there will be plenty of food, and I am baking my famous teacakes, so please come.

"Thank you, we will." They replied. They went to their wagon, got in and on the flatbed, and left with a **"Hee Haw."**

21

"Grandma, how do you like it?"

"John, things couldn't be better. This is a home. We can live here forever." She turned around and then around again. "Yes, this is our home forever."

"Mama, do you like everything, too?"

"It couldn't have been better, John, and you did such a wonderful job in getting all of this done."

"I know it's okay with Houston, but what about you, Dorothy and what about you, Mary."

"We like everything, John. We couldn't have had a better brother." Mary waved her arms around. "You've have made all of this possible."

"The next thing in order, is to get these beds made. We have plenty of clean sheets and pillowcases. I don't think all of the pillowcases were used to store things for moving. There should be enough for a while."

"This house was built over a well, so we have well water in the house. Those men thought of everything."

Charlotte ran to the faucet and turned it on over the hand -made sink. The water began to flow. Ooh and aahs were heard outside of the house. "I believe we're too loud for these neighbors." Charlotte said.

"What else do we need, Mama?"

"Nothing, John. I think all we need to do now is to make this look like a home, by making the beds."

"I will put a tablecloth on the kitchen table." She ran around to a box of kitchenware and pulled out a tablecloth. "There are a few other items that can be dressed up with some type of covering, but I'll take care of that. When we come home tomorrow from church, it will feel great coming into our new home." Elena said.

"It won't take long before we have this place looking great. We can do it." Dorothy said.

"Let's get moving. What are we waiting on?"

Dorothy looked out of her bedroom window. "The neighbors are coming out to see what all the fuss is about."

"They were looking all of the time, but they were inside, perhaps looking out of windows. They didn't want their new neighbors to know that they were nosy." Mary said.

"We're going to be the best neighbors they've ever had."

"Absolutely, John." Charlotte said.

As John gathered his bed linen, he noticed that everyone else was just standing around and gawking and walking around starring at the living room. He walked to the living room. He went to them. "What are y'all waiting on? Let's get to work. Grandma, you have time to cook our first meal. It is almost 12 o'clock."

"I believe you're right, John. Let me get started. The men were able to bring the ice box with our food inside. Let me look and see if it's okay." Elena went to the icebox opened the door, and everything was good. "Y'all are going to have the best meal cooked in Marion County." She closed the icebox.

"We know that Grandma," Dorothy said. "I can hardly wait."

"I'm going to cook Sunday meal, too. Y'all know I don't cook on Sunday."

"I know that Grandma." John said. "While you're cooking, I'll go to the train station. We might have some mail."

"Who would be writing us here in Marion County?" Charlotte asked.

"That's why I want to go and find out, Mama."

"Then, go ahead." Charlotte said.

103

John rushed out the door, and as usual, he ran all the way to the train station. When he entered the station, he was greeted with friendly voices, "Come on in John. I know you want all of this mail that's been here for days."

"That is why I'm here." He wiped the sweat from his brow. "We've had so many other things to do, until I clearly forgot the mail." He gathered the mail from the box and rushed out the door. As he trotted home, he looked through the mail and noticed that there was a letter from Natchitoches, Louisiana, and it was addressed to Elena. Oh, this is for Grandma. It's from, Grandma's cousin, so he ran home as fast as he could.

When he reached home, he flung the door opened, and almost breathless, he said, "Grandma, this is for you."

"What is it, John?"

"It's from your cousin, Helen. I didn't open it."

"Opened it and let's see what she's saying."

"Okay, Grandma." He tore it opened.

"Don't tear it apart, John."

"I won't, Grandma." He began to read.

Dear Cousin Elena,

You mentioned about coming to visit. Well, you're so welcome. My daughter, Maggie and her old man broke up, and she and her three children are here with me. She has three very fine children; a girl who is 8 and two boys. One is 11 and the oldest is 13. We have plenty room, so come on when you can.

Love,
Helen

"Well, Helen just helped me to make up my mind."

"What was on your mind, Mama?"

"Charlotte, there is no way that I'm going to raise another set of children. I might visit for a week or two, but that's all."

"When are you leaving, Grandma?"

"Mary, I haven't figured that out, yet, but I'm in no hurry. While y'all are sitting at the table, get your plates and forks out so you can eat. We have to get our clothes ready for church for tomorrow. I know they're plenty wrinkled in those pillowcases."

They quickly got their plates and tableware. "I'm ready for some food, Grandma."

"You deserve some food, John. You have done so much this week. You need to stop running and try walking. You won't get so tired."

"I'll try, Grandma."

Elena put the pots and a pan of corn bread on the table. "Y'all can pass you plates to me, and I'll dish up your food, if you want me to help you."

"That's alright, Mama. I will fix Houston's plate, and ya'll can pass your plates to me, and I'll fill them, too."

"Mama, are you going to speak for us tomorrow?"

"If you want to speak, Charlotte, you can."

"No ma'am. I just wanted to know. We need to let them know how grateful we are for their help. Also, the men who built our new home need to be thanked, too."

"Charlotte, if I'm going to speak, I know just how to do that, and who to thank."

"We know that Grandma," John said, and the other nodded in agreement.

"Grandma, when are you going to visit Aunt Anna and Uncle Mac?'

"Mary, I haven't worked that out, yet, but I will be worked that out with them. I want to be sure that y'all are in school, and Houston is in the nursery at school. I heard that school would start this year in September instead of November."

"I like that better. I don't see why it had to be in November anyway."

"Charlotte, it's because, the farmers wanted to make sure that their crops were picked, and the land prepared for the next planting."

"Well, that makes sense, but it was keeping the children further behind." Charlotte said.

"I think y'all need to hurry and eat, so y'all can get your clothes pressed and ready for church. The smoothing irons are on the stove and hot enough to begin pressing your clothes."

"I'll start and supervise that project, Mama."

"Well, Charlotte it's all yours. Y'all hurry and get those things that you're wearing tomorrow to church. Be sure to hang them in our new closet. I already have my church wear ready."

22

Sunday morning was the usual events. Everyone rose at 6:30, except Elena. She rose at six o'clock and had breakfast nearly ready for the family. "Y'all don't be late for our first Sunday morning, breakfast in our new home." She went to the front door and looked out toward the neighborhood. "I believe everyone is still sleeping, but I couldn't sleep. I was restless all night."

"What are you worried about, Grandma, the speech you're going to make this morning?"

"No, John. I have made enough speeches in my lifetime. They don't bother me."

"Since church is at eleven o'clock, I'll wait and put on my dress around ten o'clock."

"I will, too, Dorothy." Mary said.

"I know my sisters will be the most beautiful girls there."

"That's because you see us through brother's eyes."

"No, Dorothy, I know you and Mary are beautiful, and your behavior is outstanding, too. There will be some boys at church with their families, just like I'm with my family, but don't fall for them. We have to complete our schooling, before we think of love outside the family."

"That's good advice, John." Charlotte said. "I couldn't have said it any better myself. She sat Houston in a chair near her chair. Now, everything is on the table, so sit so we can bow our heads, say our blessings and began eating.

John looked at Houston and brushed his hair back from his face. "Little brother, you look good in that blue suit, and white shirt. Let me see your shoes, too." He stepped back to look like Houston raised one foot.

"See? They are blue, too, and I have white socks."

"Yes, you do. I don't have to tell you about the birds and bees, yet. When that day comes, I will tell you the same thing that I tell Mary and Dorothy."

"I like birds, John, but I don't like the bees. They sting."

"That's what I'm worried about, it's their sting. You won't have to worry about that for a long time."

Houston crawled up on his chair with Charlotte's assistance. I'm ready now, Grandma."

"So is everybody else, so let's begin." She had everyone to bow their heads while she said a long prayer.

"Whee! I hope the food is still hot, Grandma."

"You can eat it, Dorothy. This is a special day to give thanks.

"What are you wearing, Mama?"

"John, I have a new pink suit that I haven't worn before, and since I don't gain weight, I can still wear it."

"I think we will all be in pink this morning."

"I don't think so, Mary. My two-piece dress is blue. I made it myself two months before we came here."

"Houston is the only one dressed, so I think I had better get my suit and tie on, too. It's going to take you girls a long time to dress. I think you need to get started now."

"John, we have more than two hours before the eleven o'clock service. Are we going to walk, or are you taking the mules?"

"I'm taking the mules, Dorothy; however, we can walk. We're not that far from the church."

"John, I'm not walking. I've walked enough in all of my years. I'm slowing down, now."

They all laughed. "Grandma, I don't mind taking the wagon. It's time for it to be moved, and the church has plenty space in the back to hitch wagons. Our mules will be happy to be on the road again."

"When we get back, John, I want to send a telegram to Anna and Mac. I know they're waiting to hear from us, and I will send one to my sister, tomorrow."

"Alright, Grandma. He went to his bedroom, and dressed in his blue suit, black tie and black shoes, and went to the kitchen where the family had gathered.

"Whoo! John, you look handsome in your suit."

John at five feet and nine inches tall, was thin and handsome like his father. He was aware of his good looks, too.

"Thanks, Grandma. I'm going to get the wagon, and y'all can come out the front door. I will have the mules come as close to the house as possible."

"We'll be there, John." Charlotte said.

When John had the mules in front of the house, Mary and Dorothy came out first. He looked at his sisters, in their pink dresses, and waist length hair streaming down their backs. He knew they were beautiful, but he worried about the boys who would see them, too. His desire for his sisters, was to get their education, before thinking about boys. Elena, Charlotte and Houston followed the girls to the wagon and carefully climbed in.

"Is everybody in?" John asked. "Y'all look so good this morning. I know the church will be glad that we're there. I have some change for the collection. What about y'all?"

"We all have a little, John, so let's get on the way."

"Alright, Grandma. Hee Haw," he yelled to the mules. The mules moved straight ahead until they got to the corner of the block. "Hee", he yelled to them, and they turned right. "Hee Haw," he yelled, and they went straight ahead. "I see the church from here, Grandma. We will go to the back and settled the mules, and we'll walk around to the front and go in. I believe they have ushers, so we'll have to let the ushers seat us." His final yell was Haw, and the mules turned left into the rear of the church.

109

"We're here, but y'all stay in until I get the mules staked to that iron rod."

Members were walking toward the church to enter, but they noticed people that they hadn't seen before, so the men tipped their hats and the women bowed to the new family.

"This is a beautiful morning," one of the ladies said.

"Yes, ma'am, it is." John replied.

"Are y'all going inside to our church?"

"Yes, sir. We are." Charlotte said.

"Well, y'all follow us. We'll wait until you get your mules settled."

"Yes, sir. John motioned his family to follow him, as they walked behind the members.

When they entered the church, they noticed that the church was nearly packed with their members. "We'll sit here on the back row", John said to the usher. "Thank you", he added.

She stepped back until they were all seated on the back row. Moments later, the usher went to the front of the congregation, and waved her hands up and down for audience to be seated. After all were seated, she went to the rear of the church and stood at the door.

The pianist walked in from the side of the choir stand and sat at the piano and began playing. **WHAT A FRIEND WE HAVE IN JESUS.** The choir members march in and stood behind Pastor Ross. The twelve members were dressed in black and white. The women wore white dresses, and the men wore black pants and white shirts with black ties. Their harmonies were deep and rich as they sang out loudly over the piano. At the end of **WHAT A FRIEND WE HAVE IN JESUS,** Pastor Ross beckoned the audience to sit down. He looked at the back row to his right and nodded in recognition to the Frazier family.

At the end of the hymn, Pastor Ross greeted the audience with his usual greeting, "I'm glad to see y'all here this morning to worship in the Lord's house." Pastor Ross didn't believe in wasting time. He began his forty-five minutes sermon. At the end of the sermon, he said," The doors of the church are opened.' This was an invitation to join the church as new members. "Anyone who so desire to worship with us, just walk right up and take a seat."

"I guess the next thing in order is the usher's report." He nodded to the usher who was standing by the back door.

She walked up to the front and stood in front of the altar. "Good morning, everyone. We don't have any guests this morning, but we have a family who wants to say a few words to our congregation." She nodded to the Frazier family. "They will tell us what they want us to know." Everyone clapped out of respect to the family.

"Y'all can come on up or stay where y'all are and tell us what y'all want us to know." Pastor Ross said.

Elena stood. The others sat rigidly, wondering what she was going to say. She stood out by the pew, with her hands clasped in front, and for a few moments, she didn't say anything. Her family began to stir and look at each other. They had never seen Elena lost for words. John motioned to stand, but Dorothy pulled him back. "Wait." She said.

Elena began a hum that lasted about twenty seconds. Her family became concern about her. John motioned to get up again, but this time, Charlotte pulled him back.

Elena began walking slowly toward the front and began to sing: O Lord my God, when I in awesome wonder,

Consider all the worlds they hands have made.

(She waved her hands about and continued to sing.)

I see the stars, I hear the rolling thunder,

Thy power throughout the universe displaced.

When she reached the front of the altar, she said to the congregation, "This is how I feel today and every day. My family and I are here with you as free people. You saw a need and you didn't ask any questions. You came and set us free with your days of work on Mr. Nash's farm. Because of you, we're free. We're here to worship with you and give our thanks for your help. We couldn't have done it without you."

The church members nodded and said "amens" during her speech.

"Thank you again," She began walking towards the rear to join her family, and singing:

Then sings my soul, my Savior God to Thee.

How great thy art, how great Thy art.

The congregation joined Elena and completed the other two verses. The four-part rich harmony seemed to have permeated through the walls, and through the four corners of the church. At the end of **HOW GREAT THOU ART,** Pastor Ross said to the family, "Y'all are truly welcome, and that God is truly great. It was an honor to help y'all. Come back and join our choir sometime. There's plenty room."

When Elena sat down beside John, he grabbed her hand and said, "Good job, Grandma."

At the end of service, church members gathered around the Fraziers and praised them for being members of their church and invited them to take part in their church activities.

When they went to their wagon and all were seated, John yelled "Haw" to the mules.

"Where are we going, John?" Charlotte asked.

"Train station."

"Why?"

"Mama, we might have something from Uncle Mac and Aunt Anna."

"Let's go, then," Elena said.

"Mama. We were so proud of you. I was surprised when you began singing."

"Me, too," Dorothy and Mary added.

23

"I knew Grandma could do it. I wasn't surprised." John said. "We're here." He walked toward the station, as the others remained in the wagon. When John entered the station, the young man behind the counter greeted him.

"Hi, John. I see you here again, and yes you do have some mail. Your family gets more mail than anyone else in Marion County." He handed a small package to John. "Here it is."

John looked at it. "Thank you. My Grandma is going to be happy to get this letter."

"What's special about that letter, John?"

"It's from special friends."

"Then you'd better rush home and give it to the family."

John went to the wagon. When he got into the wagon, he and gave the letter to Elena.

"John, why don't you open it and read it to us all. I don't have any secrets from my family."

"Alright, Grandma." He opened it and read:

Dear Elena,

I hope all is well with you and family.

We are doing just great, especially since we found out that we are going to have a baby.

Elena shouted, "What?" She jumped and rocked back and forth. "What did you just say, John?"

"There's more, Grandma."

"What else?" She asked. "Hurry, what else?

"The baby will be here between Christmas and New Year. It will probably be here in 1887. Anna and I wish you can come. You can come anytime you want to. We have your room nice and clean just like you left it. You will be coming back home."

Mac.

"Grandma, are you going?"

"Yes, I am, John."

"When, Mama?" Charlotte asked.

"As soon as I can, Charlotte, but I will wait until school starts, and know that ya'll are safe and well."

"Who's going to be here to help me with everything?"

"Charlotte, for the first time in your life, you will have to take care of your family, because I will go to be with Anna and Mac."

"I guess I'll have to do everything myself," she said pitifully.

"You have the best help that anyone mother could have. You have three older children who can help you with Houston. You can still go to work while they're in school. I don't know that kind of help I can give you that your children can't give you."

"They're going to be busy with their studies and too busy to help with Houston."

"Houston is four years old, now. He knows what **do**, and **don't** mean. If he gets confused about the two, then it's your responsibility to teach him. You will have a chance to be a mama. I will remain with Anna and Mac as long as they need me, and John, I need you to send them my reply."

"Yes, Grandma."

"Tell them to let me know about when the baby is due. I want to be there when it is born."

"Let's take everybody home, Grandma. After we eat, I will take you back to the train station, and we will send a message to Uncle Mac and Aunt Anna."

"Can't we go?" Mary asked.

"Me, too." Dorothy said.

"Y'all don't need to go to the station just for that." John said.

When the meal was over, John and Elena went to the barn to get the wagon.

Elena gathered the hem of her dress, while he helped her in the wagon. When he stepped inside, he sighed. "Ah, Grandma, you do what you want to do. If you want to go and visit Uncle Mac and Aunt Anna, you do that, and stay as long as you want to. Mary, Dorothy and I can help Mama with Houston and the house.

"That is so kind of you, John. I believe Mac and Anna will need some help. They don't have a family near, and the family that they know don't keep in close contact with them."

John steered the mules out of the barn, steered them to the dusty road, and yelled, **"Haw."** They turned left toward the train station. "Was there a falling out in the family, Grandma?"

"I don't know, John. I have known Mac and Anna for many years. They were just young, almost like kids when they moved near us. I believe they had just married. They never went back."

"Back where, Grandma?"

"I don't know. I never asked them about their family. I didn't think it was my business."

"I don't think you would be prying, if you asked them about their family. Soon or later, someone will have to know. They just might want to talk about their family, but don't know how to start."

"John, you could be right. I just might do that someday."

"Hee," John yelled to the mules, and they turned right, and John steered them to the rear of the station. "I will stake them by this pole, Grandma, and we can go in that side door. It won't take long to send a short message."

"I don't know what I would do without you, John. You are so much help to me and the rest of the family."

John stepped down from the wagon and walked around the other side to help Elena down. "It didn't take long for us to get here. When we get settled in our new home, we will write letters. We can say more in a letter, and they're cheaper, too."

"I can do that, but I haven't written a letter in a long time, but to save money, I'll go back to writing."

John led Elena inside the train station. The young man who noticed John, again.

"I see you're back, John. What can I help you do today?"

"I want to send a telegram." John said.

"Alright. I will get the forms and pen for you. I don't think we have them out on the tables, but they should be there." He went behind the counter to get the equipment that John needed to send a telegram. He walked to John. "Here you are, John."

"Thank you." John said as he received the material. "Grandma, we can sit over here by the window, and you can tell me what you want Uncle Mac and Aunt Anna to know."

They sat down by the table. John took the forms and pen, and began writing,"

Dear Mac and Anna,

It was a surprise to hear of the baby. Let me know when you need me, and I will be there as soon as possible."

With all of my love,

Elena

"Are you writing the letter already, John?"

"Yes, Ma'am. You told me yesterday, what you wanted them to know, so I made it short and quick." He read the message to Elena. "Is that what you want them to know, Grandma?"

"You got a good memory, John, because that is exactly what I want them to know. When I get there, I can tell them more." She reached inside her purse to get some money.

"Don't worry about paying, Grandma." I will take care of that." He walked to the counter and gave the message to the young man behind the counter. How much is that?' You know, I am in here a lot, and I don't know your name."

"It's Samuel, but call me Sam. That's what everybody calls me."

"Alright Sam." He opened his pouch and gave him two or three coins. "I believe this is what you said it was. When will she get the telegram?"

"John, the telegram will perhaps reach the receiver before y'all get home."

"Well, we're on our way." He walked to Elena, and she stood when she saw him walking towards her.

"Are you through?"

"Yes, Grandma, and Aunt Gloria might have the telegram before we get home."

"Really?" She said joyfully.

"That's what Sam said.

"You know his name?"

"I'm in here so much, Grandma, I asked him his name, because he knew my name already."

They walked out the side door to the wagon.

"I noticed that Sam rubbed his right side, as if it was hurting. He probably lifted something too heavy for him."

"That's probably what happened." Elena said.

"Wait, Grandma, let me help you in. I hope everything is okay at home with Mama and the girls. I don't want them to start their families' young. I don't want them to wait as long as Uncle Mac and Aunt Anna, either, but I want them to be married." He laughed.

"I don't want them to wait that long either. I gave up on Mac and Anna having a baby, but the baby wasn't ready. I want to be there when it ready."

"You will, Grandma. I do some work at Mr. Nash's market every day, and I have saved enough money to help you on your way. After I finish my last year, I will perhaps be there, too."

"Whoa", John said to the mules, and he unhitched the wagon and helped Elena in. He got in and steered them to the road.

"Hee". He yelled, and the mules turned right. **"Hee Haw"**, He yelled again, and they went straight ahead toward their new home.

"I think these mules are going to enjoy their new home, don't you, John?"

"It looks like it, Grandma. I sure enjoy mine."

When John steered the mule's home, he saw Dorothy and Mary standing across the road talking to some boys of the neighborhood. They were turning and swaying and enjoying their conversation. Dorothy looked away and saw John. She tried to compose herself and look casual. John yelled, **"Hee"**. And the mules turned right and went toward the barn. "Whoa." he yelled at them again, and they stopped.

"Grandma, I'm letting you out here, and I will lead the mules to the barn. It only a few steps away, so you can wait on me."

"I don't like what I see, John, but I will wait and keep my mouth shut for the time being."

"I won't keep my mouth shut, Grandma. This is too soon. I know what those boys wants, and we're not ready for that yet."

"Do you think I should postpone my trip to Mac and Anna, John?"

"No, Grandma, you go right to them. I can take care of things here."

John and Elena had to walk pass Dorothy and Mary as they walked toward their home. "Y'all come on home," He said to them.

"We'll be on John, in a minute or two." Dorothy said.

"I need y'all to come on now," he demanded.

"Mama knows that we're out here." Mary said. "If it's okay with her, why are you bothered?"

John kept walking toward home. When he entered, he said to Charlotte, "Mama, this just might be harmless., but I don't like what I see."

"What do you see?"

"Mama, look out the door. What do you see?"

"Some youngsters, your sisters and some boys just talking."

"Shouldn't they be in here with you and Houston, Mama?"

"I don't see anything wrong with what they're doing, John."

"It's harmless, John." She said. "You act as if they are to be saints and never talk to boys. They are just having fun. That's all."

"Well, that's how we got started."

Elena took Houston from Charlotte's lap. "It's time for this boy to sit by himself. He's four years old, now. When he goes to the nursery school, the teachers aren't going to hold him in their laps.

"That's true, but John, what did you mean when we you said, that's how we got started?"

I know that you and dad got married, but I was born seven months after y'all got married. That's what I meant by that."

Charlotte doubles her right hand into a fist and aimed it toward John. Elena, with her five feet and two inches, grabbed Charlotte's arm and swung her onto the sofa. John jumped back to miss her fist in case it passed Elena.

"Don't you ever think about hurting John. He is the backbone of this family. He's just seventeen and that is too young to bear all of these responsibilities. You need to help him instead of trying to hurt him."

"I'm alright, Grandma. When you go to Uncle Mac and Aunt Anna, I will be there real soon. It seems like Mama's got everything under control here."

"I don't have everything under control, John, but I didn't like what you were saying."

"Sometimes, Charlotte, the truth hurts. No matter who says it. What John said is true. He wants the best for his sisters."

Dorothy and Mary came inside. They say everyone close together. "What's going on?" Dorothy asked.

"Why are y'all outside and why are you still wearing your church clothes?'

"We're just getting home, Grandma. We're going to pull them off."

"I know that y'all are going to pull them off. That's not the question. Why haven't you pulled them off?"

Dorothy and Mary rushed by the huddle. "Where y'all going? John asked.

"To our room," Dorothy said. "You act like you are our papa,"

"No, Dorothy, I wouldn't wish that on anyone, but we do need some rules here, otherwise our family's going to fall apart." He sat down at the table.

"John is right." Charlotte said. "Y'all go and pull those clothes off. When we come home from church from now on, y'all come inside with the family. If those boys want to talk to y'all, they'll have to get permission. That's the way it's going to be from now on. Do y'all understand?" She said in a demanding voice.

"Yes, 'am they said.

"John?"

"Yes, ma'am, Grandma."

"The way you spoke to your mother was wrong. People know their mistakes, because we all make them at one time or another, so you don't have to rub it in. Do you hear what I'm saying?" She said quietly.

"Yes, Grandma."

"Then you go in the bedroom where she is and do the right thing."

John obeyed her orders. He went in the bedroom where Charlotte was sitting on the side of the bed. It looked as if she had been crying. Her eyes were red, and her cheeks were wet with tears. He sat on the bed beside her and put his arms around her. "Mama, I am so sorry about saying what I said. I just don't want Dorothy and Mary get involved with guys and miss their education."

"You and I will work together, John, to make sure that they don't miss their education. You go to the girls and make peace with them, too. Let them know that you are worried about them, and want them to be concerned about their education, too."

"I'm on my way, Mama, to talk to Dorothy and Mary." Dorothy and Mary were sitting on stools by their bed. It was obvious that they were crying, too.

"How are y'all doing, now?"

"After you are doing what you did, how should we be doing?" Mary asked.

"Y'all are my sisters, and I don't want anything to happen to you. I will always be concerned about what y'all are doing. You don't stand out in the street or corner talking to boys. Y'all are disrespecting yourselves when you do that. If those boys have good manners, they will come to the house and ask if they could talk to y'all."

"What could happen to us out there in the street, John?"

"Dorothy, it was innocent, but it could someday lead to something that's not innocent and being on the streets can lead to other places."

"What did Mama say?"

"She had the same feeling as you and Mary. It's been so long since she has dated, she's forgotten everything. Things will work out. I just know they will, and I promise." John walked back to the kitchen where Elena was seated at the kitchen table.

"How did it go, John?"

"It was just fine, Grandma." He looked out the kitchen door and noticed that the boys were still hanging around, as if they were waiting on Mary and Dorothy to come out. "I got one more thing to do, Grandma."

"What is that?"

"It's across the street."

She looked out as John was walking toward the boys. "Charlotte?" She called.

"Ma'am?

"Come here."

Charlotte rushed to the kitchen. "What is it?"

"Look out across the street."

"Why is John over there with those boys, Mama?"

"Those are the boys that Mary and Dorothy were talking to."

Charlotte noticed that the boys were just about as tall as John, but larger than John. Both of the boys had stringy, blonde hair. They looked well-dressed and respectful, but John just had to see for himself.

"What do you think he is saying to them, Mama?"

John waved at them as he turned to cross the street to his home.

"We'll soon know.

John came inside and saw Elena and Charlotte standing near each other, as if they were waiting on him. "I think everything is going to be alright from now on."

"What did you say to them? Elena asked.

"I told them not to stand around and about our home. If they wanted to speak to Mary and Dorothy, knock on the door, and someone will let them in. They can ask for Mary and Dorothy, and someone will call them. Our Grandma will allow y'all to sit at the table and talk. We have a back yard with two benches, where y"ll can sit and talk, but you can't talk to my sisters on street corners or in the streets."

"What did they say?"

"Grandma, they were very nice and polite. They asked if they could come by tomorrow and talk to Mary and Dorothy, and meet the family, too."

"I told them that they could come by, but it would be up to Mary and Dorothy if they wanted to talk."

"What did they say>"

"Mama, they nodded their heads, and I walked away."

"You did a good job." Elena said.

"Thanks, Grandma."

"I think you did a good job, also, John."

"Thanks, Mama." He looked toward the bedrooms, and saw Mary and Dorothy standing in the doorway.

"Mary and Dorothy, did you hear what I just said?"

"We heard everything, John. You don't need to repeat it, because we're going to go to school and get a good education. Yes, sir, we're going to get a good education." Dorothy assured John, in a teasingly manner. They all laughed and sat down at the table to eat, as Elena had ordered them.

"Where is Houston?"

"He's taking his nap, John." Charlotte said.

"That is exactly what I'm going to do, after I eat."

"That's something we all need to do, John. I know I can take a little rest. Y'all will need all you can get, because y'all go to school Monday."

"We sure do, Grandma. That's September 5th. I will be ready."

"I know you will, John."

24

On September 5th in 1868, John and his sisters were up at 6:30. Elena heard them moving about in their rooms. "What are y'all doing? School starts at 9 o'clock, you will have plenty of time to eat and get there."

"I know, Grandma, but I can't sleep anymore. I suppose I'm nervous about going to school."

"John, you knew this day was coming, didn't you?"

"Yes Ma'am, but I wasn't this close to the date."

"It's all the same. You go and learn and come back."

"I'll go and tell Lil 'Brother that. He's still sleeping."

"I hope you have good luck with that."

"Thanks, Grandma. I believe I will. I will wake Mama, too."

John went in Charlotte's bedroom, where she and Houston were still sleeping. "Rise and shine Lil' brother."

Charlotte turned over on her back. What's going on?" She asked.

"This is school day, Mama, and Lil' brother's going to see and meet some play mates today." He shakes Houston gently and say, "Rise and shine, Lil' brother."

Houston turned over on his back and asked, "Why?"

"You go to school today for the first time, and you will learn new things and meet new friends, but you have to get up now, so you can get dressed and eat your breakfast, before we go to learn and meet new friends."

Houston rubbed his eyes and turned over on his side to resume his sleep. "I don't want to go to school to learn new things and meet new friends, John. You go."

"It won't be the same, Houston. Mama, you can get Houston up and ready for school. School begins at 9 o'clock and we want to be on time. If we walk to school, it will take about fifteen minutes, but if we take the mules, we can get there in about five or six minutes."

Charlotte sat up in bed and reached for her chenille robe. John walked to the kitchen and sat at the table. "It was hard work, Grandma, but I believe I got them up."

"Time will tell, John. Everything is ready. Do you want some coffee?"

"No, Grandma. I haven't started drinking coffee. I don't know if I want to begin drinking coffee, either."

"You will do just fine without it, John."

"I'll get up and put the plated on the table, by that time, I believe everyone will be ready. I heard Mary and Dorothy getting ready when I was in Mama's and Houston's room, but it takes longer for girls to get ready."

Elena began hitting a pan with a spoon. "Let's go, everybody."

"Grandma, what are you going to do when we're in school and Mama is at work? Won't you get lonesome being here by yourself?"

"I can find plenty to do, John. It might be pleasant jut being by myself. I haven't had that privilege in a long time."

Dorothy and Mary came to the kitchen." Good morning. We saw you earlier John, so I know you are alright."

"Good morning for me, too." Mary said. "Here comes Mama and Houston. He's all dressed for school." Mary said.

Houston was wearing blue pants and white pull over shirt. His black shoes were highly polished, and his wavy black hair was well brushed.

"You look might sharp, lil' brother," John said.

Houston turned around and around so they could see his clothes. "How do I look, Mama?" he asked.

"You look wonderful, Houston, but you always do." Charlotte said.

"Let's sit down while I say the blessing." Elena blessed the food and since here blessing wasn't as long as usual, they could eat and get an early start to school. "How are ya'll going to go to school? Are you going to walk or are you taking the wagon, John?"

"I will take the wagon, Grandma. We could walk, but it's too long for Houston."

"I can walk, John." Houston declared.

"Dorothy and Mary, what do y'all think? Do you want to walk or ride?"

"I see people walking every day, John. I don't see why we have to ride."

"Mary, if you want to try it today, we can. Li'l brother said that he could walk, too."

"Well, let's do it." Dorothy said.

"Stop talking about it and get on your way. First, wash your hands and wipe your mouth."

"Yes 'am, Grandma. "I'll take Lil' Brother's hand as we walk, just in case I have to pick him up. It's not really that far."

"Let's go, y'all." Mary shouted.

They exited the front door. There were a few other children walking to school, too. "I think we made a good choice." John said.

When they walked out the front door, Elena and Charlotte looked at them as they took their first step toward school. "That's a fine bunch of children you have, Charlotte." Elena said.

"It's because of you, Mama."

"But soon or later, Charlotte, it will be all up to you to see that they be good citizens."

"Now, that they are gone, Charlotte, I didn't know that it could be so quiet."

"It is indeed, Mama. I will go to work in another hour, and you will be alone, but I know how you can make some extra money and have fun doing it."

"How?"

There is a quilting "bee" shop beside the pottery shop. A group of ladies, about seven of them, gather every day and sew."

"How do they know what to sew?" Elena asked.

"I went inside one day and met the ladies. They showed their baskets to me. Inside each basket is a pattern of the squares, the designs are all cut and placed in a basket. Each lady has her own baskets, so when she goes into the shop. All she needs to do is get her baskets and begin to sew. They're usually working on the same quilt. When everyone has finished their baskets, they are ready to assemble it. They go to another room where all of the equipment that they need to put it together. They call it quilting."

"That sounds good to me. I believe I can do that. When do we go and meet the quilting ladies?"

"Tomorrow."

"What time tomorrow?" Elena asked.

"When we get the children off to school."

"How much do they pay?"

"They have a basket with cut outs to make ten or twelve patters of circles or squares. When you complete your baskets, you take it to the clerk, and she counts your patterns, and give you seven cents for each pattern. It's called piecing, Mama. When you have completed ten patterns, you will make seventy cents."

"When do they put the quilt together?"

"Mama, I don't know too much about quilting, but there is a room where women are sitting and over a gadget, where the backing of the quilt is stretched out. They put layers of padding over it, and then they lay the quilt pattern over it. The ladies have needle already threaded, and they begin to attach the layers. It looks easy, Mama."

"I'll try it tomorrow morning. I will fix my lunch and be ready to leave when the children go to school."

"We can all leave together. I got today off, because it's Houston first day at school, and I wanted to see him off, but I only got one day off, so I'll leave with you. We will be working almost side by side. I will be next door."

"What time will I get off?"

"Mama, you can get off whenever you get ready. You get paid only by the patterns you make in your baskets."

Sounds good and looks good. I can hardly wait. When do I pick the patterns?"

Mama, I have only seen two or three shapes, and they are squares, circles and rectangles."

"When and who put them together for the quilts?"

"When we get there, I will take you in a room where there are several Sewing machines. A woman is in front of each machine and pedaling with her feet, as she sews straight seams. There is a form for the quilts. You will see beautiful quilts hanging on the walls of that room. Those quilts were made by the women in the front room, where I showed you the baskets."

"I will meet some friends, there, too."

"Mama, the women don't have time to make friends. Their heads are down, looking at the seams that they are making. They are trying to complete their baskets by the end of the week, so they can get paid. The only time for talking, is during lunch time. They have one hour for lunch, and then back to work."

"I can do that, Charlotte. I think we'd better get back to the house, so I can begin dinner."

"Let's go. I got today off, because I wanted to see Houston off to school for the first time. You can come with me tomorrow morning, and I will introduce you to the group, and then I will rush to work."

"That sounds reasonable, Charlotte. Let's go home."

"I don't have tomorrow off, Mama, so you can go with me. I have to be at work at 9 o'clock, so we can go early enough for me to introduce you to the ladies in the sewing room."

"That sounds good enough for me. I can hardly wait to meet them."

"You will."

"I think we need to hurry home, so I can get dinner started. The children will be home from school soon."

"I saw another large room from the front entrance."

"That's the quilting room. You will see a quilt on each wall. When the ladies' complete patterns for a quilt, the patterns are passed on to that large room, where the ladies put them in the form of quilts."

"I want to go in that room and look at the quilts."

"We won't have long, Mama, because I have to go to work."

"You don't have to stay. Go on to work. I know how to get home."

"Are you sure."

"Yes, Charlotte, I do. Now, you go on to work, because I don't want to be rushed. I want to see those beautiful quilts."

"Alright, Mama. I'll see you sometime after three o'clock."

"I'm going inside the other room and see what the other ladies are doing on those machines."

"You will see beautiful quilts hanging on the walls. One day, you will see the one that you're working on."

"I hope so. You go on to work, and I will see you after you're off. It won't be too long before I leave. I will just peak inside the quilting room, and leave. I know those children will be starving when the get home."

Charlotte walked to the store to begin working. I'll see you later, Mama."

"Go on. I'll see you later. I'm going to the quilting room and look at those beautiful quilts, I see hanging on the walls. I can't see them all from here, so I'm going in."

When Elena walked into the quilting room, she saw five women at the sewing machines, peddling their feet on the bottom of the machine. Moving their feet back and forth on the pressers that gave power to the machine to function. They were so busy, no one looked up to see who had just walked in. She stood awhile and watched their dedication to their work. She looked at the walls and was a beautiful quilt on the wall beside her that had a title above the quilt that read: Riley Family Quilt. She was amazed at their feet moving back and forth on a gadget near the floor. They all seemed to have been in motion together.

After a few minutes of viewing the ladies and beautiful quilts, she left the room, and walked out through the main entrance, bowing to the ladies with the baskets, as she passed by. Elena walked past Charlotte's job at the market and went toward home. The walk was only ten minutes. When she reached home and open the door, she sat down and sighed. "I'm so glad to be home," she said in a loud voice. "But it is so quiet here alone, I can't take it another day. I will do whatever it takes to wait for tomorrow."

Elena changed her clothes, washed her hands and began making dinner. Once all pots were on the stove and cooking, she heard running and laughter coming her way. She looked out the kitchen door and noticed the path in front of her home was occupied with a few boys and girls of teen age level. School must be out and they're on their way home, she thought. Our children will be home soon.

Elena looked at the small clock on the kitchen table and noticed that is was time for the children to be on their way. It was five minutes after four o'clock. She was right. John Jr held Houston hands as Mary and Dorothy followed behind. They looked so happy, Elena thought. They must have had a great time at school today.

25

The first day of school in September 1868 was a joyous occasion. Houston came in with so much to tell, he couldn't tell it all in one sentence. "Take your time, Lil' brother." John Jr. said.

"Y'all come on in, wash up. Charlotte will be here soon, and we can all sit at the table and hear what Houston has to say." Elena said.

I believe I hear her coming now, Grandma. She's talking to someone across the road. I guess she's got a lot to tell, too."

"Everything is ready to be put on the table. I fixed a pot roast with new potatoes, turnip greens, sweet potatoes, corn bread and a few extras. This is a special day. After all, I have a new job, too."

"Doing what, Grandma?" Mary asked.

"Making quilts." She sat down at the table.

"We have enough quilts, Grandma." Dorothy said.

"These quilts will be for sale."

"I didn't know they sold quilts. I thought they were given away when people marry."

"No, Dorothy, they are for sale, too. I will teach you and Mary how to make quilts, too."

"No, thanks, Grandma. I can use what we have."

"When you marry, you will leave this house, and you will need quilts of your own."

"That's going to be a long time. I don't plan to marry soon."

"You have to find someone, first, Mary."

"John, I'm not looking."

"You have plenty of time, Mary. Take your time."

"I will, Grandma."

"Don't take too long." John said. Everyone burst out laughing.

Charlotte entered the front door to toward the kitchen. "What's going on in here?"

"Nothing much, Mama," Dorothy said.

"I told them about my new job." Elena said. "After you left me with the women, they told me, all I had to do was come in tomorrow morning and pick out a basket and begin to work on it. A pattern would be in each basket. If you can sew a straight seam, you can make quilts. I will leave every morning with you, Charlotte. I can also bring the basket home with me and sew here. The pays is only a few cents for each pattern, but I don't need a lot. I want to have enough when I visit Anna and Mac."

"Who will cook while you're gone, Grandma?"

"John, you all will not starve. Dorothy and Mary are taking home economics. They can do the cooking."

Houston began banging both fist on the table. "No, no, Grandma. They can't cook. They can't cook." He hit the table with his fist again.

"Give them a chance, Houston," Charlotte said. "Give them a chance. You have eaten their food before."

"No. I want to go with Grandma when she leaves."

"You will be in school, and you can't go." Charlotte said.

"Speaking of school, Houston. Didn't I see your teacher taking you to the principal's office this morning?" John asked.

"Yeah."

"Why?" Charlotte asked.

"That girl in front of me lets her plats fall on my desk, and I yanked both of them."

"What do you mean, 'both of them'?" Mary asked.

"Her plaits are long, and they hang all over my desk. I can't put my tablet on top of my desk. I have to move her hair to do my arithmetic."

"Well, the next time her plaits are on your desk, tell the teacher." John said.

"What did the principal do?" Mary asked.

"He said the same thing that Mama said. I have to tell the teacher."

"What is that girl's name, Houston?' Dorothy asked.

"June. Her name is June."

"Is she the little girl who was wearing a pink dress. She's the only one I saw with a pink dress on today."

"Yeah." Houston answered.

"Wow! She's pretty." John said. "Do you like pulling her hair."

"Yeah!" Houston answered with delight. "I like pulling her hair."

"I bet you do." John said. "But no matter how pretty June is, don't pull her hair."

"Don't pull her hair anymore." Charlotte demanded.

"Oh, shucks, I like pulling her hair."

"I mean it, Houston."

"Oh, alright, Mama. I won't pull her hair again." He said unconvincing.

"Now that that settles everything, let's eat." Elena said.

"I'm ready for that, Mama." Charlotte said. "We haven't had a pot roast in a long time."

"I know that." John said. "I am ready for everything on the table. Let's eat well, because when Grandma starts working, we might not see this during the week. I call this meal, Sunday meal." He waved his hands back and forth over the table.

"Do the women sell those quilts, Grandma?"

"The women don't sell them, they just piece them, but the store manager sells them, and the manager is Mr. Nash. I saw such beautiful quilts on the walls yesterday, and they all have names."

"Can you remember some of the names, Grandma?"

"I believe I can, John. I saw one named Peacock Quilt on the back wall, and beside it was Riley Family Quilt. I saw Prairie Star Patchwork quilt and Underground Railroad Quilt on the other two walls. The quilts seem to decorate the walls, because they are so beautiful. Charlotte, when we get to work tomorrow, let's go early, so you can see them, too."

"Do y'all have homework to do for school tomorrow?" Charlotte asked.

"I don't." John said. "I can help Houston with his A, B, C's."

"I know my A.B. C's. John. I learned them a long time ago."

"What about your arithmetic?"

"That's hard. You can help me with that."

"The dinner was delicious, Grandma, and we will clear the table and wash the dishes. Won't we Mary and Dorothy."

"John, are you speaking for yourself?"

"No, Mary. Grandma has a job now, and she is tired when she gets home, but she makes the dinner just the same, so we can and will do something."

"You're right, John." Mary said.

"Lil Brother, you can scrape the plates in that can over there." He pointed near the side of the stove.

"I can do that." Houston said.

"I know you can. When we get through with the kitchen, I will help you with your schoolwork, and then I can do my assignments. I have some writing to do in my English class."

"I brought a basket of patterns from the quilting room. I will try to do as many as I can tonight and finish up with this basket and bring another one home."

"Do the women sometimes take patterns from other baskets, and use them as their own?'

"That's possible, Charlotte, but when I leave for the day, my baskets come with me, and stays with me until I complete the baskets of squares."

"What do you do with the squares when you finish them, Grandma?"

"John, I take them to Mr. Nash and get paid for each square."

"How much do you get?"

"Not, much, but enough for me to have some spending money on my trip to see Anna and Mac."

"Grandma, I will have some money for you, too. I work in the pottery room, and I get paid a little for that. One of these days, I'm going to be the best pottery in the world. People will read about me, and by my pottery. I will use my full name with my middle name."

"That's John Milligan. Frazier." Dorothy said.

"Yes, that's it."

133

"I like the sound of it." Charlotte said. I am going to do some ironing, while y'all do the kitchen. Mama, you have done enough. Why don't you sit down and rest before you begin your quilting work?"

"While I'm sitting down resting, I can make several squares."

"I want to see the room with those quilts handing on the walls in the morning." You can go inside with me. The ladies are friendly, and they can tell you all about them, if they're not working. But if they're working, they don't lift their heads for anything."

"Grandma, I would like to see them, too. They're not too far from the pottery room. I can go by there after school."

"Is this your last year in school, John?"

"Yes, Mama. It is."

"What do you plan to do when you finish school?"

"Mama, I just said that I want to make the best potteries ever. I can learn that, just where I am, so I will be around here for a while."

"You're welcome to stay as long as you like." Charlotte said.

"You can stay here forever." Elena said.

John laughed. "Thanks, Grandma, but I don't want to stay here forever."

"In the meantime, I need to work with Houston with his arithmetic."

"I didn't know that those little children had arithmetic." Elena said.

"Another grade has been added to the school classes, and it is called Primmer. This grade prepares the little children for first grade when they are six. Houston has a year and a half before he gets to the first grade. That's not far off. I'd better get him before he takes a nap. I know he's tired and sleepy."

"Get on the job," Elena teased. "I can sew some more on the quilt and be ready for another basket tomorrow."

"I will finish my basket of ironing, and then I'm going to go in for the night."

"Mama, you have to wait on Houston. I will take him over his ABC's, and then he will be ready for bed."

"Hurry with that, John. I have to go to work in the morning, too."

John went to Houston's and Charlotte's room. Houston was lying across the bed, asleep.

John went to Elena and Charlotte. "He's asleep already, so I will leave him alone. He said he already knew his A B C's. We will just have to trust him on that. I will go to my room and do a little studying, so I'll see y'all in the morning."

26

"RISE AND SHINE," John yelled. "It's time to get up."

Elena rushed to the kitchen, wearing her white chenille robe. She tightened the long belt around her waist. "What time is it, John? It's still early. You have plenty time to get ready for school."

"I want an early start. I have made the breakfast, Grandma. You won't have to do that. You have done enough for us. Now we can do something for ourselves, and something for you, too. You just keep working on those quilts. I'm going to continue to work on pottery. The men in that shop are so helpful. After school, I can drop Houston off at home, rush to the pottery shop, and get a lot done, before I begin my homework."

"Seems like you've got everything already planned." Elena said and sat down at the table.

"I have, Grandma. When I can't fall to sleep right away at night, I lie awake and make plans. I also want to be able to go and visit Aunt Anna and Uncle Mac. Let me get you a cup of coffee." He reached inside of the cupboard, got a cup and filled it with coffee. Here, Grandma, drink and enjoy.

Elena took a sip. "Yum," she said. "This hits the spot."

"I knew it would." John went to the stove and placed a pot of hot grits on a wooden block in the center of the table. "How's that Grandma?"

Elena put her cup of coffee on the table. "Let me help you, John. I hear everyone in the back. It sounds like they are just about ready." She went to the stove and placed the bacon and hot scrambled eggs on a platter. When everyone is seated, I'll brown the bread on top of the stove. It will be good and hot when they're ready for it. They can get their own grit."

"I hear them, too. They will be seated in a little while. Grandma, I still miss Uncle Mac and Aunt Anna."

"Speaking of Mac and Anna, I think it's time to go to the train station and see if they've sent a telegram. The baby is on the way, and I know they're busy, but they might have a little time to send a short message."

"Alright, Grandma. I'll go to the train station. Dorothy and Mary can bring Houston home."

Dorothy and Mary came to the kitchen, already dressed for school. They stood at the table beside Elena. "What are you doing, John?"

"Dorothy, I've already done it. I have made ya'll some breakfast."

"It smells good." Mary said.

"Take your seats and we'll wait for Mama and Houston."

"We're on our way. You won't have to wait long." Charlotte walked in the kitchen, holding Houston's hand. "We'll sit at our same spot, Houston. We're all washed up and ready to eat."

"Yum!" Houston said.

"That's what I say, too. This is a real treat. What's the occasion?" Elena asked.

"Just giving you a break, Grandma. We can cook, too."

"Speak for yourself." Dorothy said.

"Lil' Brother, you will have to come home today with Dorothy and Mary."

Houston banged his fists on the table and yelled, "No! No! No! I won't come home with Mary and Dorothy. I want to come home with you."

"I am not coming home right after school, so you will have to come home with Dorothy and Mary."

"No, I don't." Houston yelled.

137

"Yes, you do, Houston." Charlotte assured Houston. "You can't come home alone. John has something he needs to do after school, so he's not coming home until later."

"I can come home later with John. I don't have anything to do."

"Yes, you do, Houston. You will have some school assignments to work on. When John gets home, you will have them all done."

"I can wait on John." Houston cried.

"Lil' Brother, I will bring you a few gumdrops when I come home. You won't miss anything." John assured him.

"Well, alright, but hurry home." Houston said slowly.

"I'll do just that. I promise."

"What's so special about gumdrops?"

"Mama. Gum Drops have many colors and different flavors. You can eat many flavors at the same time. Also, we celebrate **NATIONAL GUMDROP DAY** this February 15. That's a special day, especially for children." John said. "Houston and I will celebrate it in a big way. I like gumdrops, too."

"You will have to wait five more months to celebrate **NATIONAL GUMDROP DAY**." Elena said.

"We can wait. Can't we Lil' Brother?"

"I can wait." Houston promised.

"How do we celebrate **NATIONAL GUMDROP DAY?**"

"Mary, we just eat all the gumdrops our bellies can hold. Won't we Lil Brother?'

"Yeah." Houston yelled.

"Y'all hurry, dig in and eat your breakfast. John made breakfast this morning, and it's delicious." Elena said. "He even made biscuits for our sorghum syrup." She pointed to the large can of syrup in the middle of the table. "I'll put the platter of bacon on the table. John should be through with the eggs, so let's eat."

"I agree to it being delicious, Grandma. I have watched how you fry the bacon to be dry and real crisp. That's how I like it, and I haven't heard anyone complaining about it. I want to get to school early this morning, so let's hurry." Mary said.

"What are y'all learning in school?"

"We are in the same history class, and we're learning about slavery, Grandma."

"Why?"

"Grandma, our father died because he could read, and he told a friend, who told everybody what John told him, because John could read."

I want to know, what was the big secret that the masters didn't want the slaves to know."

"Hurry, and go on to school and learn that lesson, and come home and tell me what was the big secret."

"We can give you a full report when we get home, Grandma." Mary said.

"How will you know what John just said?"

"We have history together, Grandma. It's all the same, no matter what grade you're in." Dorothy said.

"I will be here, waiting on the report."

"I want to hear the report about slavery, too, Charlotte said. I will leave early, when you leave the sewing room, Mama. I'll leave with you."

"I'm almost through with my basket. When I leave the sewing room today, I will turn in a basket that is complete. I don't know if I want to continue this project or not, but I will be paid for what I have done. I want to have enough money to visit Mac and Anna and see the baby."

"Don't worry about money, Grandma," John said as they were leaving for school. "I'm going to help you. When school is out, I will visit Uncle Mac and Aunt Anna and the baby, too."

"They will be glad to know that you're coming, too, John. Y'all rush on."

John grabbed Houston's hand, and Dorothy and Mary followed them out of the door. "We'll see y'all later, Grandma." John called back to Elena.

"Y'all come back with a full report. I want to hear everything that took our John away from us."

"We will, Grandma." John called back.

"Houston. Don't yank that girl's hair again. You hear me. The principal might not be so kind again."

"I won't, Grandma." Houston promised.

"Y'all hurry and go to school and learn that lesson and come home and tell us what was the big secret."

"We can give you a full report when we get home, Grandma." Mary said.

"I will be here waiting on the report," Elena said.

"I want to hear the report about slavery, too, Charlotte said. "I will leave early with you Mama."

"I'm almost through with my basket. When I leave the sewing room today, I will turn in a basket that is finished. I don't know if I want to continue this project or not, but I will be paid for what I have done. I want to have enough money to visit Mac and Anna and see the baby, too."

"Don't worry about money, Grandma." John said as they were walking out the door for school. "I'm going to help you. When school is out, I will visit Uncle Mac and Aunt Anna and the little one, too. I will be graduated from high school, too." He called back.

"We're so proud of you John. You have a good head on your body. I know Mac and Anna will be glad to see you."

John grabbed Houston's hand and walked out the door. Mary and Dorothy followed behind them. "We'll see y'all later, Grandma." John called back to Elena.

Elena stood at the door and watched her grandchildren walk to school. "I hope they do well in school and make something of themselves."

"They will, Mama. I know they have had good home training, and they're determined to have a good life."

"I know you're right, but I was just thinking." Elena closed the door and went back to the kitchen.

"Don't bother about the dishes, Mama, we can wash the dishes when we come home from the market."

"No, Charlotte, I don't want to come home to a dirty kitchen and have to start dinner. I will take care of everything before I leave. If you have to go early, go on. I don't have a particular time to be there."

"How are you doing with your quilting, Mama?"

"I have almost completed my baskets. When I leave there, it will be completed, and I'll take it to Mr. Nash so I can get paid. I plan to take the train back to Nacogdoches to visit with Anna and Mac. I want to be there when the baby gets here."

"When will that be, Mama?"

"About six more weeks."

"We're going to help you go, Mama, so don't worry about money."

Thanks, Charlotte."

"You're so welcomed, Mama."

"It will be just about time for Anna to have their baby, and I want to be there." Elena said.

"You will, Mama. You will." Charlotte assured her. "We need to get on our way to our jobs. You will probably finish up with your work before I finish in the store."

"I believe so, Charlotte. If I do, I'll just go home, start the dinner and wait on you and the children to come home."

"That's sounds good, Mama. I don't know what I'd do without you, Mama."

"You'd manage, Charlotte. Mac and Anna need me, too. You have your children here to help you. John, Jr. is good help."

"I know he is, Mama, but he plans to go to see Mac and Anna, too. He just might stay."

"He might, Charlotte, but you are their mama, and these girls are here with you, and they will help you with Houston. I know that Houston is a hand full, but he's young and he will grow out of being a problem."

"I will have to just cope with things, Mama."

"You have to do more than cope, Charlotte. You have to be their mama. You haven't had to do much mothering, because I have always been here to help you. That will end someday, and the children will grow up and won't need our help. Prepare yourself for that, but in the meantime, be their mama."

"I will, Mama."

"Let's get on our ways to work." Elena said.

27

Elena completed her basket that she had started the day before and began a new one. Toward the end of her workday, she decided to go home early, and take her new basket with her. She would start dinner early and wait on John Jr. to bring her some information from Mac and Anna.

On her way toward the market, she went inside, and saw Charlotte slicing meat for the meat trays. She waved at her, and gestured that she was leaving, and mouthed that she would see her at home. Charlotte lifted one bloody hand and waved a good-bye to her.

Elena rushed home as fast as her short little legs would take her. She knew that John would have a telegram from Mac and Anna. When she reached home, she was there alone. She forgot that John had to work on some pottery at the pottery shop. When she reached home, she undressed and put on her housecoat, and began preparing the evening meal.

Thirty minutes later, she heard children running and laughing, so she went to the door and looked out. She turned around and looked at the clock on the table. It was exactly 4:00 o'clock. Elena rushed to the pantry and pulled out pots and pans to begin preparing the meal. "Hi, Grandma."

She looked around, and saw John Jr. Why are you home soon? I thought you were going to be late today. I haven't started dinner, yet. Did you get Houston's gumdrops?"

"Yes, ma'am, I did. He wouldn't let me rest without his gumdrops. I will get dressed and help you. I can set the table. Oh, yeah. I went to the train station and got a telegram from Uncle Mac and Aunt Anna."

"You did?" Elena jumped for joy. "What did it say?"

He reached inside his back pocket and gave the telegram to Elena. "The baby is coming earlier than they thought. It will probably be a Thanksgiving baby."

Elena held the telegram in her hand. "I see here where Anna wants me to come before the baby gets here. I will plan to get there two or three weeks before Christmas. We can celebrate Thanksgiving here. When Charlotte comes home, we can begin making plans. You will have to give your mama a lot of help, John."

"Grandma, Dorothy and Mary can help, too. I'm not going to be around all of the time, so they need to start helping."

"You're right, John. You do what you want to do."

"I want to own a pottery shop and make beautiful pottery. I can do that any place. When I visit Aunt Anna and Uncle Mac, I'll look around, and see if I can find a good place to do pottery right there in our old hometown."

"When you finish school, are you going to teach?"

"Yes 'am. I'll will need to make enough money to put in a neat little shop. When I begin to make money off of my potteries, I can retire from teaching and just do pottery."

"Seems like you have everything well planned, John, but you always do."

"I hear Mary and Dorothy laughing. I know Dorothy's laughing anywhere. She sorts of squeal with her giggles." John said.

"I hope they have Houston with them." Elena said.

John walked to the door and looked out. "Mary is holding his hand."

"That's good." Elena said. I was able to heat up enough food for the day. I only had to make some corn bread. We had plenty left from yesterday."

"I can make lemonade, Grandma."

"That sounds good. You need to finish putting the plates and tableware on the table. When they get in, and wash up, they can sit and eat and tell us about their lessons. We'll hear from Houston first. And then y'all tell us about **EMANCIPATION PROCLAMATION** and slavery."

"I took a lot of good notes, Grandma, so our table talk will be long today. Are we going to wait on Mama? She seems to be working longer than usual."

Elena looked at the clock, and it was five o'clock. "She probably on her way."

"What is the first thing we should tell her; the lesson on slavery or Uncle Mac and Aunt Anna's baby?"

"We'll test the water and see how it flows. If she's happy, we'll talk about our lesson on slavery. If she's just, so so, we'll tell her about the baby.

Dorothy, Mary and Houston pushed the screen door open and rushed in.

"Whee, I'm so tired," Mary said.

"From what?" Elena asked.

"I'll take charge of Houston tomorrow," Dorothy said.

"Thank you."

"You're welcome, Mary."

"John, did you get my gumdrops?" Houston whined.

"Yes, Lil Brother, I did, but you have to wait until we eat dinner."

"Then, I'll be too full."

"You'll have plenty of room, Houston. It won't be too long."

"Well, when do we eat?"

"When Mama gets here." John said.

"She's working late today. She's usually home by this time." Elena said.

Elena went to the door and looked out. "Here she comes. She has a package in her hands. I wonder what she's carrying."

"My gumdrops, Grandma."

"No, Houston. I always bring your gumdrops. Remember?" John Jr. said.

"Yeah." He said slowly. "But if you tell Mama about them, she'll bring me some, too."

"Then, you'll be known as the **Gumdrop Kid**." John teased.

"I don't mind being The **Gum Drop Kid**." Houston said.

"Y'all hurry and get ready for dinner." Elena scolded.

Charlotte opened the door and walked in. "Whee, it's getting hot so early."

"This is Texas, and the weather gets hot here faster than some other places. We just have to adjust to it. Get comfortable, and we can sit down and have dinner." Elena said.

When they were comfortable, they sat at the table, and waited for Elena and John to put the food on the table.

"What did y'all learn today in that history class?" Charlotte asked.

"A lot, Mama," John said. "In fact, I took a lot of notes. Our history teacher is really smart. He just talked about Emancipation and slavery as if he was there."

"This sounds like it's going to be interest." Elena said.

"I took notes, too." Dorothy said.

"Me, too" Mary said. "I almost filled my little notebook." She held it up.

"The dishes are on the table. When we get our plates full, we'll begin the lectures."

"It won't be a lecture, Grandma. We will give facts that were given to us." Dorothy said.

"That sounds good to me, but first, let's hear how Houston is doing." Elena said. "How are you and that girl in front of you, getting along?"

"You mean June." Houston asked. "Her name is June."

"Yes, June." Elena said. "Are you still yanking her hair?"

"Yea, but she won't say anything. She likes it when I yank her hair, Grandma."

"Lil' Brother, how do you know?"

"John, she keeps flipping her braids back on my desk, and I keep yanking them."

"Well, try to stay out of the principal's office." John said.

"I will." Houston promised.

"What was the subject today in y'all's history class?" Charlotte asked.

"EMANCIPATION PROCLAMATION, PROCLAMATION." They repeated.

"Sounds like ya'll have rehearsed your answers before we could ask." Charlotte said.

"From my notes, President Abraham Lincoln issued the **EMANCIPATION PROCLAMATION** on January 1, 1863, as the nation approached its third year of the bloody Civil War. The proclamation declared, "That all persons held as slaves" within the rebellious states" are hence forward shall be free."

"What do you mean by the rebellious states?" Elena asked.

Houston got up from the table. "I'm tired," He yawned.

"Tired of what?" Charlotte asked.

"I don't know. I'm just tired." He yawned again.

"Lil Brother wants these gumdrops that I have for him."

"What's so good about gumdrops?' Mary asked.

"They're sugar coated, and very sweet." John said.

"Won't that hurt his stomach?" Dorothy asked.

"So far, Lil Brother gets along very well with his gumdrops."

"What is the subject tomorrow in ya'll history class?" Elena asked.

"Some of the same thing, but I think we'll talk about slaves when they became free." John said.

"That's sound good. I can hardly wait to hear about that."

"We'll take notes again, Grandma." Dorothy said.

"I still want to know who were the rebellious states." Elena repeated.

"There were ten states that were in rebellion. According to my notes, Grandma, some of the states were Missouri, Kentucky, Maryland, and Delaware. We'll talk more about it tomorrow. Let me take care of Houston."

"Go ahead. John" She said. "In the meantime, stop giving Houston so many gumdrops. He soon won't have a tooth left in his head."

"Let me know what we will talk about today." Elena asked.

"Quite a bit, Grandma," Dorothy said. "We're going to talk about how the slaves came to America, and who owned them. We have a list of presidents that owned slaves."

"Our first president, George Washington owned a lot of slaves." Mary said.

"Did Abraham Lincoln owned slaves, too?" Elena asked.

"No, he hated slavery, but he had to abide by the rules of the nation for a time."

"I can hardly wait to hear your lessons. You see, when I was growing up, we attended a school for Indian children, and they didn't teach us about slavery in my school. In fact, babies were sometimes snatched from grieving mother's arms, and separated from parents for life. I don't know my parents. I never did know them."

Dorothy gasped, "You didn't know your parents, Grandma?"

That is why I make it my business to help Charlotte to raise y'all. I want ya'll to know your family and be proud of your family. I hope separating children from parents never happens again. That is so cruel and inhuman, but that was all we knew."

"That will never happen again, Grandma."

"I hope you are right, John. I hope you're right."

"Do you think the government will allow children to be separated from their parents again?' Mary asked.

"Not during my lifetime, nor after. I will fight it to the day I die." Elena said. "After our mother died Gloria and I were sent to an orphanage for a while. Several months later, a white couple adopted me and my little sister, Gloria .and gave us a nice home in Ohio. They never owned slaves. They hated slavery. When they died, they left us with some property and some money. Our cousin rents some of the property out, and that is how we get extra money. She rents two houses, and sends money to me and Gloria, often. The rest of the money is used for upkeep and her use, too."

"You all didn't have such a bad time, Grandma." Mary said.

"Unless there is some form of abuse, no child should be separated from their parents. That should never happen again in this civilized world." Elena said. "But we couldn't do any better, because our mother was dead, and our dad was perhaps a slave somewhere."

"I hope that never happens again. I don't believe it will. We're too civilized for that to ever happen again."

"I hope you're right, Charlotte. There were mother with piercing screams, as their children were ripped from their arms. That was called **THE WEEPING TIME.** They didn't forget the mothers, though. The mothers were sold to the highest bidders."

"That time is over, Grandma." Mary said. They all breathed a sigh of relief.

"If you forget about those times, they will surely repeat. The only way you can avoid that ever happening again, is never forget it, and do something about it.

"I have some homework to do for next week, Grandma. So I'd better get to it, so I can have plenty of time to get the information that you want."

"We'd better eat first." Elena said.

"I know y'all have done a lot of work to get your report ready for me and your mama. Why not take a little rest today, and y'all can do it later?"

"That sounds like a good idea, Grandma. I will have time to get everything that you need. I'm learning a lot about slavery and the civil war."

"I can wait patiently, until tomorrow for y'all reports. I want to know about those subjects, too."

"Dorothy and I have some notes on the subjects, too, Grandma."

"Mary, I can certainly wait. Can't we, Houston?" She nodded at Houston.

"Yeah, Grandma."

"What's your history teacher's name?" Charlotte asked.

"Professor Benson."

28

After school, John found Houston standing in the hall. Let's go Lil'
Brother. Who are you waiting on?"

"I thought Mary and Dorothy were going home with us."

"They are, Lil' Brother, but they might be talking to some of their
friends. They know the way home. Let's go. I had a busy evening today."

"Why?"

"I am going to Mr. Nash's shop and do some more work on some
pottery. I am making some bowls. That's what I'm doing."

"What kind of bowls?"

"Two or three for us and two for Mac and Anna. The small bowl
will be for their baby. I will take it when I go."

"When are you going to see them?"

"After I graduate, Lil' Brother."

"I want to go with you."

That might not be possible." He looked toward the end of the hall.
"I see Mary and Dorothy, now. They are on the way."

"Let's go, John."

"We can wait a few seconds. They'll be here, and we can go inside
the house together."

Mary and Dorothy joined them near the principal's office.

"Who was in the office today?" Mary teased.

"We were waiting on you and Dorothy. The principal's office is near
the door where we exit."

"Let's go. I have some good notes, but I want to tell mine first, so I can go to the pottery shop, and work on some bowls."

"I have some good notes, too, John." Dorothy said.

"Me, too." Mary added.

Houston grew impatient and pulled John toward the door. "Let's go."

"We're on our way, Lil' Brother."

'Grandma is going to make us eat, clean the kitchen, and then tell her about our notes." Mary said.

"Maybe not," Dorothy said.

"We'll be ready either way," John promised. "Let's get a move on it." They followed him out of the front door.

Dorothy looked back at the school. "John, how old do you think our school is? It looks old, but in good shape."

"It's been around a long time. I believe it was a public building for farmers who sold their crops and farm animals to buyers. When they no longer had many buyers, they sold it to the city, and the city made a school for free slaves. That's what I've heard around here."

"That sounds right John. It's a nice building." Mary said. "Grandma might want to hear that in our report tonight."

"We'll tell her someday, but today, we're going to talk about the Civil War and slavery. She has plenty of time to learn about the school building." John said. "Lil' Brother, you have to walk faster. We're almost home."

"I know how to go home, John."

"But not by yourself." John told him.

"You can always come home with me," Mary said.

"And me, too," Dorothy said.

When they reached home, Houston pulled his hand away from John, and ran home and pushed the door opened with a bang. He stumbled in and wobbled to a chair at the dining room table.

Elena saw sweat on his face. She grabbed him, and asked, "Are you by yourself, Houston?" She released him and rushed to the stove, grabbed a broom that was leaning on the wall behind the stove. She grabbed it and raised it above her head. She was ready to attack anyone who came through that door for Houston.

Houston began to laugh. "Grandma, I'm not by myself. They are behind me."

Elena grew alarm. "They let you come home by yourself?'

"I know how to come home, Grandma." He puffed some more.

Elena began to pace the floor. "Something's not right." She said.

The door opened, and John, Dorothy and Mary entered, and began laughing.

"How did Houston get home first?" She yelled at them.

"It's all a joke, Grandma. He wanted to show us how he could come home alone, so we let him try it, and he fooled you by coming inside first." Dorothy said.

"He's too young to come home alone. I thought he was by himself."

"That will never happen, Grandma. He's got a lot of growing to do before he can come home alone."

"I hope you're right John. Elena put her right hand over her heart. Y'all will be the death of me. I don't want this old heart to give out before I go back home to see Mac and Anna."

"You will be just fine, Grandma, when you visit Mac and Anna."

"I hope so, John. Did y'all take good notes today?"

"Yes, Grandma, and we're ready," Mary said.

Now, y'all get ready for dinner."

Elena put the broom handle back in place behind the stove.

"I'll put the food on the table, while y'all wash up. I set the table an hour ago."

"Everything looks and smell good, Grandma.

"John, that's what I want to hear. I put lots of time and effort in this meal. You see, what we will be doing for the next few days is for John, your dad. He didn't die for nothing."

"That's what I think, too, Grandma. We should be proud of him. I am."

"I am, too," Dorothy said.

"Me, too." Mary added.

"Why are y'all just standing around, doing nothing? Get ready for dinner.

"Grandma?"

151

"Yes, John. What is it?"

"Since everyone is tired, and Mama had to work late today, why don't we do the report tomorrow? Tomorrow is Saturday, and we will have plenty of time."

"We can also sleep a little longer, too." Dorothy said.

"That's fine with me, and I know your mama will be alright with that, too. It seems like she's working late today."

"Maybe I need to go and see what's keeping her." John said.

John rushed to the door and opened it and saw Charlotte walking toward the door. "Here she is." He called to Elena and others. She's smiling. She must have some good news."

Charlotte was close enough to hear John. "Yes, I have some good news." She said as she reached for the handle to open the door.

John opened the door for her. "Come on in, Mama, and tell us the good news."

"I got a raise." She waved some papers back and forth. "I got a raise."

"How did you get a raise?" Elena asked.

Mr. Nash hired a new worker this morning. She will take my place and I will move a notch up, so I got a promotion, too."

"What do you do on this new job? I know you sliced meats with the old job. What do you do with this new job?"

"I am the manager of my department. In other words, I see that everyone is at his or her station when we begin the mornings. If everyone is in their places at the right time, we can have a good morning, and ready to serve the public."

"I hope you treat them well, Charlotte. Don't yell and scream at them when they make mistakes, just because you are the boss." Elena warned.

"I would never do something like that, Mama. We all get along. Everyone was glad that I am their manager. When do we eat? I thought we were going to hear more of y'all notes."

"We thought that since you'd be tired when you got home, we would wait until tomorrow. Since tomorrow is Saturday, we won't have to rush for anything."

"John, I would like to hear your notes today. Tomorrow, I want to do something else. I don't want to hear anything about books and learning."

"I'm ready with my notes." Mary said.

"Me, too." Dorothy chimed in.

"Let's get started. Y'all sit down at the table. The food is already on the table. All ya'll have to do is serve yourselves."

"We can do that, Grandma." John said. Charlotte reached for Houston's hand and the others followed her to the table.

"Grandma?"

"Yes, Dorothy. What is it?"

"What did the fathers do when their children were taken?"

Enslaved mothers and fathers lived with the constant fear that they or their children might be sold away. Nights and days, you could hear men and women screaming. Many mothers and fathers died from broken hearts."

"Grandma, I don't want to ever see that again."

"Dorothy, we hope not. Now let's get to the table."

"Grandma, our teacher is having seminars all next week, where he will talk about slavery. I think he can give all the information that y'all will need. It's too sad talking about how children were wrenched from their parents' arms. Let's talk about something that's not about slaves' holders taking little children away from their parents."

"You're right, John, but power gives people the power and the will to take children away from their parents. Let's promise, John, to never let power get in the way of human rights. Every child has a right to a mother and a father. Let's stop the sadness and let's eat."

"I'm ready, Mama." Charlotte said.

"Before we begin eating, let's start on a good note about the slaves. Some African men resisted slavery by joining the army, to fight for their freedom. Some slaves claimed to be too sick to work. When they did do work it was poorly done. They didn't take care of how their work was done. The slave holders labeled them as slovenly, and lazy. The Negro didn't go into slavery without a fight.

153

"We'll continue tomorrow. I want to go to the pottery shop and talk to Mr. Nash."

"We can wait, John." Elena said.

"Thanks, Grandma."

"Can I be first?" Mary asked.

"Of course." Elena said.

29

"You're on, Mary." Elena said.

"I'm ready."

"Well, get started. I have something I have to do today."

"Okay John. I will. The first thing Professor Benson wanted us to know is that many of the slaves were brave. They didn't go into slavery without a fight."

"So, did African American slaves' rebel?"

"They certainly did rebel." Mary said. They rebelled in many ways."

"But, how?" Charlotte asked.

"In many ways, Mama, but I will name a few ways that they resisted or rebelled against being enslaved. Slaves didn't consider themselves as victims, who accepted their situation. Instead, they proved their strength and determination in fighting for their freedom.

Slaves stole from their owners, robbing them of his property and profit. They could damage machinery, so that it was put out of action and needed lengthy repairs or costly replacement. They could avoid work by claiming to be ill. There were other ways of attacking the slave owners. The children of a slave woman were born as slaves. Some women would end a pregnancy or kill their new born babies rather than bring a child into the world to be a slave.

Many resisted being slaves by running away. Enslaved Africans also fought against slavery by keeping their African cultures and traditions alive in words, names, music and beliefs.

Grandma, you will hear of many more ways that the slaves rebelled."

"You did a good job, Mary. I didn't know all of that."

"Neither did I." Charlotte said.

"One more thing," Mary said. "Slave women knew a lot about herbs and plants that would cure some ailments. Slave owners were in constant fear that they would be poisoned by some of their medical treatments. I'm sure I have missed some important things that the slaves did to rebel against their owners, but you will probably hear some more later on."

"You've done a great job, Mary. I didn't know all of that."

"Thanks, Grandma."

"Me, too," Charlotte said. "I can also understand that John died for a good cause. He's up there smiling."

"Where is Benjamin?" Elena asked.

"Grandma, he is somewhere still running. He's more afraid of John than the masters."

"You're right," Mary said. "'If John told him to cross his heart and hope to die.' He meant that, and Benjamin knew what John meant."

"I believe that someone has killed Benjamin for causing John to leave and lose his life, just because he was trying to finally get the news to all slaves."

"I believe Benjamin is somewhere alive." Elena said.

"I hope so," Charlotte said.

"Why, Mama?"

"Dorothy, I want Benjamin to know that I have forgiven him."

"Why?" Mary asked.

"It's the right thing to do, and we all must forgive Benjamin. He didn't know that he was harming John."

"Whether he knew he was harming John or not, it is the right thing to do. We all can forgive Benjamin."

"Grandma, how can we forgive him, when we don't know where he is?"

"You don't have to know where he is to forgive him, Mary. When you see him again, let him know that you have already forgiven him."

"That is a hard thing to do, Grandma, but if you say it's the right thing to do, I will forgive Benjamin. I know he regrets what he has done, and is probably afraid to meet us, and let us know how he feels."

"Somehow, John, we'll meet Benjamin again.

"I know we will, Grandma. I would like to talk about the end of slavery. The end of slavery brought about many concerns for the ex-slaves. There was a man named Hawkins Wilson, who was enslaved from the region outside of Galveston, Texas. When he realized that he was free, the first thing he wanted to do was to find his family. He knew that he was sold from a plantation in Carolina County, Virginia twenty-four years ago. To help him find his family, he had some to write a letter for him that said:

'I am anxious to learn about my sisters, from whom I have been separated many years. I am in hopes that they are still living. I was sold at a Sheriff's sale to a Mr. Wright of Boydtown Court House, and that he hoped that an additional letter that he enclosed could be delivered to his sister.'

The pain of his separation and the strength of his desire to find his family are evident in the second letter. 'Your little brother, Hawkins is trying to find out where you are and where his poor old mother is. I shall never forget the bag of biscuits you made for me the last night I spent with you." He added that he had lived an honorable life, so that if they did not meet on earth, we might indeed meet in heaven.' He ended his letter by asking his sister to write back quickly and said she should not be surprised if he should drop in on you some day.'

There is no evidence that Wilson's letter was ever delivered or that he ever reconnected with his family. To the newly emancipated, freedom was never all that they had hoped, but it was much more than they had ever had.

During the depression, an elderly African American man, Cornelia Holmes, was asked by a WPA historian, if slavery should still matter in the United States? Cornelia labored most of his life on rice plantations in South Carolina, said, "Though the slavery question is settled, the race issue will be with us always. It is in our politics, in our courts, on our highways, in our manners, in our religion, and in our thoughts, all the day, every day."

"Remember, Mama, our teacher, Professor Benson, has a speaker coming Thursday evening. That's tomorrow night. I hope y'all are going, and all that we don't get answered today, the speaker will answer tomorrow night. Write your questions on a pad or piece of paper, so you won't forget them. Our chapter on slavery ends after his speech.

"We can wait, John," Charlotte said. "You can go on with your report, Mary."

"Thanks, Mama."

'MY interests were the states that were involved in slavery and those states, that weren't involved. I thought, for a long time, that all states had slaves. It seems like this war was an economic war, but I'll get to my notes.

"Well, who were the states?" Elena asked.

"Grandma, there were eleven slaves states in 1861-1865. They were Alabama, Arkansas, Florida, Georgia, Louisiana, Mississippi, North Carolina, South Carolina, Tennessee, Texas and Virginia."

"Who were the other states?" Charlotte asked.

"There were quite a few free states during 1861-1865, and they were: California, Connecticut, Illinois, Iowa, Kansas, Maine, Massachusetts, Michigan, Minnesota, Nevada, New Hampshire, New Jersey, New York, Ohio, Oregon, Pennsylvania, and Rhode Island.

Before and during the Civil War, much of The United States was made of farmland, unsettled territories and small areas. Most of the people lived on farms or in small towns in the south. Unlike most of the small towns, there were many who lived in cities, like New York, Philadelphia, Boston, and New Orleans. These cities were heavy populated with people, businesses and factories. The South was more rural with farms and plantations, and while the North had its farmers and rural places too, it had more cities.

The division of slavery would split the union of the states and bring on a Civil War, that would kill hundreds of thousands of people. The Civil War changed the lives of the people and the geography of the states."

"I have more information on that subject." Dorothy said.

"You're on, Dorothy," John told her.

"I will only be repeating what you and Mary have said. We need to talk about Benjamin, and what are we going to say to him, when we see him again."

"I will probably see him before long," Elena said.

"How's that, Mama?"

"Charlotte, I turned my trays in today to Mr. Nash, and got paid. I plan to leave next week to see Anna and Mac."

"Why are you just now telling us, Mama?"

"I just made up my mind to go. You have your family here with you to help out. John is a lot of help. Mary and Dorothy can help you with Houston, too. You don't have anything to worry about. All you need to do is just be their mother."

"When is the baby due?"

"Soon, Charlotte, and I want to be there when the baby is born. I will take the train and get there in two or three days. I wish y'all can come later on. There's plenty of room, because Mac and Anna's house is still vacant. They have our old house with plenty of room."

"We can make plans for that, Mama."

"We'll all be there waiting on y'all to come."

"We'll be there, Mama."

30

Elena kept her promise. Five days later she boarded the train for Natchitoches to see Anna and Mac. Mary, Dorothy, Charlotte and Huston stood by watching Elena get on the train. John held her bag until she was aboard, and he gave it to the train helper. The clerk at the train station ran on board and gave a bag to John. "Here, John, I kept it for you. Now, do you want it beside you or with the other baggage aboard?"

"Put it with the other baggage, please."

"What are you doing, John?"

"I'm going with you, Grandma. I would never let you make this trip all by yourself." He teased.

"Did you tell your mama what you were going to do?"

"No, I didn't Grandma. I knew what she'd say. She will learn that she has everything under control. We just have to let her learn."

"The school principal said so many good things about you on graduating night, and he was right."

"Thanks, Grandma."

Elena felt a pleasant aura about the trip. She is going home for a pleasant trip. Other trips were due to deaths, this trip is a birth, Mac and Anna's baby. Also, she has John beside her, and he always sees that everything is alright.

When the train began to move with John aboard, Charlotte began to run toward the train to let them know that her son, John was still aboard. The doors closed and the train picked up speed.

"How did you pull that one off, John?"

"Grandma, with a little help from my friend, Sam at the train station. He had me to bring my bag a day before leaving, and he would put it safely with the other bags. No one would know that I was leaving."

"I wonder what they're doing now, that you are gone, John?"

"Grandma, they'll survive. I need a vacation. It is time for Mama, Dorothy, Mary and Houston to be together. They don't know that they can get things done together, but they can."

"They'll have to, John."

"I can hardly wait 'til we get there. It will only take a half a day by train from Natchitoches, Texas to Marion County. The distance is a little under a hundred miles. The train is faster than Coco and Dapper. We won't be tired of traveling when we get there. By the time we get there, Anna and Mac will be well rested. She saw Dr. Rivers and he has her resting during the day."

"Who is going to meet us at the train station, when we get home, Grandma?"

"Mac will be there."

"What about Aunt Anna?"

"She will be surprised to see us. He's keeping our arrival a pleasant secret. She needs some good news for a change. We want talk about the children's history classes. We'll talk about the future of the new baby."

"That sounds good to me, Grandma."

"I was just thinking, John. How are the mules going to get from the train station, where we left them. Who's going to take the mule's home.

Sam has a friend who is good with wagons, and he promised to take them home. In the meantime, they're enjoying the green grass at the train station."

"I don't think we could have selected a better day to leave, than this day. Everything seems so perfect. I had no idea that you were going to go with me, John, but I am so glad that you are going. Anna and Mac are going to be surprised, and happy."

"I wonder what Mama is doing now, that she has everything to do by herself."

"The girls will help her. I'm sure they have skills that they didn't know that they had."

"I hope so, Grandma, and I hope those skills are not with those boys."

"They are smart girls, John. After all, they were raised well. I don't doubt them at all. I do worry about Houston when he grows up."

"Whoa", John said. "I guess the train is stopping at another train station to let some off and some on. We won't have to wait too long, Grandma."

"I'm in no hurry, John. The ride is so smooth, I believe I can sleep through the whole trip."

"Do that, Grandma. I will wake you when we get to Nacogdoche."

The train pulled out again. Perhaps they were loaded and ready to go. "I'll go back to sleep and depend on you to wake me when we get there."

"I will, Grandma. Your nap will be a short one, because I believe we will be in Nacogdoche real soon."

"I hope so, John, because I am tired of riding."

"Go back to sleep, Grandma, and I will wake you when we get there. You don't want to go on with the train. Do you," He teased.

Elena obeyed John and went to sleep again.

After a few clangs and train puffs, the train came to a sudden stop.

"Nacogdoche, Texas, everyone. We're here," a loud voice yelled over the train compartments. John looked to his left and noticed that Elena was still asleep. He nudged her in her left arm. "Grandma, wake up. We're here."

"Where?'

"Wake up, and you will see. Look out the window. Do you see the tall pine trees, that you loved so much?"

"Oh, I see." She said.

A train assistant came to their section. You may stand and stretch your legs, if you like. I know you're tired of sitting." He smiled.

"Let's do that, John."

John stood and moved in the aisle so Elena could get out and stretch her legs, too. She moved near John but stumbled. John grabbed her. "I got you, Grandma."

"Always remember, John, that I love you." I guess I will go back to sleep."

"I know, Grandma, and I love you, too."

A train attendant came through their section and helped everyone off the train. When John and Elena were away from the train, they looked around to see if they saw Mac. "I think Uncle Mac is going to meet us, Grandma. You stay here, and I will get our bags."

"I'm not going anyplace, John." She teased.

John looked forward. "I think I see Uncle Mac on the way."

Elena looked in his direction. "That is Mac, and he's alone. I hope Anna is alright."

"Hee," Mac yelled to the mules, and they made a right turn toward the train station.

"They're coming our way, John."

"I know, Grandma, but it's only Uncle Mac."

"That's enough."

When Mac recognized John and Elena, he got out of the wagon, and ran toward them. "It's so good to see you home again. I know Anna will have a good day, because she's going to be happy all day. Let's get your bags in the wagon, but first let's get Elena in."

"I can get her in, Uncle Mac."

Elena gathered the hem of her dress as John lifted her in the front seat of the wagon. When she was inside the wagon, John and Mac loaded the bags. "Is this everything?" Mac called.

"That's everything", Elena said.

"John, get in and we'll be on our way.

"How is Anna, Mac?"

"Elena, you will soon see for yourself. Her stomach is so big, until she's afraid to move around too much. The baby might decide to come."

"It waited all the years, Mac. It will come when it's time."

"We'll see Elena." Mac said.

Elena stumbled, as she looked back at the train.

John grabbed her arm. "I got you, Grandma."

"I know."

31

As they approached their home, Elena yelled, "Thank you, thank you. We're here. Who is that man sitting on the porch?"

"He's an old friend, Grandma. You will meet him. I'll pull around the back and the mules will go in their old barn. They haven't learned the new barn yet." John said.

"Well, they have time," Elena said.

"Whoa," Mac yelled to the mules. We'll get out here.

John jumped down and helped Elena to the ground. "This feels so good, but I want to meet your guest."

"You will Elena. You will."

"I believe I will, Mac."

As they approached the porch, the guest stood, and extended his arm out for Elena to hold as she climbed the three steps. "Thank you, but you look familiar. Do I know you?"

"Yes, Ma'am, you do. I'm Benjamin."

"You're who?" Elena asked.

"Elena, that's Benjamin." Mac said.

"Benjamin, I didn't recognize you with that hair on your face."

They laughed. "Let me help you in. Anna will be so happy to see you. John, how have you been?"

"As well as I can, Benjamin. I just graduated from high school, and I am working on pottery."

Mac opened the front door. "Let's go in and sit down. Then we can talk about our past and present. Elena was the first to enter. Anna ran to her and gave her a big hug.

"Take it easy, Anna." Don't hurt the baby.

"I won't, Elena, but I am so glad you're here. Y'all come on and sit down at the table. You can wash up while I am putting the food on the table."

"We can do that, Aunt Anna. I am so glad that I'm going to be an uncle. I can hardly wait."

"John, I can hardly wait, too." Anna said.

After everyone had washed their hands and were seated, Elena addressed Benjamin.

"Benjamin, we were just talking about you before we left."

"I hope it was good." Mrs. Elena."

"It was, Benjamin. We want you to know that we forgive you for telling John's secret. You didn't mean to harm him, but you were so glad that the slaves were free, that you wanted our little village to know that they weren't slaves anymore. It wasn't' meant to hurt John. John would want us to forgive you, too, because he was always a forgiving person."

"Ms. Elena. I came here to ask for forgiveness. It seems like we had the same thing in mind. I am so sorry that John had to die. He was my best friend, and I miss him so much. Being around his family gives me some comfort. Please tell Charlotte that I have asked to be forgiven, too. I meant no harm."

"She knows that already, Benjamin. How long are you going to be here in Nacogdoche?

"I don't know. I'm looking for a place for me and my family to stay. I would like to raise my children here in this village with y'all."

"You have a family, Benjamin?" Elena asked.

"Yes, Ma'am. I do. I have a wife and two young children."

"How old are your children.?"

"Elena, they are six and eight. I know you want to know how I got children that old, so soon. Well, when I married their mother, I married them, too. I don't know how I could love them more. My little daughter, Katie, is six, and my son, Roy is eight."

"I have a peach cobbler for dessert, but I feel so tired," Anna said. "I think I will rest before I serve it. I'll go to the back room and rest."

165

"We can serve ourselves, Anna, but I will go to the back room with you and stay while you get some rest. A little rest will help me, too." Elena said. She followed Anna to the back room and had her to put on a loose night gown. She noticed that Anna was grimacing as if in pain. She went to the kitchen and told mac to put on a kettle for hot water. When she returned to Anna, who was lying across the bed. "Get straight in the bed, Anna. I believe the baby is on the way."

Elena had several towels and a dish pan. "I'm ready when it gets here. She pulls Anna's gown up around her waist and felt her stomach. It has fallen so low; I won't leave the room. I want to protect it while it's on the way."

Anna gave out a loud moan. Elena looked again and say a head full of black silky hair. She caresses the baby tenderly and tenderly, pulled it out. The baby cried out. "It's a little Mac," Elena called to Mac and Benjamin. Mac, take those scissors there on the pillow and cut the cord."

"What cord, Elena?"

She held it up from the baby. "This cord."

"Won't that hurt Anna?"

"No, it will not hurt Anna. I want you to cut the spot that I am holding."

Mac cut the cord, and it fell onto the bed. "Is that it, Elena?

"That's it, Mac. You did a good job. I will take this short piece that's left and make a navel."

She washed the baby and dressed it in clothing that Anna had made for the blessed occasion and placed the baby in Anna's arms. Anna couldn't stop smiling. "He's so beautiful she said."

Mac couldn't stop dancing. "Let me see my son, Elena. Let me see my soon."

Anna lifted the baby to Elena. She wrapped a soft white band around the baby's body to hold the umbilical cord in place. Then, she wrapped the baby in a soft tiny blanket and gave him to Mac. Mac, here's your little son."

Tears dripped from Mac's face as he reached for his son.

"Why are you crying, Mac?" Benjamin asked.

"I don't know, am I crying? I'm so happy."

"My friend, you're going to have a lot of help with the baby. What is the baby's name?"

"I know Mac wants the baby to be a junior. Don't you Mac? Elena asked.

"You bet I do."

"What is your name?" Benjamin asked.

"It's James McDonald."

"A baby had to be born before I knew your name, Mac." Elena said. "I like the name."

"Uncle Mac, I want to hold my nephew, too."

"Yes, you can hold your nephew, John." He reached toward John with the baby. John grasped the baby tenderly. "I don't want to let go."

In the meantime, Elena had washed Anna's face and cleaned her bed for the new arrival. John reached over to Anna with the baby in his arms. "Here, Aunt Anna. Here's your little son."

"Somebody should send a telegram to Charlotte and let her know that the baby is here." Elena said.

"I think I should go and get Dr. Rivers. He would want to see if Anna is alright."

"You're right Mac. In the meantime, send a telegram to Charlotte, and let them know that the baby is here, and it's a boy."

"I'm on my way, Grandma."

"John, send the telegram to Charlotte, and I will get Dr. Rivers."

"I'm on my way, Uncle Mac."

Benjamin looked at the baby as Anna held him. "He is so beautiful, Anna."

"Thank you, Benjamin.'

"I am on my way to get Dr. Rivers. I won't be gone long." He left the front door running down the road towards Dr. Rivers.

"I thought he would have taken the wagon," Elena said.

"Mac is faster than the wagon, Elena. He's just about there now. Dr. Rivers will bring him back in his wagon."

"How far is Dr. Rivers from here?" Benjamin asked.

"About five blocks," Anna said.

"Well, he's there by now, Benjamin said.

32

D_{r.} Rivers was standing in the front door, when he saw Mac running toward his house. Mac ran up the three steps to the porch and stopped.

"Mac, what's wrong?"

"Nothing is wrong, Dr. Rivers. The baby is here, and we need you." He began to pant as if out of breath.

"Come on in Mac, and I'll get my black bag and we'll be on the way."

"I can run back, Dr. Rivers."

"Mac, I'm ready. You don't have to run back. You will soon give yourself a heart attack, and the baby won't have a father. Let's go and see what the fresh vegetables and fruits have brought. Follow me out the back door."

Mac ran to Dr. Rivers, and they went out the back door to his barn. Dr. Rivers prepared the mules for the trip. He climbs into the wagon. "Hop in Mac. We'll be there in a few minutes."

Mac jumped up into the wagon, and Dr. Rivers gave the signal to the mules to leave the barn.

"Dr. Rivers, I could have been there already."

"Of course, you could, Mac, but what could you do? You came for me to do what you couldn't do. I will take care of Anna and the baby, so you just settle down. I'll be with you soon."

Mac stood on the porch, moving about, while he waited on Dr. Rivers.

"Let's go," Dr. River said. "We can rush to the back and get the mules and wagon. Follow me through the kitchen to the back door.

When you get to the wagon, just hop in, and I'll get in and steer the mules toward your home."

Mac ran to the wagon and followed Dr. Rivers' orders. Dr. Rivers got in and steered the wagon towards Mac's home. "We're here Mac, and I will stake the wagon on the side of the house."

Mac didn't answer. He jumped out and didn't stop running until he was inside the house.

"Where is Dr. Rivers, Mac?" Elena asked.

"He's on the way."

"I thought y'all were coming together."

"We did," Mac said, and ran back to the door to let Dr. Rivers in.

"Good morning, everybody. I understand that we have a new arrival today."

"Yes, Dr. Rivers, we have. I have a teapot of hot water for you to scrub. You can have a peep at our new arrival."

"Let me scrub first, and I will take a peep. I know everything went well with you in charge, Elena."

"I think so, Dr. River, but we need your final words."

"You got it. He walked to the bed and looked down at the newborn. "Let me take a look at the umbilical cord." He gently pulled the band from the navel. "This is perfect. Who cuts the cord?"

"Mac did, Dr. Rivers." Anna said proudly.

Dr. Rivers laughed loudly, "You mean that Mac stood still enough to cut the cord?"

"That's my little son, Dr. Rivers. I wouldn't harm him for my life."

"I know you wouldn't, Mac. You did a good job. He pull out his instruments and examine the baby heart. He pulled the band from his navel. This is neat and perfect. I will need to see him a week from today. Thereafter, I will need to see him three months later. After his third visit, I'll see little Mac as often as needed."

"Thank you, Dr. Rivers," Anna said.

Dr. Rivers grabbed his bag, and looked toward the front door, where Benjamin stood. "Who is that young man, Mac?"

"That's Benjamin, Dr. Rivers."

"Oh," Dr. Rivers uttered, and proceeded toward the back door.

"Dr. Rivers," Benjamin called. "I came to ask the family and friends to forgive me. I meant no harm."

"That being the case, Benjamin, we all can forgive you. Where are you staying?"

"I'll find a place for my family soon as possible."

"You have a family?'

"Yes, sir."

"Mac?' Dr. Rivers called. "Since y'all staying in Elena's home, why can't Benjamin and his family have your home? If no one stays there, it will soon fall down."

"That's a good idea," Anna called from her bed. "Benjamin, y'all are welcome to stay there. Have your family to come on."

"You really mean it? I will send a telegram right away and let them know."

"John, you've been really quiet, when are you going to send a telegram to your mama, and let her know about the baby and let her know that Benjamin is here?" Anna said.

"I'm on my way, now." He ran out the door to the wagon, jumped in and led the mules to the train station where he would send a telegram to Charlotte. "I know she's going to be surprised and happy about both; the baby and also about Benjamin."

"I will go with you, so I can send a telegram to my family, too."

"Let's go, Benjamin."

"I'm ready.' Benjamin said.

"I don't know how we can thank you and Anna for letting us live in your home. We will certainly take care of everything. My wife is a neat housekeeper, and I help, too. Y'all don't have to worry about a thing." Benjamin promised.

"Benjamin, I know all of that. Y'all are welcome."

Benjamin followed Mac out to the wagon. "Hop in, Benjamin. We'll get there sooner than you think."

"I can hardly wait, Mac. I know my wife is going to be so happy. Her Uncle Jim will help her get everything packed and ready to go."

"Who is Uncle Jim, Benjamin?"

"Uncle Jim is my mother's brother. He lives in the same house with us. Of course, my mother, Beulah, will probably come with her, to help with Roy and Katie."

"Will Uncle Jim want to come and stay, too? There's plenty of room over there. With these children and a baby, we'll need plenty of help."

"That's a good idea, Mac. I hadn't thought of that. Uncle Jim is the best handy man in town. Y'all will like him a lot."

"I like Uncle Jim already. Tell us about your family, Benjamin. We know about your son and daughter."

"You already know about Uncle Jim, and my folks."

"Alright, Benjamin. We're here at the station. Get a good look, Benjamin, because you will need to know how to get here to send quick messages to your family and friends."

"When I send the message to my wife about our home, how soon will she get the message?"

"Right away, Benjamin."

"How will I know that?"

"She will answer right back, so you need to have everything ready for her and the rest of the family. Sometimes, a clerk from the train station will meet you with the reply in his hand when we return."

"Mac, you mean Ruthie will get the message that soon?"

"Yes, she will, and her reply will probably be waiting for you, when we return."

"That is fast. I like your method, Mac."

"Charlotte will know about the baby that fast, too."

Mac steered the mules to the rear of the train station. **"Whoa,"** he yelled to them. "Let's get out here, Benjamin. We can go around to the front door. The mules will be alright here until we get back."

Benjamin jumped out and waited for Mac to steady the mules and follow him toward the front door. "This was a short trip, Mac."

"I know, so let's go in and send our messages. I will ask the clerk to please notify us with a hand delivery."

"What is a hand delivery, Mac?"

"That means that someone will bring it to the house."

"Your method is getting better and better, Mac."

171

"I know," Mac said with a chuckle. "Our replies will probably be waiting on us when we get home. It's that fast."

"I bet Ruthie and Uncle Jim are packing everything now. The children have a lot of toys. I don't know how he's going to get everything here at one time."

"It might take more than a day to do that, Benjamin, but we have nothing but time." Mac opened the door. "Follow me, Benjamin."

"I'm right behind you, Mac."

Mac walked to the only clerk behind the desk. He was tall, thin and a head covered with red bushy hair. "Good afternoon. My friend and I want to send a couple of messages to some family friends."

The clerk brushed his hair from his forehead. "How soon do you want them sent?" He asked.

"Soon."

"Then, I'm your man. Let's get started. Who's first?" The clerk asked.

"Benjamin, you can send your message. I can wait to tell them about the baby."

Benjamin jumped for the opportunity. "I'm ready." He rushed to clerk with pad and pencil in his hand. "I know what I want to say to Ruthie."

"Then, write it down and I'll see that your wife gets the message right away."

Benjamin jotted down exactly what he wanted to say. He also mentioned the new baby.

"I can hardly wait to hear from Ruthie. I believe this is her first telegram."

"You did a good job, Benjamin. I will do mine, now and let Mama and my sisters know about our baby."

They gave the messages to the clerk, and paid the fee, and left out of the front door.

"Mac, do you think they'll get these messages today?"

"Benjamin, they might already have the messages in their hands."

"Now, that's what I call fast." Benjamin said and laughed.

"Before we go home, I want to stop by the fruit market on the way and take some fresh fruit." Mac said.

"I'd like that, too. I can get some collard greens, too. I know that is the first thing that my Mama wants when she gets here with Ruthie and the children."

"I'll get enough for everybody. We like collard greens, too." Mac said. "Elena can really cook them."

33

Benjamin, we'd better get to the wagon and head toward home. I bet they're wondering about us."

When they reached the wagon, Benjamin put his vegetables and fruits in first, and then, he hoped in. "Let's go Mac."

Mac put his two bags in and got inside and began to steer toward home. "How many bags of greens did you get, Benjamin? I like greens, too, but I don't want to eat them all week."

Benjamin laughed. "Just eat what you want, Mac. That's what I'm going to do."

As they approached the house, a tall bushy head guy was standing near a horse at the front door. "Do you see what I see, Benjamin?"

"Yeah. That looks like the guy we saw at the train station. What is that in his hand?"

"It's probably a reply from your wife, Benjamin. We'll soon know."

"That is what I call fast, Mac. We just sent the message."

"Hee," Mac yelled to the mules, and they made a right turn toward the side of the house. The young man on the horse rode toward them and gave the message to the first hand that he could reach, and he sped off.

When Benjamin and Mac reached the tall, shaggy head guy, he reached the message to Mac on the left side "Here's your message."

"We just sent it." Benjamin said.

"They got it as soon as you sent it. I got to get back. Come back to the station when you need to send another message." He said. He tapped his horse on the rear and rode off.

Mac reached the message to Benjamin. "Open it, Benjamin." They both got out of the wagon.

Benjamin tore the envelope open nervously. "It's from Uncle Jim, Mac."

"Well, what did he say?"

"Benjamin, I'm putting Ruthie and the children on the train today. Of course, their Grandma Beulah will come with them so she can help with children. Ask Mac to meet you tomorrow at 2:00. I'll leave tomorrow with the rest of our belongings. Meet me at 2:00 on Friday.

Bye,

Uncle Jim

"I can hardly wait to meet Uncle Jim. Will he mind us calling him Uncle Jim?"

"Of course not, Mac. Everybody calls him Uncle Jim. Let's go inside and give the message to everybody."

"Let's go in and tell them the news, and I want to see my baby again. I'll get them to the barn, and meet you inside, Benjamin. I want to see their faces when you read the message."

"Hurry up. I don't want to wait too long." Benjamin said.

Benjamin opened the message and noticed that it was from Uncle Jim. He read: Got your message, Benjamin. Everyone is so happy. I will put Ruthie and the children on the train tomorrow at 2:00 pm. Mama will come with them, so she can help with Roy and Katie. I am sending a few clothing and toys. Everything else will come with me Friday. I will leave tomorrow.

See you soon,

Uncle Jim

"Uncle Jim didn't waste any time. He gets things done right away. I believe we're going to get along with Uncle Jim just fine. Does Uncle Jim like to fish?"

"Does he like to fish?" Benjamin said. "He could fish everyday including on Sundays."

"Then, Uncle Jim is going to get along just fine with the neighborhood. Everybody likes to fish and show them off by giving them to those who don't fish."

"Uncle Jim keeps what he catches, because he likes to eat them, too."

After a short visit in the wagon, Benjamin and Mac got out. "I can hardly wait to give the good news" Benjamin said.

"What did the message say?" Elena asked.

"How do you know we got a message, Elena?" Mac teased.

"I saw the guy from the train station standing out there with something in his hand. He was waiting on y'all. He didn't see the wagon, so he knew his horse beat y'all here. So he just waited."

Benjamin read the message loud enough for all to hear. We will have a full house by Friday, because Uncle Jim will be here with all of their belongings. I believe we're going to like Uncle Jim, as well as Ruthie, her mother and the children. So let's get ready for them, Grandma. Their Grandma is Grandma Beulah."

"I like her already, Mac. I had a best friend with that name.

Ruthie, the children and Beulah will be here tomorrow."

"That's Wednesday, Mac. We'd better get things ready for them."

"Mac, if you and Anna don't mind, I can add three more rooms and a" built in" back porch to our new home. I am a pretty good handy man, so I don't mind at all, and my labor and material will be free to you. All you have to do is sit and look."

"Benjamin, I'm good at that. Anna and I are okay with you adding to the house."

"I can also add to this one, too, if you need more space."

"Do as you like, Benjamin. I might be able to give you some help, too."

"That'll be fine, Mac."

"Benjamin, I am taking you to my job Monday, so you can see what I do at the mill. You might like the work, since it deals with lumber. The pay is descent, and you can make a living working there. With your skills, you will be hired right away."

"Mac, that sounds great. I can do that. As long as it's working with wood, I am comfortable."

"You will be very comfortable, Benjamin, because the whole job is about wood."

"I can purchase the wood and supplies that I need to build the extra room from my job. That sounds great, Mac."

"You can do just that, Benjamin. Your Uncle Jim can help, too."

"If you knew Uncle Jim like I know him, he will probably do the whole job."

Elena reminded Mac that they had to send a message to Charlotte and let her know about Benjamin and his family moving here with us. She will be so excited."

"I know she will be, Elena. It seems as if she is doing a good job with taking care of the family. At least she hasn't sent any complaints. If she's not complaining, everything must be alright."

"I hope you're right, Mac."

"I think Christmas will be a great time to have everybody here. We don't have to worry about buying gifts for everyone. We grownups know about Christmas. We'll just get gifts for the children and enjoy each other."

"Elena, I like that idea," Anna called from the bedroom. "I'm going to get up and move about, so I can do something for this occasion. Lil' Mac just sleeps. I can do as much as I can until it's his feeding time again.'

"You'll get your strength back, too," Elena said. "Having a baby is a lot of work."

"I found that out, Elena. I can fold whatever is needed, as long as I can sit for a spell."

"You'll work out just fine," Elena said.

"I can go out into the woods and cut down a Christmas tree. I saw a lot of firs that would work out just fine. We have three more weeks before Christmas. I might be able to build some rooms before that time, so let's get the wood today, Mac."

"Let's go. In the meantime, I can get you hired." Mac said.

Benjamin followed Mac to the wagon, and they went on their journey to get lumber and a job for Benjamin. When they entered the door, Mac was greeted by the manager. Mr. Gibbs.

Mr. Gibbs, tall and round belly, pushed his silvery gray hair from his face. "Mac, congratulations on you baby. Yes, I heard about it. News gets around in this little town in no time. Who's your friend?'

"Mr. Gibbs, this is Benjamin. He's an old friend of my, who is going to stay and help me out at the house. He has a family, and we need some lumber to build three rooms onto out house, so they'll have plenty room."

"Which house are you going to add on?"

"Anna and I live in Elena's home. There's plenty room there for our family, but Benjamin and his family will live in our home, next door to Elena. He has a wife, mother, uncle and two children. Anna and I didn't have anybody but the two of us when we lived there, so we didn't need a lot of room."

"I see. Benjamin, do you know how much lumber you'll need? Of course, you'll need hammers, nails and other supplies, too."

"Yes, sir. I have that all figured out." He reached his list to Mr. Gibbs.

Mr. Gibbs studied Benjamin's list for a few seconds. "You have everything in place. I believe you know what you're doing. You can come in a pick out what you need. We'll talk about price later."

"Mr. Gibbs, why don't we do that now? Benjamin needs a job. As you can see, he's a good handy-man and can do whatever is needed. I thought you could hire him here at the mill?"

"That's a good idea. When can you start working, Benjamin?"

Benjamin clasped his hands. "I can begin working right now, Mr. Gibbs."

"Alright, Benjamin. Mac can take you around the mill, and you get everything you need for the rooms. If you can't get everything today, you can come back and get more."

"Mac, you can use that flatbed truck to deliver all of the equipment. I don't think your wagon can take everything."

"Yes, sir. We can do that today. Benjamin, when do you want to start on the rooms.?"

"Today." Benjamin said. "Today.

When Mr. Gibbs left, Mac said, "You know you will have to work for free until this is paid off."

"I can do that, Mac. Is Mr. Gibbs always that friendly?"

"I've never seen him any other way, Benjamin, but he wants work done on time and the right way. Any boss would want that."

"I can do that, Mac. I know that Mr. Gibbs and I will get along just fine."

"Then you're hired, so let's start getting your supplies. I can drive the flatbed truck and you can steer the mule's home. We can put some of the materials in the wagon, too. We have one more day before I pick Ruthie and others from the train station. I will be in the process of building when they get here."

"How would you like for me to be your boss, Benjamin?"

"What do you mean?"

"You can work in my department where I am the boss, and you can work off your debt for the lumber and materials that you need to build the rooms. I'm going to help you with those rooms, too."

"Well, boss, I like you already.

34

Benjamin and Mac went to the train station Friday to get Benjamin's family and their belongings. Their children, Roy and Katie ran to Benjamin, crying Papa, Papa. He dropped to his knees to hug them. After their hugs and kisses, Ruthie pulled him up and hugged him tightly. "I am so glad to see you. Your mother is on the train. She wanted to wait awhile before getting off."

"We've been standing here waiting for the doors to open. This is Mac, but I'll introduce him when I get Mama off. I'll go in."

After a few minutes, Benjamin and his mother, Beulah came to the door or the train. Mac went to the door and helped Benjamin assist his mother off the train.

"Mac, I want you to meet my family before we start home."

"I'd like that, Benjamin. I feel like I know y'all already."

"Mama, this is Mac. He's the one I always tell you about. Mac, Mama's name is Beulah Branch, and this is my wife, Ruthie."

Mac shook Ruthie's and Beulah's hands. "Now, I guess these little ones are son and daughter?"

"You're right. This is Roy." He rubbed his head, and this is Katie. Now, I guess we'd better get home and meet the others there."

"Follow me to the rear of the station, everybody. That's where our mules are waiting on us."

Mac noticed that Benjamin touched Ruthie's stomach. "Are you carrying something in there?"

"Yes," Benjamin answered. "I didn't tell you, because we had so much going on, but we're expecting in six months."

"It seems like y'all will have a spring baby. My son will be about six months about that time. We have two little Grandmas ready to handle them.

When they reached home, Mac jumped out of the wagon and gestured to the others. "Get out. We're here and everybody's waiting on y'all inside. Benjamin, you can help them out. I'm going to see my little son."

"He's got a little son?" Beulah asked.

"Yes." Benjamin said. "And he's only a few days old. He is so pretty. You'll like him, Mama."

"One more little one won't hurt. Yes, I will like him and welcome him into my heart."

Benjamin helped Ruthie down from the wagon. "This wagon is a little higher than ours, so you just can't jump in and out of it like our wagon."

"I'll catch on," she promised. "Let's go. I want to see our new family."

Benjamin led the way toward the house. We'll all be here by tomorrow."

"Yes, when Uncle Jim gets here with everything. We'll meet him at the train station tomorrow by four 0'clock." Benjamin said.

Mac ran back to the group. "Come on in and meet everybody. We'll unload everything later."

Beulah and Ruthie opened the door, and the others followed behind them. They went to an opened room, where they saw Anna and the baby. "Come on in," Anna said. "And meet our new family member."

Ruthie reached for the baby. "May I hold him?"

"You sure can. He is only three days old, but he likes to be held."

Ruthie lifted him tenderly from Anna's arms, and held him to her chest. He is a perfect fit. I've held many little ones here in this same spot. I don't know if I told you my name, but I am Ruthie, and this is Beulah Branch. She's Benjamin's mother."

Elena rushed to her and grabbed her hand. "Mrs. Branch, we're so proud to have you and your family with us. When Mac settles down, he will tell you about our arrangements."

Beulah held Elena's hand for a few seconds. "Elena, I'm Beulah."

"Yes, Beulah. I'm glad to meet you. You will have a chance to meet everybody before the day is over."

Elena looked out the back door and saw a few things left in the wagon. "I see y'all are traveling with only enough."

"Not really, Elena. My brother, Jim will come tomorrow and bring everything. He's even bringing the children's dog."

"They have a dog?" Elena said. "I like dogs, too."

"That is the only way that we could get them to want to come. They would never leave their dog, Spot. He's a member of the family."

"There's plenty of room for him." Anna said.

"I see Ruthie, Benjamin and Mac taking things over to the other house. I'd better get out and help them." Beulah said.

"Pardon my manners," Elena said. "Take a seat anywhere in here."

"We'd had better help and limber up some of these joints from traveling so long."

"Y'all have plenty of help over there. I have supper almost ready. I have everything in the warmer, but I wanted to wait until everyone was here, before I baked the corn bread. When y'all get worked up and freshen up, it'll be time for supper."

"It smells like it's ready, Elena." Beulah said. "I cook, too, so if you ever need help over here, let me know. I know I will have plenty to do over there, but I will have a little time sometimes."

"Y'all sit down anywhere in here. There's plenty of room. You just have to find it." Mac said.

After Beulah and Ruthie were seated, Benjamin sat down at the kitchen table. "Mac, I thought there were more members to this family."

"Yes, we have plenty members. John Jr. gets up early and goes to the pottery shop to work on pottery. He got his own place. Charlotte and her two daughters and son, Houston are in Marion County. She promised that they will be here for Thanksgivings."

"We will have that house ready by that time. Uncle Jim will be here tomorrow with all of their belongings and the dog, Spot."

"Dog?" Elena asked.

"Yes, the kids have a dog. Elena, you'll like Spot. He's friendly to everybody, so you know he's not a watch dog. He likes everybody."

"That's my kind of dog," Elena said. "We'll get along just fine. Tell us something about Uncle Jim before he gets here."

"Elena, he's another Mac. You can hear coins jingling in his pocket when he gets up from his seat."

"Benjamin, we've got a real problem, then."

"No, Elena. You'll like him. He's handy and willing to work."

"I'm excited about Ruthie's baby," Anna called from her bedroom.

"Who's this coming towards us?"

"That's John. Somebody at the house told him where we were, and he came to help. That's how he is." Mac said.

When John reached them, he walked around and shook all unfamiliar hands. "I'm John. John Frazier."

"Good evening, John." Benjamin said. "We arrived yesterday, and we're waiting on the last to arrive in a few minutes. When we get back to the house, we'll have a good introduction party. There are more at the house."

"Who are we waiting on today?" John asked.

"Uncle Jim and Spot, the dog. He's also bringing all of their clothes and belongings."

"Sounds like y'all will need as many hands as you can get. Count me in. I have two hands, and I'm willing and able to work."

"You're in," Benjamin said.

"Who are we waiting on?" John asked.

"Uncle Jim. He's coming on the 4 O'clock train." Benjamin said.

"Well, here he is, 'cause the train is in view. I can hear it, too. It's coming around the curve and will be here in a second."

"That's it. Y'all will get to meet Uncle Jim in a few seconds. Let's walk over to the sheltered spot over there. It will stop there."

The train will let people out there." Benjamin said.

They followed Benjamin to the sheltered area and waited for the door to open. "Here they come," Mac said.

"When these people move on, Uncle Jim and Spot should be next or not far behind." Benjamin said.

Benjamin looked back where he heard a wagon coming their way. "Who is this coming this way, Mac?"

Mac turned a looked at the wagon. "That's John."

"He's got a wagon, too?"

"No, he probably knew we would need help, so he borrowed our deacon's wagon. The mules are Coco and Dapper. He came to help us."

Benjamin looked back toward the train station. "Here comes Uncle Jim and Spot."

The children began to yell, Spot, Spot."

Ruthie held their hands, because she knew they would run after Spot. Spot heard them and began to pull Uncle Jim. Spot soon pulled away from Uncle Jim and began to run toward Roy and Katie. Roy and Katie pulled away from Ruthie and began to run toward Spot. When they met, Spot had a lot of wet kisses, and Roy and Katie had many hugs to give Spot. They rolled around on the grass with Spot until Ruthie called them to calm down.

"You'd think they were away from each other a month. They were away only two days." Mac said.

John pulled his wagon nearby. "Y'all need some help?"

"Yes, John, we need help." Mac said. "You came just in time."

Benjamin rushed to Uncle Jim. "Uncle Jim are you alright. I saw Spot pulled away and you were left reeling."

"I'm okay. I need help when they open the unit to get our things. Roy and Katie got Spot, so we don't have to worry about that. Come on y'all the unit is open and I see all of our things. I guess we're the only ones who have a lot of bundles. Ruthie, if you don't mind, just see after Roy, Katie and Spot."

"Yes, Dear. I can do that."

"I guess we need to know everybody. Benjamin, will you introduce your family?"

"Of course, I will." He put him arms around Ruthie. "This fine lady is my wife, and those little ones out there running in the grass are our children and dog: Roy, Katie and Spot, our dog."

"We will introduce ourselves when we get home. In the meantime, let's get packed." Mac said.

Mac, Benjamin and John loaded both wagons with all of their belongings. They even had Spot's eating and drinking dishes.

"Is everybody okay and ready to go?" Mac asked.

"Yes, we're ready, Uncle Mac." John said.

35

The wagons didn't stop until they reached their homes. Mac steered his wagon to the rear of their home and gestured to Benjamin to follow him. "We're going to unload everything on the ground, first, and then we'll decide where to put things in the house." Mac said.

"It looks like everything is going to fit in just fine." Benjamin said.

"Let me go over to the other house and see what's going on. It's awful quiet over there." Mac said. He rushed to the house, and noticed Elena and Beulah sitting on a couch and working on quilt squares."

"Do you quilt, too, Mrs. Branch?"

"Yes, I do Mac, and you can call me Grandma, too."

"We're unloading the wagons and it seems as if everything goes to your house over there. We also have Spot with us."

Beulah got up and ran to the door. "Where is he? I don't see him."

Grandma Branch, he's with Roy and Katie. They're out there somewhere playing with him."

"Alright Benjamin. Why don't y'all take a little time off, and eat some dinner? I thought y'all would eat as soon as you got back and then, we'd unload I can help, too." Beulah said.

"I'll tell them to leave things alone for a while, and we'll take care of things later." Mac said. "But first I want to see my baby."

"Mac, he's asleep." Anna said. "I've been up stirring around. I feel strong enough to set the table. How many do we have eating?"

"Anna, there are six of us and a dog. We can take food over to the other house and eat. There are only four of you over here."

"Benjamin, we can seat ten people at our table. Let's eat here. I will feed Spot. You need to find a safe place to tie his rope, where he can't get loose." Grandma Branch said.

Elena was already placing the plates on the table. Anna, you can put the spoons, forks and knives by the plates, and we're all set. I'll also put the food on the table, so no one will need to get up."

Anna was already placing the utensils where they were needed. "What else do we need?" She asked.

"I'll put glasses on the table, and everybody can get their own water," Elena said.

"Do we have ice for the water?" Beulah asked Elena.

"No, Beulah, this is well water, and it comes ready to serve. It's always cold."

"Who's going to call them to dinner?" Anna asked.

Beulah took a pie pan from a shelf and a long handle spoon and went to the door and began hitting the pan with the spoon. "I know they heard this, and I know they know what it means. Ann, you need to take a seat on the corner of the table, in case you need to tend to Lil' Mac."

"That's a good idea, Grandma Branch.

Benjamin entered the back door. "Looks like I'm just in time. I am ready for everything that I see on the table. Do you want me to call the others? I tied Spot to that old oak tree out there by the gate. I'll feed him first, and he can wait for the scraps, too."

"When you get Spot in the right spot to eat, then you can call everyone. As you see, we're ready."

Benjamin looked around at the table and noticed that everyone was seated, and the other six seats were for his family. "I want y'all to meet Uncle Jim before we eat."

Uncle Jim had just entered and stood by the door. His change was jingling in his pocket. "Is he nervous?' Elena asked.

"No, he's another Uncle Mac." John said. He's never still. "Come on and sit by me at the table, Uncle Jim." John said. "I'll take Spot's food to him, and I'll be right back."

When they were all seated, Benjamin blessed the food. John began passing bowls and platters of food around. "Let's keep things moving." He said. "After we're through, I will go to the train station, and see if Mama, Dorothy, Mary and Houston will be here for Thanksgiving. They know y'all are already here, and they're waiting for some kind of information."

"It's hard to leave this good food, but we'd better take care of business, too. I have had two servings of everything, so I'm ready to make plans on building more rooms onto this one, too."

"Jim, do you think we'll need more room,"

"Elena, these children are growing up, and pretty soon, they'll have some little ones to bring home, too. We don't want to wait until we need more room, let plan ahead."

"Uncle Jim, you're right," Benjamin said.

"That's a good idea, John. When they get here, we'll have the entire family together." Grandma Beulah said. "I can hardly wait to see everybody. "How are y'all doing about adding more rooms to Mac's and Anna's house?"

"We got everything covered, Grandma." Benjamin said. "We'll get to the other house later."

They will have plenty of entertainment while they're here. There's a rumor that a big powwow is planned during thanksgiving. Someone needs to let them know about the powwow, so they can bring something to wear to it. We have enough here for everybody."

"I can do that," Mac said. "I haven't been to a powwow in a long time."

"Did y'all see that blue bag that I brought along with my luggage." Grandma Branch asked.

"I saw it," Mac said.

"Well, it filled with powwow stuff. Y'all will have to wire a message to our guests and tell them to bring what they have for the powwow. I can dress them all."

36

"Mama? What is a Powwow" Benjamin asked.

"Ben, a powwow is a gathering of Native people. It is usually a religious gathering, but the Natives dance and march around having a good time with one another. There is always plenty of food to share. Elena and I are preparing our food. I see y'all have made room for Charlotte and her group, but John has a big house with three extra rooms. He says some can stay with him."

"I like that idea. Mac and I were thinking about turning the back porch into two rooms, but I don't like that idea, because you and Grand Ma Elena like sitting out there. If we used that porch, y'all wouldn't have a place to sit outside."

"I have a feeling, Benjamin, that we're going to have one of the best times of our lives. We have a new baby and another one on the way. We can manage that, too."

"I know we can. Mac and I are going to the train station today to help John get his family."

"What time, Ben?"

"4:00 o'clock. They're to arrive exactly at 4. John's wagon might not be able to bring them all, so we will help them. They'll have a lot to do before tomorrow, because tomorrow is the powwow. I hope they brought enough clothes for the powwow."

"Ben, if they didn't bring enough, I have the rest. Don't worry."

"Thanks, Sir."

"I'm going in the house to see what Elena is doing."

"Go ahead. I will wait on Mac. We have about twenty more minutes before we leave for the train station."

Branch goes inside and find Elena working in the kitchen. "Is everything about ready, Elena?'

"I hope so. I have a big peach cobbler for the family, and anyone else who might like peach cobbler." Elena said.

"That's everybody," Branch said.

"Branch, did I hear you say that Jim was your brother?"

"Yes, he is."

"Now, how did that happen?"

They both roared with laughing. "You see, Elena, my folks wanted a boy, but they kept having girls. There are four girls. I am the last one. After I came along, they decided to give up. But when I reached fifteen, they discovered that another baby was on the way. My mother said that she wasn't excited, because she believed that she could only have girls, and this was going to be another girl. When the baby was born, she found out immediately, that she had given birth to a son. There was jubilee all day and all night. Jim had four older sisters, and he didn't have to do anything. I am fifteen years older that Jim. He's my baby brother."

"I've never seen him act like he was spoiled." Elena said.

"He's not. He's the best little brother ever."

"Branch, I believe you're right. I hear the wagons. I guess they're on their way to the train station."

Branch and Elena went to the front door, and saw Mac and Ben pulled out to the road. Mac was steering the wagon. "When they get here, the food will be ready to serve. All they have to do is wash up and dig in."

"After we eat, we need to get the clothes out for everybody to wear for the powwow. All I know is they have to be colorful and beautiful."

"They will be, Elena."

After an hour of waiting on their guests, Elena began to worry. "I wonder what happened to them. I have warmed the food up two times. After while, it won't be fit to eat."

"Don't worry Elena, they will eat it."

"How long do you think this powwow will be?"

The powwows have lasted all day. Some people come and stay two or three hours, and then go home. Some will come back, and then some will stay home. They probably tired out early with all the dancing and parading around. If you get tired, we can leave and come back later or we can stay home, and let the young folks stay as long as the want to."

"I like that idea, Elena."

After about forty-five minutes, Elena went to the door. "I thought I heard a wagon. Here they come."

Branch rushed to the door and stood beside Elena. "You have good ears, Elena. I didn't hear anything."

"You will soon see them, because they're almost here."

"I can see that, Elena. Is that Charlotte in the center?"

Elena pushed the door open. "Yes, that's my girl. That's Charlotte."

"She's pretty. I see two more young ladies beside her. They're pretty, too. Who are they?"

"Charlotte's daughters. They are Mary and Dorothy. They had a brother named Paul, but he died about a year ago. Now, the only brother they have is John. He's a good brother, too."

I see they are pulling up in the back, so they can come in the back door. I'll see if it's unlatched." Branch went to the back door, and just stood, with one hand on the screen handle.

"I'm behind you," Elena said.

"You should be in front Elena, because you know who they are. I don't."

"The wagon was silent for a few minutes. "I wonder what they're doing. Why don't they get out and come on to the house.?"

"They're taking their time." Benjamin said, while standing by his mother. "They might be getting a lot of things out."

Finally John got out of the wagon and walked to the side in front of the wagon to let Charlotte out. He opened it and helped her out. "Did you get your bags, Mama?"

When they all got out and began walking toward the house. Benjamin and Beulah Branch stood mid-way and didn't move until Charlotte and the girls reached them.

191

Elena began running toward Charlotte, crying, "My baby, my baby.' Mary and Dorothy began calling; Grandma, Grandma."

They noticed some new faces. Charlotte saw Benjamin and Beulah standing near beside each other. She didn't know either, but she asked, "Who are you?"

Since she looked at Benjamin, he answered her.

"My name is Benjamin, and this is my mother. Her name is Beulah Branch."

She bowed to them. "I'm glad to meet y'all, but you look familiar."

"I was John Frazier's best friend. He told me a secret, and instead of keeping it as a secret, I t old it to many, and it got him in trouble. I am so sorry, and I miss John so much. I came to ask y'all to forgive me. I know that it's hard to do, but that is my wish."

"Benjamin, hating you won't bring John back. He would want us to forgive you, and I do forgive you, and my children do, too. I will take a little more time to get back to normal, but we will."

Benjamin went to Charlotte. He leaned down to her and hugged her tightly.

Dorothy and Mary nodded in agreement. "Yes, sir. We truly forgive you. We know our dad can rest now."

Benjamin went to Mary and Dorothy and hugged them, too.

John and Jim walked to join them.

He held out both arms and said, "Now it's time for your hug, too, John."

"No, Benjamin. We don't need to hug. A handshake is sufficient, and we have already done that." They both laughed at the joke.

"This is Uncle Jim, my mother's brother." He pointed towards Jim. And waved his arms around. He came with us. "Of course, you know that Beulah Branch is my mother."

"Let's go in and meet the new baby and the rest of the family." John beckoned.

"It's about time, John."

"But wait a minute." Jim said. "Where are their bags?"

"They're staying with me," John said. "And we took their things to my house first."

"Do y'all mean that we did all of that work for nothing? We worked day and night adding extra room to Mac's house, so y'all would be comfortable."

"We're grateful, Jim, but John asked us to stay with him, and we couldn't refuse. Maybe another time, we can stay in the new rooms."

"Think of it this way," John said. "The children will have all the room they'll need. Your efforts want go to waste."

"Let's go in," John beckoned to the group. They followed him through the back door where Mac stood holding his baby, while Anna stood near him. Katie and the two children stood beside Mac and the baby.

"Now, we're all here, so let's sit down wherever you can find a comfortable seat, and we'll eat and talk about plans for tomorrow."

"John, you're like your dad. You already have everything well planned." Benjamin said.

"After we eat, we'll talk about the powwow, and what to wear and what to expect." Elena said. "But first, we have to introduce our newest member to the family. Mac, you are holding the newest member. Why don't you introduce him?"

"Gladly. This is my first and only son, Mac Junior. You will have a chance to see him a plenty while you're here."

"A good introduction, Mac. Now, let's eat."

"Grandma, I'm ready for that." Dorothy said.

"And so am I." Mary agreed.

"After we eat, I will show y'all some pictures of a Powwow we attended when I was younger, but know, when I go, I sit on the sideline and watch. Some of the performers will bring their acts to those of us, who can't walk around and follow their acts.:

"Let's hurry and get through eating, so we can see the pictures," Mary said.

Elena pulled out some photos from her apron pocket. "Here are a few from the past," she said.

"You can see the people who attend the Powwow, and wonder Where did all these people come from in this little village. Well, they come from far and near. Many travel many miles to get here. The Powwow is the biggest celebration we have to demonstrate and share our culture with others. It also helps us to teach our young people about their culture."

A solo performer showing off his many feathers while dancing.

"You see, some of us old people can't walk, dance and parade like these young people, so some of the performers bring those talents to us. While we can't get up and dance, we clap our hands, and laugh at some of their stunts. They have many of those for our entertainment."

"Do y'all ever get up and join them?"

"Sometimes they will reach for one of us. Whoever they choose to get up and dance with them have no choice but to get up and give it their best. It's all in fun, anyway."

"That sound like a lot of fun, Grandma." Mary said.

"You will see for your self tomorrow, Mary."

"Charlotte? Elena called. "When are y'all leaving?"

"Tomorrow is Thanksgiving, and the children will see their first Powwow. We will leave Friday, the next day after Thanksgiving."

"Why so soon?"

"Mama, school starts Monday. They only had Thursday and Friday off. They missed a day getting here, so we can't have too many absent days."

"Y'all need to come during the summer, when y'all have longer vacation time." Elena said.

"Those are our plans for the next vacation. We don't want the new rooms that Mac and Ben built to go to waste." Charlotte laughed. "I have to be on my job, too. I have been made manager of my department, and I get a little more money, and I certainly need it."

"If y'all can't come to us, we might have a chance to go to you, but I don't know when that will be, because we have a lot of little ones in school and need our attention." Elena said.

"That will work out just fine." Charlotte said.

Drummers

"The drummers sat in a circle and tap gently on one drumhead. They set the crowd in motion for the entire event. While we sat on our blanket on the ground, a solo performer came to us, and show his outfit. They are all beautiful."

Elena showed a few more Pow wow pictures and then she put them into a little folder for safe keeping. "Do y'all have your Powwow clothes ready for tomorrow?" She asked.

"We brought a lot of things with us," Charlotte said. When we finished eating, we will go to John's and put things all together. When you see us in the morning, you will wonder, 'Who are they.'"

"I know we can count on you, Charlotte," Elena said. "What about you men? What are you wearing? You know you need lots and lots of colors and feathers."

"We got everything covered, Grandma." John said.

"I think we need to get these names right. Who is John?" Branch asked.

"John is my oldest son," Charlotte said.

"Then, why is his name John if your husband was named John. I get this confused."

"He was named after his father. Sometimes we call him little John, and then again, we call him John Jr." Charlotte said.

"Now, I got everything right in my mind." Branch said.

"What do you want us to call you?" Dorothy asked.

"I like that question. Y'all can call me Grandma Branch." She laughed. The old folks can call me Beulah. We call Benjamin Ben most of the time."

"What time do we eat Thanksgiving's dinner?" Charlotte asked.

"I think 11 o'clock will be fine enough. We can be through by 12 o'clock, clean the kitchen and be on our way by 1:30." Elena said.

"I like that idea. I won't stay there long, 'cause Anna can't go, and I need to be with her and our baby. But y'all go and have a good time."

"Mac, you can enjoy the fun for a little while. Next year, Anna can bring the baby and enjoy the Powwow."

"That's a promise, Elena. She will like knowing that."

"We need to go to bed early tonight, so we can eat and get ready for the Powwow tomorrow as planned." Elena said.

"Yes, Grandma. I'm ready for bed already." Dorothy said.

"What are we waiting on? Let's go." Elena said.

"Dorothy, y'all get in the wagon and let's go. We'll be here early in the morning, Grandma."

"Alright, John," Elena said.

"I was sorta disappointed," Elena said. "I thought we were going to stay together."

"We will be together in the morning, and then we'll all be together at the Powwow."

"You're right. They will all meet here. I will make enough breakfast, just in case they don't have breakfast at John's."

"That's a good idea, so let's go to bed. I told y'all that I wasn't going, because I will stay here with Anna and the baby."

"You should go, Mac. I'll be alright, the baby will be alright, too. We'll stand on the porch and look at as much of the Powwow that we can see. It will be almost like being there."

"I have all night to think about it. Since I haven't seen one in a long time, it might be a good idea to attend this one. How often too they come here?"

"There is a Powwow, every year, Mac. Sometimes we might have to travel a short distance to them, but they're nearby."

"Well, Elena, I might give it a try. Y'all might need me to come along, too. I know John will be there, but he needs help, and Benjamin will be there to help Beulah in case she needs help. Let's go to bed."

"We're ready for bed too, Mac."

"Let's go and get in our beds."

"We'll be here early in the morning, Grandma."

"What do you call, early, John?" Elena asked.

"Real early, Grandma, but I'll bring some cooked breakfast to add with what you're going to cook. We'll have enough."

"Y'all go on, and we'll see y'all in the morning. Good night."

All responded with, "Good night."

37

John set his basket down on the porch, near the door, and opened the door with his key. He picked the basket up and walked in. All was quiet. He put the basket on the kitchen table, and walked to the hall between two bedrooms, and yell, "Rise and shine!"

Elena jumped from her sleeping position. "Is that John, I hear."

No one answered. They were still asleep. John went back to the kitchen.

Elena rose from her bed, wrapped her robe around her and went to the kitchen. She saw John standing there by the table and laughing.

"John, why are you here so soon? I just went to sleep."

"It's time to get up Grandma. The others are still in the wagon. They wanted to be sure that they could get in, before getting out of the wagon."

"How did you get in?"

"You gave me a key, Grandma."

"I remember, now. Tell them to come on in, but I haven't made breakfast, yet."

"I have Grandma. I made lots of breakfast. Mama will bring it inside in a basket, and y'all can reheat it, it needed."

Charlotte and the girls got out of the wagon wearing their Powwow clothing. "I feel awkward wearing all of this stuff," Charlotte said.

"I hope we don't have to stay all day. I want to get into something that's comfortable." Dorothy said.

"I do, too." Mary said.

"We haven't made it to the Powwow yet, so stop complaining. Y'all might like it and want to stay all day." John said.

John lifted Houston from the wagon and carried him a few feet toward the house. Houston had to be carried from the wagon, because he was still asleep and didn't want to be disturb. "I'll take care of Houston," John said. "Y'all just go on into Grandma. She's holding the door open for y'all."

Charlotte and the girls went toward the house, while John took care of Houston. "Come on Lil' brother. You need to walk so you can wake up and eat a big breakfast."

"It's too soon to eat, John, but if I have to, I will eat."

John grabbed Houston's hand and walked toward the house and joined everyone in the kitchen. "What did you fix for breakfast, John?" Houston asked.

"You'll have to wash up and come back and see. Some of your favorite is waiting on you."

"Houston rushed to the bathroom and washed his face and hands and rushed back to the kitchen to eat some of his favorite, bacon and eggs.

The house was loud with ooh's and aah's over the Powwow clothing that Dorothy and Mary were wearing. They were dressed as Indian princesses.

Jim, Benjamin, and Beulah Branch heard all the noise at the other house. 'Something is going on over there," Beulah said.

Benjamin rushed to the kitchen. "Where?" He asked.

"Over at the big house."

"You have given their house a name. Now what is this house name, Mama?

"Benjamin, we'll call it, The other House. I believe we can all tell them apart."

"I have done enough work on this house to know it, Mama."

"So have I," Jim said.

"Let's go. I think we're eating breakfast there, and then go on to the Powwow. I see y'all have dressed for it. I am wearing what I wore the last time. No one will remember." She laughed.

Members of the 'Other House' went over to the Big House and joined in the fun and breakfast. After eating and introductions, the Grandmas gathered the children and all walked out to join the parade of people going to the Powwow. Both Grandmas had a blanket wrapped around their arms. They knew that they would soon need them.

As they walked down the road to the Powwow, they were admired by many, who stood inside their door, and looking out. Someone yelled, "Y'all look really good."

Elena yelled back, "thank you a lot."

Mac walked to the front door and looked out at his family going to the Powwow. He was fully dressed for the Powwow event, but he promised Anna that he would stay with her and the baby.

Anna stood in the hallway between the two bedrooms, but she could see Mac shuffling his feet to his own imaginary music. Anna observed Mac. "Mac?"

"Yes, Hon. What is it?"

"You're dressed for the Powwow, why don't you go?"

"No. I need to be here with you and our little son."

She noticed that Mac couldn't stand still. He moved his elbows up and down in rhythm with his feet.

"Mac, I want you to go right now. You're making me nervous>"She scolded.

"Alright, Hon. I'm on my way." He pushed the screen open and ran to join his family.

"I thought you didn't want to go?" Benjamin said.

"Well, I changed my mind. I didn't want y'all to have all of the fun. You need a little help, so I thought I'd come alone."

"Did Anna throw you out?" Elena asked.

"She thought it would be a good idea for me to come alone and be with y'all. Y'all might get lonesome."

"I bet she did." Benjamin said.

"I see a small knoll just in the right spot where we can sit and see everything." Elena said.

"Where?" Beulah asked.

"Right over there," Elena pointed.

Benjamin took Beulah's blanket and Mac took Elena's blanket and they went to the knoll.

"How do y'all like this spot? It flat enough where y'all can get up and sown and keep your feet out of the way. I believe it's safe here." Benjamin said.

"I think so, too." Elena said. "Now, y'all get the two of us settled, and y'all can go and join the commotion. They usually bring entertainment to us sitters. Go on and enjoy yourself."

Charlotte, Mary and Dorothy were in the middle of the commotion. John held Houston's hand and took him through the entertainment. They did their little dances and yells along with the crowd.

"How do you like the Powwow so far, Houston?"

"It's fun. I like it. Can we come again?"

"Perhaps next year, but we leave tomorrow for home. You have to be in school Monday. Mama, Mary and Dorothy have to be at work, and I have to be in my shop." John said.

"Well, let go back to the fun, John. I like over there." He pointed at the drummers and dancers. "When I get bigger, I'm going to play one of those drums, and let the girls dance."

"That won't be long, Houston. You're growing so fast, now, I believe you will be able to join the drummers next year." John said.

"I have to have a drum, John, before I can learn to play one."

"Trust me, Lil' brother, you will have a drum."

"Alright. Let's go. I want to see some more dancing."

"Why don't you join them?" John asked.

"When I come back again, I will join them, but for now, I just want to watch them."

John looked toward the knoll. "Is that Mac over there, Houston?" I thought he wasn't coming to the Powwow."

"I guess he changed his mind. Everybody wants to come to this Powwow. It's fun."

"You're right, Lil' brother. Let's go over there and see for ourselves."

Houston started in that direction. "Wait on me. We're not in a hurry. We'll get there."

"I want to hurry so we can come back to see the dancing."

"We can come back and see the dancing any time. There are plenty dances all around."

Houston hesitated, "Well, let's hurry."

Toward the end of the day, people began to gather up their things and prepare for leaving.

"We'll come back tomorrow." Elena said.

"What time?"

"Benjamin, we'll have to think about that later."

"Alright, Mama."

"We're leaving tomorrow morning, Mama, so we won't be back this evening."

"I want to come back." Houston yelled.

"Lil' Brother, you heard what Mama said. We have to get up early in the morning for y'all to get on the 8 o'clock train. You have to be in school Monday morning at nine o'clock."

"We can still get there, John at 9 0'clock if we stay a little longer and see the dances and parade." Charlotte said.

"It's alright with me, because I don't have to catch a train in the morning. If y'all want to stay for the evening events, it's okay with me."

"John, we'll stay for a little while for Houston." Charlotte said.

"Yes, Mama, we'll stay, but just for a little while."

Houston was able to get his way, as usual, and they stayed for the evening activities. At the end of the evening, Houston was tired, and said loudly, "Let's go home. I'm tired."

Charlotte asked John to get everyone's attention, so they could get to him home and prepare to leave the next morning.

John located Mary and Dorothy among the crowd and brought them to join the others at his home. "Y'all get ready to leave in the morning on the 8 o'clock train."

"We'll be ready, John," Charlotte said.

"Let's give our hugs to all and say our goodbyes." Charlotte said.

"No, Charlotte," Elena said. "We'll give out our hugs and say, "Til' we meet again."

"Yes, Mama, it's 'til we meet again."

"We'll walk over to the wagon with y'all and help y'all in>"

"Mac, y'all have done so much already. I believe we can get in the wagon. We will be back again. We've had so much fun. We can't stay away too long."

"I hope you are telling the truth, Charlotte. We need to keep in touch."

"We can do that Mama." Charlotte and her family walked away toward their wagon, while Elena and the others looked on.

"I enjoyed them." Beulah said.

"You will see them again". Elena promised.

As Charlotte and her family walked slowly to their wagon, Elena, Mac Beulah and their families stood in a line, facing the backs of Charlotte and her family. Benjamin noticed that Charlotte had a tight grip on Houston's hand. "I hope she keeps that grip on Houston for a long time, because he's going to need it."

"What do you mean?" Elena asked.

"I notice that Houston tells her what he wants to do, and what he not going to do."

"When did you notice that?" Elena asked.

"Charlotte gave him a plate of scraps from the table and told Houston to go out in the yard and feed Spot. He told her he didn't want to feed Spot, so she went outside and found Spot and fed him herself. I couldn't imagine telling my mother that I didn't want to do what she asked me to do. He's eight years old now. What will he do when he is five or six years older?"

"Time will tell, Ben. Time will tell." Elena promised.

When John and his family reached the wagon, they turned and faced Elena and the group. They waved slowly to them and turned and climbed into the wagon.

Elena had a sad feeling about their departure. "Let's wait until they leave." She said.

Beulah noticed tears flowing from Elena's eyes. "You'll see them again, Elena. You can also go and visit them."

"I know I can, but I don't feel that everything is alright with them."

"If not, they can handle it, and with John's help they will be alright."

"John has given enough of himself for a young man. He needs to take care of himself."

"He's doing that, Elena. We can go to his exhibits next week and see for ourselves." Beulah said. "He invited us when he was at the Powwow, while we were sitting on the blanket.

"John is going to be a famous businessman someday." Beulah said. "I just met John, and I notice how dedicated he is about his work."

"I believe you're right. In fact, I know you're right." Elena said.

After a few moments of silence, John yelled, **Hee Haw**.

38

There have been many changes since the 1871 Powwow. There have been many Powwows, but the family didn't attend, because of the distance. Also, the children were growing up, and didn't won't to go to another Powwow. Elena and Beulah were busy helping the young families with their growing children. After eight more years, Spot was still having more fun with his friends. Baby Mac was up and running and chasing him. Spot made him welcome to the chase.

Charlotte and her family were too busy to travel. Mary and Dorothy had beaus and were busy courting them. They all taught in the same school that they once attended. The only problem with their family was Houston. Charlotte was staying out late every night. Charlotte sat up every night by the door, and worried that she might get a bad report about him being hurt. She thought nine o'clock at night would be a good time for a teenager to be home. Houston was fifteen, but looked older, because he was more than six feet tall.

One night, Charlotte confronted Houston about his late hours. He came home each night after ten o'clock. "Houston, where are you at this time of night? You have to be here, in the house every night at nine o'clock. We've been through this once. I don't want to go through it again."

Houston didn't respond. He just walked away to his room.

That night of the same day, Houston wasn't home at ten o'clock. Charlotte got up and looked out the door to see if she could see him walking toward home. The night was quiet, and no one was walking in the streets. She sat up until 12 o'clock waiting on Houston. Finally she went to bed, because she had be at work early the next day. Sleeping wasn't on Charlotte's mind. She had no idea where to find Houston. She only knew one of his friends, and that was the little girl, June. He had to go to the office at school for pulling her hair. Finding June wasn't easy. She and her family moved away years ago. Furthermore, she is a young lady now, and might have a family of her own.

Many thoughts came to mind for Charlotte, but she didn't know where to start. The only help she could think of was John. John has his own life, but he will stop and help her find Houston. Charlotte dozed off with that idea on her mind.

Early the next morning, Charlotte got up and prepared a quick breakfast. Mary and Dorothy were married and living away from home. They have their own lives, and she didn't want to worry them. Mary and Dorothy were teachers in the same school that they had attended through grade school. They had to be on the job at eight o'clock, so Charlotte was on her own.

When Charlotte finished her day's work at the store, she sent a telegram to John. "John, I need your help. I know this is a busy time for you, but Houston ran away. I have looked everywhere for him. He's only sixteen. Where can a sixteen-year-old child be? I need your help, please. Mom."

John stayed late at his pottery shop, because he was preparing for a showing of the pottery done by the beginners. This show will take place there two weeks from the present date. When he reached home, he saw his friend from the train station by the door, holding a letter in his hand. He rushed to him, because he knew something was wrong for him to be there waiting on him. He rushed his mules and staked them outside beside the shop. He rushed to the guy holding the telegram. "Whee, something must be wrong."

His friend gave him the letter and rode away on his horse. He opened the telegram slowly and read Charlotte's message. His anxiety and worries seem to disappear. He said to himself, "I can't help with this. He went to his wagon and got in and steered them to the train station. When he went in, he saw his friend standing by the counter, as if he was waiting on him.

"Is everything alright, John?"

"No, but it soon will be. I need to send a telegram to my Mama."

The young man got a sheet of paper and a pencil and gave it to John. "Take your time, John. I'm in no hurry."

In the meantime, Charlotte realized that she was alone for the first time in her forty-three years. She walked to the front door and saw Mary and Dorothy walking toward home. She realized that she would have to tell them, but what could they do. She would wait on John. If anyone can find Houston, it will be John. As Mary and Dorothy got near the house, Charlotte rushed out to meet them.

"What's the big rush Mama?' Mary asked.

"Houston ran away." She said softly.

Dorothy and Mary began to laugh. They opened the door and went inside. Charlotte went in behind them.

"It's true, y'all. Houston ran away, and it's no laughing matter. I just sent a telegram to John. I hope he can find him."

"Mama, John can't find Houston, and neither can we. He knows where we are and how to contact us. When he gets ready, he will do that. You will have to let go for a while. When Houston is ready to come home, he will. He will perhaps never come back to stay, but at least we'll know where he is. Don't worry. He is well and safe." Dorothy assured her.

Charlotte saw another figure coming down the road toward them. "I wonder who is that man coming here?"

"It looks like something important that he's bringing." Mary said. They stood in a huddle together until he reached them.

"Charlotte Frazier?" He announced.

"Yes, I'm Charlotte Frazier."

"Here's a telegram for you." He reached it to her, turned and walked away.

"Thank you," she said. Charlotte smiled as she opened the telegram. She knew everything would be alright, and John would help. She continued smiling as she opened the telegram, hoping to receive some good news from John. When the telegram was opened, her smile turned to an expression of disbelief.

"Mama, what did John say?" Dorothy asked.

Charlotte reached the telegram to Dorothy, and Dorothy read it aloud.

Mama,

I am in full charge of my business, and I cannot leave it. Houston knows the way home. When he is ready, he will come back. You don't need to go out hunting for him.

Love,
John.

Charlotte began to cry. "I thought John would come and help me find Houston." She sobbed.

"Mama, John is right. Leave Houston alone, do something for yourself." She motioned with her hands. "There are a number of things you can do to keep busy."

"Like what?"

"Do you remember the man who was in charge in building our home? He made sure that it would please us, and I think he was trying to please you."

"Mary, what are you talking about."

"You're so busy trying to keep Houston, you haven't taken time to do anything for yourself."

"Like what, Dorothy?"

"Dress up. Put on some makeup and walk out of the house for a change." Dorothy said loudly.

"Don't be so loud, Dorothy."

"Well, somebody needs to hear it. You don't seem to want anything but Houston. He's letting you know in his own way, that he wants a little freedom. You can't hold his hands forever. He is showing you his way."

"He's only fifteen. Where can he go and work to take care of himself at that age."

"Mama, Houston will find a way. We all have a part in spoiling him, but he's letting us know that he can do everything on his own. When he realizes that he needs help, he'll find us. He knows where we are, but we don't know where he is. Everything will work out soon or later."

"I hope you're right, Dorothy."

"I know I'm right, Mama. Houston likes to be comfortable. When he's not, he'll find us for his safety and comfort."

"I wonder what John is going to do to help find Houston?"

"He told us what he wasn't going to do in his telegram, May. I don't think he's going to change his mind."

"You're right, mama." Dorothy said.

In the meantime, John took the telegram, got into his wagon and went to the Big House. There, he would see everyone, and he would tell them about Houston. Benjamin went to the back door and looked out. He saw John coming toward them with something in his hand. "Y'all, I see John coming with a letter in his hand. I wonder what could that be."

"We'll wait and see," Elena said as she joined him at the door. She opened the door wider for John. "Come in, John. What's that in your hand.?"

"A telegram from Mama. I thought I would bring it and let y'all see what's going on."

"Well, open it," Elena urged.

John opened the letter and read slowly what Charlotte had written. "It seems like she needs help in finding Houston."

"Whoopee!" Benjamin yelled. "I believe someone made a $10.00 bet to me. Who made that bet?"

"No one, Benjamin. Nice try, but no one made a bet to you."

"I guess I was dreaming, then. What is she doing to find Houston?" Benjamin asked.

"She wants me to find him. I can't and I won't quit my job jut to look for Houston. I sent her a message and let her know that. In the meantime, I am inviting y'all to come to my shop next Thursday night and see our exhibits."

210

"John, I like pottery and I can hardly wait to be there." Beulah said. The others agreed that they would be there, too.

"I'll see y'all there." John said, and he walked toward his wagon.

Elena ran to her bedroom and put on her walking shoes. She ran back to the kitchen, and to the back door. She saw John walking hurriedly to his wagon. "Wait, John. I'm coming."

John turned around and saw her running towards him. "What is it, Grandma?"

"I want you to take me to the train station."

He noticed that her eyes were filled with tears. "Why, Grandma?"

"I want to get a ticket."

John didn't ask any more questions. He knew that Grandma Elena would always make everything better. He helped her in the wagon on the passenger's side and went to his opening, got in and said, Hee Haw, and the mules were steered to the train station. He helped Elena out and they went inside the station. Elena pulled out a handkerchief from her bosom and asked the clerk to give her a ticket to Marion County. "I want to leave tomorrow as soon as possible."

"We have a train leaving at 8:45 to Marion County tomorrow morning. Is that okay?"

"That's fine with me. John, can you get me here by 8 o'clock?'

"I can bring you here at any time, Grandma." Are you going to help her find Houston?'

"No, John, I'm not. Houston knows how to find use and he will, when he wants to. Charlotte is my baby, and I want to comfort her. I don't want her to go through this alone. There might be a time when I will want all of my things sent to me. If so, John, I will ask you to get them together take them to the train station to be shipped to me."

"I will do that, Grandma."

"Let's get back to the house, and you can get back to your job.

"I'm ready, Grandma. How are you going to take care of yourself? I notice you frowning a lot when you get up from a chair."

"That's a sign that I'm getting older, but I'm alright."

"I hope so, Grandma, but if you get sick there with Mama, will you let me know?"

"You'll be the first to know, John."

"What time do you want me here in the morning, Grandma?"

"7:30 will plenty of time, John."

"I'll be here at 7:30, Grandma.'

Elena was up at 6 o'clock and ready to leave. She sat at the kitchen table with her hands on her bag. "No breakfast this morning, Elena?" Beulah asked.

Elena noticed that Beulah had a bag with her. "Where are you going, Beulah?'"

"With you."

"You can't go with me, Beulah." They both stood as to face each other in a duel.

"What and who is going to stop me?" Beulah asked.

"Somebody needs to stay here with this bunch. Someone needs to help take care of the children and little babies."

"It won't be me, Elena. These are their children and babies. It's time that they take care of them. Anyway, Elena, you would do the same for me."

Charlotte's girls and me will be enough to help her during these times."

"I'm not talking about Charlotte and her girls, Elena. I'm talking about you. You need help, too. I notice that you frown sometimes when you get up from a chair. You can't fool me. I will be there to help you."

"Charlotte needs help in finding Houston, Beulah."

"If that's the case, we both need to unpack our bags and go back to bed. Houston will come home when he gets ready. It will be soon or later, but he will be back."

"I know you're right, Beulah, but I need to get Charlotte to understand that."

"You don't need to get Charlotte to understand anything, Elena. Houston is doing a good job of that himself."

Elena got up from the table and went to the back door. "I see John pulling up to stake his mules.: Elena said. "I thought I heard him."

Beulah go up and joined Elena at the door. "that's John. I wish we had more John's. He is so faithful."

"He is, and I don't know what we would do without him."

"Someday John will show y'all what you can do without him. He's got his own business, and he's going to grow and grow."

"I believe you, Beulah. I know he will be a success at whatever he set out to do."

As John came walking toward the house, Elena and Beulah opened the door, closed it, and began walking toward John.

"Good morning," He said. "I thought we bought only one ticket. Grandma Branch, where are you going?"

"With Elena."

"You have to have a ticket."

"I'll get it when we get to the station. I brought money with me."

"You won't have to use it; I'll get it for you. Let me help y'all in the wagon and get on our way."

After they were settled in the wagon, John steered the mules to the train station. When they went inside with their bags, John's friend at the desk, said, "John you bought two tickets yesterday. I see two passengers and two bags."

"I know, but I'm buying another ticket."

"Here's your ticket, John." He accepted the money from John for the ticket. "Let me help y'all in. I'm not busy now."

"Thanks, Tim. Thanks very much."

After they were seated, Tim rushed to the office, and noticed that everyone was seated. "All aboard?" He yelled.

He pulled the rope that signaled to the engineer that all passengers were in and ready to go.

"I guess we're on our way." Beulah said.

"Yes, we are." Elena said. "We're on our way."

The two little Indian Grandmas sat silently for a while. After a moment, Beulah asked Elena, "How did we get ourselves into this?"

"What are you talking about, Beulah?"

"I don't know, but I will figure that out later. We will not try to solve their problems. If we stay out of their problems, they will learn how to solve them."

"You think so, Beulah?"

"We learned how to solve our problems, and they will do the same, if we stay out of their business."

"I can certainly do that." Elena said.

Beulah reached for Elena's hands and held them in her lap. "I am leaving all of my family behind. I only have my brother, Benjamin and his new family."

"You've got us," Elena said. "You've got us."

"Thank you so much for that, Elena."

After a brief nap, the conductor yelled. "Marion County, Texas"

Elena nudged Beulah, "Beulah, we're here. We have to get off. An attendant will help us with our bags. We will stand near the door when we get off, so he'll know where we are."

Beulah followed Elena off the train and stood by the door outside until the attendant could help them. Finally, he came running towards them, pushing their bags. "Here you are. You see I remembered them. I hope y'all enjoyed your trip and will enjoy your stay here.'

"We will, and here are fifty cents for helping us." Elena said.

"And here are another fifty cents," Beulah said.

"Oh, thank you both so much."

"Look over yonder, Elena."

"Where?"

"Do you see those two young women coming this way?"

"Yes, I see them now. One is Mary and the other is Dorothy. Those are my granddaughters. They came to meet us."

"They came to meet you, but what about me? Do you think they'll be glad that I came along?"

"Of course they will, Beulah. We'll be one big family."

"I hope so, because I don't know where to begin to find Houston."

"Neither do I, Beulah, and I'm not going to try."

Mary and Dorothy came running toward Elena and Beulah, calling out: "Grandma Beulah, Grandma Elena."

After greeting Mary and Dorothy, Elena asked, "Where is Charlotte?"

"She is getting the wagon ready, and she'll be coming down the road soon." Mary said.

"I hear her now," Dorothy said.

"Clang, clang, clang."

"Do you hear that, Grandma?"

"Everybody can hear that, Dorothy. I believe she know we're here. Oh, here she comes around the curve." Elena said.

They all rushed to meet Charlotte as she got out of the wagon. "I'm so glad to see y'all. You've made my day."

"We are here to help you with days ahead, not just this day, only."

"I'm so thankful. Y'all get in the wagon, and we'll go home."

Dorothy and Mary helped Elena and Beulah inside the wagon, and Charlotte steered the wagon toward home.

"Grandma Beulah, I'm so glad that you came alone with Grandma. Now, we have two Grandmas."

"Mary, I'm glad that I came, too. I was worried at first, that y'all wouldn't want me here."

"Never worry about that, Grandma." Dorothy said.

Charlotte steered the mules in the rear of their home and got out to hitch them to the stump of a tree. "We can all get out here. There's the house." She pointed toward the house that was built for her family.

"That looks like a house that a slave master owned. It's wonderful. How did y'all get that beautiful house.

"Tomorrow is Sunday. You will meet the men who built this house, and also the pastor and members who helped us to end s our Slavery soon than expected."

"Charlotte, I can hardly wait to see these find people that y'all talk about."

"You will meet them tomorrow at church. You will find, that these are some of the friendliest people on earth. When they say 'You're welcome', they mean it."

I believe you, Charlotte," Beulah said.

"We'll get up early enough to make breakfast, eat dress and on our way to church about 10:45. We'll get there in time for 11 o'clock service."

"It seems like you have everything all figured out, Charlotte."

"Yes, Mama, I have."

"Do these people at church look like us?" Beulah asked.

"What do you mean?" Elena asked.

"Are they Indians, too?"

"Some are red, some white, some are black, and some are brown Beulah. You will like them. They helped us to get out of slavery, and some built the house that we will stay in. Wait until you meet them."

"I like them already, Elena. I was worried about them liking me."

"They will. Don't worry. Let's go to bed, so we can get up early in the morning for church."

39

"Rise and shine," Elena called out.

Elena had dressed for making breakfast and church. She had a chenille robe over her clothes that she was wearing to church. She called again, "Rise and shine."

Dorothy came out of his room fully dressed. "She bent down and hugged Elena. "Good morning, Grandma. I'm up and ready for the day. What do you need?"

"You need to get your mama and Dorothy up, so they can eat and get ready to leave for church about 10;30. Beulah is already up and working in the kitchen."

"What is she doing, Grandma?"

"Putting out the plates. The forks, knives and spoons are already out and in place."

"When did y'all do all of this, Grandma."

"While y'all were sleep last night."

"I'll go and get them up, Grandma." Dorothy went to the kitchen to see Beulah. "Good morning, Grandma. I see you're up early, too."

"Yes, I didn't want Elena to do everything by herself, so I got up when I heard her getting up."

"I'll get the others," Dorothy said, and she went to the back where they were still asleep.

"I believe you are right, Elena."

"Right about what, Beulah?"

"That they will like me, too." Beulah said, and laughed.

"You don't have to worry about anything, Beulah. I told you that they will like you, too."

"I believe you."

Beulah began setting the table for the family of five. "We are really growing. We have five to get ready."

"You're right, Beulah. Let's keep it that way. I don't think Mary and Dorothy plan to marry soon and have babies. I love babies, but I've had my share for a while. I am willing to help out, when necessary, though."

"So am I, Beulah. I have a feeling that something good is going to happen today. I don't know what it is, but I have that feeling." Elena said.

"Elena, I have that same feeling, so let's get everybody up and out on time, so we can find out what kind of feeling we have." Beulah said.

"Good morning, "Charlotte said as she entered the kitchen.

"Good morning," they replied.

"Since everybody is here, be seated and I will say grace. After we eat, I will warm up the Sunday dinner that I cooked and kept cool for today,"

"What did you cook Grandma Beulah?"

"A pot of collard greens, beef pot roast and I will make the hot water corn bread when we get home from church."

"What is hot water corn bread, Grandma?"

"You'll see when I make it, and some day you will make it, too." Beulah said.

"I'll have to taste it first, before I know if I want to make it or not."

"Dorothy, you will like it. I've never seen or heard of anyone who didn't like hot water corn bread."

"I'm going to make it someday," Charlotte said. "I ate some hot water corn bread years ago, and it was so good."

"I made that batch that we ate years ago, Charlotte."

"Mama, why didn't you make more."

"I don't know. I'm already dressed for church, and I see that everyone is, too. I have a good feeling that something good is going to happen today, so let's hurry and get on our way." Charlotte said.

Beulah wiped her hands on the kitchen towel and grabbed her straw hat from the corner rack. "Let's go and see what that good feeling is all about." She said.

Elena led the family to the door and outside to the road. "We're safe in case if someone comes alone in a wagon. We won't get dusty before we get to church."

"I hope you're right, Elena, 'cause I spent a lot of time ironing this long skirt that I'm wearing today."

"Beulah, the ushers will have you to stand as a guest. Do you mind standing? You might be asked to make a statement. Do you mind?'

"Not at all. You see, I was an usher for our church back home for more than twenty-five years. I know what to expect, but thanks for reminding me. Jim, you're so quiet. Did you get enough to eat? I promised myself that I was going to put some more pounds on you."

"Sis, I'm just fine. I feel like today is going to be a day to remember."

"Everybody is saying that. Let's get out of here and see what that good feeling is." Dorothy said.

Their feelings gave them the idea to dress up to their feelings. They out dressed their Powwow fashions. Dorothy, Mary, and Charlotte wore long skirts, with long sleeves, tucked in blouse. Each wore a long flowing scarf to drape over their heads, Charlotte and Elena had similar dressing, but Beulah and Jim wore their Powwow clothes. They stood around in a circle to view each other. Benjamin and Jim wore the same outfits that they wore for the Powwow.

"I think we look great for church." Elena said. "What do y'all think?"

"I agree," Dorothy said.

"Did anyone tell Mac and Anna about today?"

"I did, Grandma, but they said that they would miss today." Dorothy said.

"Well, let's go. Do y'all want to walk or ride in the wagon?" Benjamin asked.

"I'd rather walk," Dorothy said.

"Let's shut the door and get on our way." Jim said.

219

When they reached the church, they hesitated for a few moments before going in.

"What's wrong?" Benjamin asked.

"I still have that good feeling," Charlotte said. "I don't want it to go away."

"It won't go away, Charlotte. Let's go in."

"Alright, Mama. Let's go."

When they reached the door, there were several members waiting to enter, but they stood back and let the Frazier's family enter.

"I remember y'all from the last time you were here," one member said. "We are so glad you came back."

"Thank you so much." Elena said as she entered the door.

"We also have some more guests today." The members pointed toward a large wagon. "They will come in later," She said.

"Who are they?" Charlotte asked as she followed Elena to their seats.

"They're loggers. They come through here every year and visit our church.".

The usher opened the door wider and beckoned the members and guests to come in. When they were in, Elena led them to their same seats on the back row on the left of the aisle. The men, who were visiting too, sat four rows down to the right of the aisles. They looked back at Elena's group, briefly before sitting down.

When the usher stopped seating members and faced the front, the pianist began to play for the choir to enter. Their pastor was already at the pulpit and looking over the audience. He raised his hands for the audience to stand and join in singing their opening hymn., What A Friend We Have in Jesus. Their pastor probably had a good feeling, too, because he couldn't wait for the usher to introduce their guests. "I know this is a bit unusual, but I want to introduce our guests before we began our service. So I am asking you men to stand, please and give us your names. We met the Fraziers a few weeks ago." When he mentioned the name, Frazier, three or four of the men standing, turned and looked back at the Fraziers. After they identified themselves as loggers just passing through their town, the pastor greeted them, and asked them to be seated.

One man took out a pencil and a piece of paper from his pocket and wrote a few lines. A friend beside him, asked, "What are you writing?"

"A few notes that Houston gave me before we left."

"Let me see them."

"No, I have to see them first."

"You have them already. What else do you need to see?"

"Houston described his family, and I want to check this list to see if he was right. Let's be quiet."

The pastor began services with a hymn led by the deacons. After the morning services, the usher opened the door and assisted the members out of the church. The men wanted to find the Fraziers. Elena and her family left first, because they were seated on the back row near the door. Three of the men pushed their way through the door, but they didn't see the Fraziers.

"Where did they go?' one of the men man said.

"I don't know, but we have to find them. We don't have a lot of time, because we leave tonight."

"I see them over there in the road. They're walking home. Let's follow them and call them."

"We don't know their names. How are we going to call them?"

"Another man called to them Frazier? Frazier?

Elena looked back and all stopped and waited on the men, who were running toward them.

When the men finally reached them, their leader said. Good morning. I believe we have some good news for you this morning."

"I hope so," Elena said. We have had a feeling that something good was going to happen today. We didn't know what it was, but the feeling was good."

"We are loggers headed to the Oklahoma territory. We have a new member of this group name Houston Frazier."

Charlotte began to scream, "That's my boy. That's my boy. Where is he? What is he doing?"

"Hush, Charlotte." Elena said. Give them time to answer your first question."

"He's on his way here, and he should be here some time tomorrow. We left early. He will be here. He wanted us to find y'all and let you know he's alright and will see y'all soon."

"He has been gone for more than fifteen years. Can you tell us something about him.?"

"Ma'am, we certainly can."

"Can y'all go home with us? We have a big dinner ready for today's special feeling. I know y'all like pot roast and collard greens."

"Yes, ma'am we do, but we have promised to eat with another family today. I might can cancel and let the other two men go."

"Will you do that, please?"

The man, who seemed to be their leader, ran to the other two men, and talked to them. He ran back toward the Fraziers.

"I can go and stay for a little while."

We walked to church this morning. I hope you don't mind. We don't live too far from here." Elena said.

"I don't mind at all. We have been riding for days. Walking will do us some good. Houston will be on his way to see y'all in a little while."

As they came near their home, Elena said. "this is the home that the men of our church built for us. As you see, we help each other."

"They did a good job, ma'am."

Charlotte opened the door, and invited the man in. "We don't know your name, sir." She said.

"Just call me Henry. That's what everybody calls me. My name is Henry."

"Y'all wash up and get ready for dinner. I will wash up and put the food on the table." Elena said.

When she began to open the pots and pans on the stove, the aroma filled the kitchen. "Oh, I can hardly wait for these collard greens and roast."

"We also have candied yams and hot water corn bread. I'll make the hot water corn bread in a little while."

"Mrs. Elena, I can give y'all plenty information about Houston. He has done well considering the hard times he's had."

"Let's sit in the living room. When Mama gets the bread ready, she will call us." Charlotte said.

They all sat in the living room as directed. "How did you meet Houston?" Charlotte asked.

"I met him at the home of my best friends. Houston was widowed two times. Each wife had three daughters. He wasn't able to tend to three babies, so their grandparents took over. When I met Houston, he and three young daughters were living with our best friends, who happened to be his in-laws of his second wife.".

They liked him but felt that he needed to find work to help take care of his family. They asked if I could help Houston find work that he could do. I am a Mason and a lodger, so I discussed those things with Houston.

"What happened to the first three little girls?" Charlotte asked.

"Their grandparents took them and Houston in their home. Later, Houston left and left the girls with them. They're loving grandparents, too."

"That means that I have six granddaughters. I want to see them."

"Charlotte, let him finish telling us about Houston. Houston is the only one who can help us see his daughters."

"I know, Mama, but I can hardly wait."

"You can and you will wait, Charlotte."

"Yes ma'am."

"Y'all can come on in the kitchen, and sit at the table, while I put the food on the table." Elena said.

223

40

Henry was the first to sit down. "I can eat and talk, too, Miss Elena. Everything smells so good; I'm going enjoy this feast."

"Henry, you are welcome. Eat as much as you please."

"Miss Charlotte, you won't have to beg me. I'm ready." He sat down at the table and stretched his long legs under the table and began to eat. After Henry had eaten three pieces of hot water corn bread pones, He told Houston's entire story. "Houston and Ruth dated when they were in their early teens. He used to pull her hair in school. When they found out that she was going to have his baby, they didn't know what to do. They were afraid to tell their parents, so they ran away together."

Charlotte began to cry. They could have told us. We would have helped them. Where did they go?"

They went to Minden, Louisiana. There they met a widow named Mrs. Sadie Lewis. She was alone and lonesome, so she took them in as her own. "I'm not a mid-wife," She told them. "But I have a friend who is, and y'all will be in good hands."

"Thank you so much, Mrs. Lewis." He told her. "I can help with your chores around the house. I know how to repair things, and I see a few things here that need repair."

Houston said Mrs. Lewis laughed and showed them their room. Ruth was young, but she knew that she couldn't lift heavy things, so she said. "I'll do the dishes, and I can help with some of the cooking, too, Mrs. Lewis."

"Ruthie? Can I call you Ruthie?"

"Yes. ma'am. I like that."

"Then you will be Ruthie. Do you know when the baby is due?"

"No ma'am, I don't. But I believe it will be in four or five more months."

"You might be right, but I will call my friend over this evening, and she can tell."

"How can she tell?" Houston asked.

"She's a mid-wife, and she knows things like that."

"What is a mid-wife?" Ruthie asked.

"She can and will perhaps deliver your baby. She will also know when or about when it's done."

"I will work hard to find a job so we can pay her and help out here." Houston told Mrs. Lewis.

"Y'all raised Houston right. He's concerned about paying his way."

"We will help him, if we know where he is.' Charlotte said.

"If he needs your help, he will let you know. As I said before, Houston will probably be walking down that dusty road tomorrow. You will see him."

"How long will he be able to stay with us?" Charlotte asked

"Oh, just over night. He will be leaving early the next morning, and we will meet up together two or three days later in the Oklahoma territory. I have to leave now, so I can get a little rest before I we leave. I sure did enjoy dinner and especially that hot water corn bread. When y'all come to see Houston when we get back, please show my wife how to make hot water corn bread."

Henry, I'd be glad to do that." Elena said.

"Then, it's a deal." Henry said and he rushed out the door. "My child had some hard times in his life, and I couldn't help him." Charlotte cried.

"Houston is a grown man, Charlotte. You can't hold his hands anymore. Henry said that Houston was doing fine. He's going to have some hard times in life. We all do, but we survive."

"I just want to see my brother." Dorothy said.

"Me, too," Mary said.

225

"Tomorrow we'll get up early and look down that dust road to see if we can see a long, tall lanky man, named Houston. That is the way Henry described him. Also, Houston is good looking, too. That is the cause of so many marriages. He's attracted to the women."

"As he works with the men in the logger group, he will learn how to survive in the love department." Beulah said.

"How do they live and sleep on their journey to a logging location?" Elena asked.

"We asked Henry that same question. He said that they had enough cots for everyone. We camped in the largest camp and put our cots on the floor. We sleep until the next day. Then we roll them up for the next night. It works out just fine." Henry said.

"It's getting late. I have a kettle of water on the stove for the dishes. When we clean the kitchen, it'll be time for bed."

"I am ready for bed, Grandma." Mary said.

"I can't wait to see my six granddaughters," Charlotte said. "You have enough grands, here in Nachedochee. You will see those granddaughters soon enough. In the meantime, they're with their other grandmothers and doing fine. Let's take care of things here first. Houston might be doing fine considering how he was doing in the past, but he will still need our help. Don't go out looking for me problems, Charlotte."

"Mama, those are my granddaughters, and I want to see them."

"You will, Charlotte. Let's take care of matters here before we invite someone else into it. I want to see Houston and see if he's alright. I'll think about other problems later." Elena said.

Elena was satisfied that everything was clean and neat by eight o'clock. "Let's hit the sack, y'all."

"I'm ready," Dorothy said.

The night seemed long and quiet. Their dog, Spot, didn't seem to have a worry at all. He just slept through the night. Although he had been protected of the family at night, they were safe without his help, so he slept through the night and woke up only when it was time for his breakfast.

"I guess we were tired last night. No one woke up for anything. Spot was quiet all night." Mary said.

"Maybe he knows something that we don't know."

"Dogs can sense things sometimes. I hope he's right." Elena said.

"Henry said that we should look out the door toward that dusty road anytime doing the day. We will see Houston on his way."

"I have looked out several times already," Dorothy said.

"So have I." Mary said.

"I couldn't sleep just thinking about Houston, and what will we talk about when he gets here."

"Charlotte, there will be plenty to talk about when Houston gets here. He will let us know how and when we can see his six daughters. They're with their other grandparents, now, but maybe they can visit us sometimes."

"I hope so, Mama, but not all at the same time." Charlotte said.

They all laughed. "I don't think we have enough space for six more girls. How old are they, anyway?" Dorothy asked.

"According to Henry they're from three years old to thirteen. There won't be any lap babies." After giving a moment of thought, "Well, the three-year-old might have to be held at times, but she will probably be chasing after her older sisters." Elena said.

Charlotte went to the kitchen door and looked toward the dusty road. She did see a tall, lean, and lanky figure coming toward the house. "I think I see him," She shouted. "I see him, Mama."

Everyone ran to the door. "That's him", Elena said. "You're about to see the rest of the family, Beulah."

"I can hardly wait." Beulah said. She joined the others at the door and looked at this tall figure coming toward them. He didn't seem to be in a hurry. He knew his destination and he knew he'd get there soon enough.

Spot woke up barking. He knew his family was anxious about something. He ran from the back yard into the dust road toward the tall figure. Spot jumped into Houston's arms and they both fell to the ground. It's as if they already knew each other. When they got up, Houston patted Spot on his head, and hugged him for a few seconds.

"What is that in his hand?" Elena asked.

"It looks like a bag, Mama. I hope he can stay for just a little while," Charlotte said.

Mary and Dorothy had stood in the door long enough for Spot to complete his greetings. They both burst out of the door and ran toward Houston. When they reached him, they jumped in his arms, and began to cry. "We've missed you so much, Houston. Where have you been?" Dorothy cried. "Where have you been all this time?" She asked.

"I will tell y'all all about it before I leave."

"Where are you going and when?"

"I have a job working as a logger. We're headed to the Oklahoma territory, and that's where I'm going. Come on and let's go to the house. I want to see Grandma Elena and Mrs. Branch. I know they are wondering about me, too."

Spot had begun to feel rejected and jumped up on Houston, for his attention. Houston began to rub Spot heads and give him the attention that he wanted. "Let's go Spot. We don't have a lot of time left."

Before they reached the gate to their yard, Mary asked, "How long can you stay, Houston, before leaving again?"

"I'm leaving tomorrow morning at 8 o'clock. I hope John can take me to the train station."

"You don't have to worry about that. We have mules ready to go at any time and we all can steer the wagon." Dorothy said.

As they walked close to the door, Elena opened it. Houston ran to her and hugged her tightly. It seems as if he would never stop., "I'm here, too, Houston." Charlotte said and laughed.

"He released Elena from his embrace and held Charlotte. "I saved you for the last, Mama. I know you'll always be here." Houston reached down and hugged Beulah. "I'm glad to see you again, Mrs. Branch. How have you been?"

"Tolerably well. We're all doing great now, that you're here. I spent the night here last night, 'cause I wanted to see you again."

"Come on in and sit at the table. I know you're hungry. How long are you going to stay?" Charlotte asked.

"Over night. I will leave in the morning on the 8 o'clock train."

"Where to?" Beulah asked.

"Oklahoma territory."

"It seems like you met a good friend, when you met Henry. Who is he anyway?" Elena asked.

"He' the best friend of my late wife folks.

"I'll tell y'all all about it before I leave in the morning."

"What does he do?" Dorothy asked.

"He's a logger, Dorothy. He was probably logging before y'all were born. He's a real pro."

"Y'all sit down. I have the food on the table. We can eat and talk." Elena said.

"I'm ready for that, Grandma." Houston said.

After dinner was served and eaten, they gathered in the living room. "Do y'all know that the men who built these houses were loggers?"

"No, I didn't know that, Houston." Charlotte said.

"Trees have to be cut down and processed into lumber. Then, houses can be built. All of these houses you see in this area and about were once logs until loggers cut them down and processed them into lumber."

"How long are you going to be a logger?" Charlotte asked.

"Not long, Mama. I asked our manager if I could have a job there in the lumber yard, instead of traveling. I want to stay near my children."

"What did he say, when you asked him that?" Elena said.

"My wish was granted. This is a hard life. Many of the men and some of their family members died because of the cold winters. I don't like this life, but it's the best that I can do at this time. When I finish this run, I will be going back to Louisiana to stay."

"Will you let us know where you are when you leave here?" Charlotte asked.

"If it's possible, I can do that. We don't always have telegrams offices near, but I'll do what I can."

They talked into the late hours of the night. "I think I will turn in for the night, y'all. John, will you be here in the morning about seven o'clock? I have to take the train at eight."

"I can be here whenever you want me. I'd better get home and get a couple of hours of sleep, too."

"See y'all in the morning." John said as he left out the back door.

"let's get some sleep, too, so we can go to the train station with Houston in the morning." Charlotte said.

"I can do that." Mary said, and they all agreed.

41

"Rise and shine!" Elena called softly.

"Grandma, it's only five o'clock. Can't we get another hour of sleep?" Mary asked.

"If you're going to the train station with Houston in the morning, no, you can't get another hour of sleep. I have already started breakfast."

"Grandma, Houston can eat breakfast on the train when he gets there." Dorothy said.

"You don't know that, but if he eats here this morning, I'll know that he had breakfast. There is something about sitting down as a family and eating together. Y'all don't have to do the cooking, I'll do it all myself. Are we going to the train station with Houston?"

"Yes, Grandma." Dorothy said. "After I eat, I will be wide awake, and I don't mind traveling."

"Me, too.: Mary said.

"Houston is still asleep, Grandma."

"I'd better wake him. I know he's tired, but I don't want him to oversleep.:

"I'll wake him, Mama." Charlotte.

"I think I hear a wagon." Elena said.

Charlotte looked out toward the back yard. "That's John. He probably got up before we got up." Charlotte said.

"Well, he's just in time for breakfast. I suppose y'all have washed up and ready to eat."

"Yes 'mam, Grandma." Mary said.

"Well, take your seats at the table. Save the end for John, put his plate there, too." Elena said.

John got out of his wagon and secured the reins to a tree. He rushed in the back door. "Good morning, y'all. Are y'all eating before we leave?"

"Yes, we are John. Take that seat there at the end of the table. We have everything planned. After we eat, we will go to the train station with Houston. If you don't mind."

"I don't mind, Grandma. I have plenty of room in that wagon to take us all.

Houston jumped up from his seat and hugged John. John jumped back in surprise. "Is this Lil Brother?""

"Yes, this is Lil Brother." Houston said.

"You have grown a lot, Lil Brother. He hugged Houston again. Let's sit and eat. Our trip is short, but we want to be there on time."

Elena put the fried bacon, eggs and boiled rice on the table. "Now, y'all pass everything around, eat and talk later. I believe we need to leave here by seven o'clock. We can have a few minutes with Houston before he boards the train.

The platters of food were passed around to everyone, and they began to eat, and thanked Elena for the treat.

"Y'all are welcome. You know that."

"Houston, when will you have a steady place to stay? I hope it's soon, then we can all see each other often. Our family is small, and we need to get together often."

"We're not that small, I have six daughters." Houston said.

"You are kidding us, aren't you Houston?"

"No. I'm not. I have been married two times, and both wives died from the cold weather. I don't want to take a family on these harsh trips of logging again."

"I'm so sorry to hear of your loss, Houston." John said. "We will do whatever we can to help you and your daughters."

"Thanks, John. I know we're in good hands with my family."

Dorothy and Mary got up from the table and began to move left over food back to the stove. Elena got up and began to help. Let's hurry and get on our way."

"Are y'all going with me?" Houston asked.

"Yes," Dorothy said. "We're going to the train station to see you off."

Charlotte was ready and at the door. "Don't try to get rid of me so soon, Mama."

"It's close to seven o'clock, we don't know what the mules have in mind, so we'd better get on our way."

"You right, Charlotte." Elena said, "Everyone get out and go to the wagon. I will close the door."

They rushed to the wagon. Jim, who had been silent during their discussion, said, "I'll help y'all in the wagon, and then I will go back to the house and clean up. You don't have to take care of the door, I'll do it." He nodded to Elena.

"Thanks, Jim." She followed everyone to the wagon. Since Houston was their guest, He was invited in to sit in the front passenger's seat. The others followed as they Jim helped them in.

John yelled, "Hee Haw" to the mules, and they followed his orders. The train station was only a thirty-minute trip. When the red train station was in view, John pulled back on the reins for the mules to slow their journey.

"Why get slower, John?" Charlotte asked.

"I don't want to rush Lil Brother away so soon. He will have plenty of time to stay in the station before the train arrive."

"I don't want to miss the train. Your mules can't chase the train fast enough for me to get on, so let's get a move on, and wait on the train. I'd rather wait on the train, than have it to wait on me."

"I do, too, 'cause the train is not going to wait on anyone. It's got a schedule to keep." Elena said.

John yanked the reins, and the mules rushed toward the station.

John saw a huge oak tree only a few yards from the station. I'll go to that old tree over there and settled the mules." Houston said, and laughed.

"That old tree looks like it can handle your mules, John."

John was successful in settling the mules. "We can get out here and walk to the station."

"You're right, John. This is the right spot." Houston said, and he began to walk toward the train station.

When he was near the gate, He hugged and kissed everyone except John. We'll shake hands, John."

"I like that idea, Lil Brother."

When Houston looked back, he saw his family following him. "Where are y'all going?"

"We want to go to the gate with you and say goodbye," Elena said.

"No, Grandma." He bent down to her and held her by her shoulders. "It's not goodbye, Grandma. It's "Til we meet again." Remember, Grandma? It's 'til we meet again.".

They stood motionless while Houston ran to the station. When the train was loaded with passengers, it pulled out of the station to begin its journey. Houston was seated by a window, where he could look out and wave to his family, and he waved to them until he was out of sight.

Charlotte began to cry. "I don't know when we'll see him again."

"At least we know where he is. We don't have to worry about where he is." Elena said.

Dorothy and Mary cried out loudly. "When will we know where he is."

"Soon," John said. "We'll get back to the house and see what Jim is doing."

"I'm ready to get back." Charlotte said. "I don't know what we'll do, but we can find something."

Houston reached his destination at 1:00 AM. Unlike Charlotte, he was in an unknown place. He didn't know where to go for the night, so he sat on a bench by a door in the station. H decided to remain there for the rest of the night.

"Houston?"

He heard a familiar voice call his name. He looked back and saw Henry and another friend standing beside him. Tears of joy streamed from his face. He ran toward Henry. "I am so glad to see y'all."

234

"We're glad to see you, too, Houston. We've been here three times already. We knew that you had to be on this trip, because it's the last trip for two more days."

"I was so worried, Henry. I don't know anyone around here, and no one knows me."

"I didn't forget you, my friend. I found a wonderful place for you to room and board."

"Where?"

"Not far from here. There's a young lady named Ollie Jefferson. She has a two-year-old son, named Jonas. Mrs. Jefferson's husband was a logger, but he was killed when a falling log fell on him. He died suddenly, which was two months before his son was born. Mrs. Jefferson lives pretty well, but a little income once a month would help out. She can give you a room to sleep every night and three meals a day, but you have to wash your own clothes."

"I can do that." Houston said. "When do I get to see her?'

"We're on our way. She's not too far from here, so you know, we have to walk."

"I know how to do that, Henry." They all laughed. He looked at the other friend. "Doug, how have you been?"

"I'm doing just fine, Houston. We've been worrying about you. I hope you will like our group. You are new to the group, but I know they will like you, too."

After walking about ten minutes, they walked in a large yard, with a beautiful house."

"This is a beautiful house." Houston said. "Who built it?"

"Her husband. Remember, he was a logger, and had been one for a long time. He was a bit older that Mrs. Jefferson."

"I know we'll get along. I can help with a lot of repairs. Most homes need repairs at sometimes or another. I can do that."

"Y'all should be a good match." Doug said.

"I bet y'all will." Henry said. "Come on. I'll knock on the door. I bet she's been waiting on us."

"Do you know where she lives, Henry?"

"Yes. I saw her house as we passed by. She's not far from here. You'll see her soon." Henry said.

"Who stays with her?" Houston asked.

"She has a two-year-old son. No one else stays with her. Her mother, Mrs. Greggs stays down the road, and I see them, sometimes walking from house to house; especially on Sundays." Henry said.

"Why on Sunday?"

"They belong to the same church, and when church services are over, they have dinner for the family at one or the other's house. Mrs. Jefferson got two or three sisters and one brother, so that family is larger than small." They kept walking until they reached Ollie's house.

"Who's going to knock on the door?" Houston asked Henry.

"I will." He answered. Just as he raised his hand to rap on the door, Ollie opens the door.

"Howdy, she said. Y'all come in."

"Thank you. I have a boarder for you, Mrs. Jefferson. I think you will like him. This is Houston Frazier." He nodded toward Houston.

"Good morning, ma'am." Houston said with a nod.

"Why are we standing here at the door? Y'all come on in and take a seat."

They joined her in the living room. "I have an extra room, Mr. Frazier. You can see it, if you like. I also can prepare three meals seven days a week, but you have to do your own laundry."

They all laughed. "I can do that." Houston said.

"Let's go to your room." She beckoned. "Followed me, she led him to the back room with an outside door. He noticed that he could come and go without disturbing anyone. The bed was large enough for his tall body. He didn't see anything about the room that he didn't like. How much do you want for rent, Mrs. Jefferson?"

"II don't know. I have never rented a room before. Five dollars on your pay day will be fine."

"I can do better than that Mrs. Jefferson. I will go over some larger fingers that five dollars. Where is your little son?"

"He's with his Grandma today. He'll be home before bedtime."

"What is his name?" Houston asked.

"Jonas. That was his father's name, too."

Houston turned to Henry and said, "I want to thank you for finding this place here with Mrs. Jefferson and little Jonas. I know we're going to get along just fine."

"Houston, you are welcomed. You are worthy, too."

"Pardon my manners, Mrs. Jefferson. He turned to his friend. "This is my friend, Willis. He went to the train station with me to get Houston. I believe we can go and leave y'all to work out your business about the room. We will come by tomorrow morning at eight o'clock to take you to the job sight, Houston. Get plenty of rest, because tomorrow id going to be a hard day. This is new territory." He grabbed Houston's hand with both hands. "Take care."

"Thanks, Henry and thanks to you, too, Willis. I will be ready at eight o'clock."

"We can work everything out to our satisfaction, Houston. You can call me Ollie."

"Well, Ollie, I don't mind calling you Ollie.:

42

It only took three weeks for Houston and Ollie to know that they were meant for each other. Little Jonas had already accepted Houston, because he thought Houston had the best lap ever. He waited for bedtime, so Houston could rock him to sleep. Ollie had noticed Jonas's love for Houston, and Houston's love for him. Everything seemed to be going well in their household.

Before making breakfast for the morning, she looked out the kitchen door, and saw several men walking towards the grove of trees. "What time do you have to be on the job, Houston?"

Houston looked at the clock on the kitchen table. "It's seven o'clock now, and we begin working at eight. I can get there in ten minutes. We can't get our tools until the exact time, so getting there early won't help us to get started before time."

"You can sit down and eat now. I have your eggs and bacon ready. The coffee will be ready in a minute."

Houston saw a young man walking toward the door. "I wonder why is he coming here. He got up and met him at the door and was given a telegram.

"What is that?" Ollie asked.

"It looks like a telegram." He opened it. "It is a telegram from the home company. Remember I told you that I might be able to work at home in the home office."

"Yes, I do, but I didn't think it would be so soon."

"When I go, you and Jonas can come a few days later. It will only take a few days for me to get the house aired out and ready for guests." He laughed.

Houston read the telegram again. They want me there as soon as possible, but we need to take care of a few things here, first."

"What kind of business?" Ollie asked.

Houston knelt down on the floor. "Will you marry me?"

Ollie dropped down and hugged Houston. "Of course I'll marry you."

Houston stood and lifted Ollie up from the floor. "We need to take care of that right away. Let's make it as simple as possible, because we need to leave as soon as possible."

"Mama would want a big wedding, because I will be the first to have a big wedding. My first wedding was at home and simple."

"That makes sense. It will save our little money, and we'll still be married just as if we had a big wedding." Houston said. "How soon can you get ready?"

"I can pack some things for me and Jonas today. It won't take long. How soon can we leave for Minden?"

"Tomorrow." Houston said. "Who will take care of the house and things in it?"

"My sister, Ruby. "She can stay here and send things as we need them."

"I thought she stayed with your mama. How will your mama get along without Ruby? Can she live by herself?"

"She will get along just fine on her own. Ruth can still see after her during the day. They'll do just fine."

"Then, we'll leave tomorrow afternoon." Houston said.

Houston looked out the back door and saw Henry coming toward the house. "I wonder what he wants."

"Who?" Ollie asked.

"Henry. That's him coming toward the house. He must have some good or bad news to bring." Houston said.

"It could be good news." Ollie said.

"We'll soon know." He opened the door. "Come on in, Henry. What's the news?"

"It's good new, Houston."

Then, what is it?" Houston asked impatiently.

"I will be going home, too, to work in the plant there in Minden."

"Really?" Houston asked. "I am so glad. I won't be alone."

"We might be working on the same shift. I have done that work before, so I might be able to help you."

"Where is your friend? Is he going, too?"

"Yes, he will go and work with us. When are you leaving?"

"Tomorrow afternoon." Houston said. "Ollie and Jonas are going with me."

"She's going to have a great time there with my wife and folks."

"Thank you so much, Henry." Ollie said. "We just got through eating, and I'm putting food away. Would you like to eat something?"

"We just got through eating, too. I just came over to let y'all know that I'm leaving tomorrow, and I'm glad to know that we can go together. What about Jonas?

"Henry, he's going, too. We would never leave him." Houston said.

"Miss Ollie, you will have a lot of help with Jonas. We three men can help a lot. I guess I'd better get back and finish packing my bag and get some sleep."

"What time do you think we can meet at the depot tomorrow afternoon?" Henry asked.

"The train leaves for Minden at 1:30 PM. We can leave early enough to get there by 12:30. That will give us an hour to get our tickets and get our bags checked." Houston said.

"Why don't y'all go now and get the ticket? That will save some time tomorrow" Ollie said.

"I like that idea. Let's go, Houston."

"I'm ready to go Henry." Houston said.

"In the meantime, I will make arrangements with Ruby about taking care of things here." Ollie said.

"We'll be back soon." Houston called to her.

"I will probably be packed by the time y'all get back, but first, I need to talk to Ruby, before I make that decision." Ollie closed the door and went back to the bedroom to get Jonas. "Do you want to see Grandma and Aunt Ruby today?"

"Yeah." He said

"You don't sound like you want to see them, Jonas."

"I don't, Mama."

"We want them to take care of our house, while we go to Houston's house. They will take care of everything while we are away. Don't you like that?"

She picked him up and held him close to her.

"Okay, Mama. They can take care of everything."

"That's good, Jonas. You will have your birthday there soon. Do you know how old you will be?"

"I'm two."

"I know, but your next birthday, you will be three.'

'Can I go to school with the big kids, then?"

"No, not with the big kids, but they will have school for the little kids, and you can go with them."

Ollie picked Jonas up in her arms. "We're going to see Grandma and Auntie Ruby."

"Yeah, "Jonas cried. "Can we go now?"

"Yes, and we're on our way."

Ollie walked outside with Jonas in her arms. "I will carry you for a while and then you can walk. Is that okay?"

"I like to walk, Mama."

"It's not far, but your little legs will get tired before we get there. Let's get on our way."

Ollie followed her plans. She carried Jonas and then, he walked for a while. The distance was close for grown-ups, but quite a distance for little tots."

When Ollie and Jonas reached her mother's porch, Ruby met her at the door. "Y'all come in. What's the big rush?"

"We thought we'd take a little walk and talk to you about something."

"What is the talk about?" Her mother said as she came out of the kitchen.

"Houston and I are going to Minden for a little while, and we need someone to see after things while we're gone, I thought Ruby could do that. We also might need some things sent to us, and maybe Ruby could do that, too."

"Why would Ruby need to send things to y'all?"

Ruby looked at Ollie and smiled as if she knew what Ollie wanted. "I can take care of things for you, Sis. When are y'all leaving?"

"Tomorrow?"

"That's soon, but I can do it." Ruby knew that Ollie and Houston were going away to get married and stay in Minden.

Ollie reached inside her apron pocket and got a set of keys. "Here are the keys to our house. You can go to the house whenever you like. I don't know exactly what time we're leaving tomorrow, but it will be early."

"Don't worry. I will take care of things.

"Mama, I will let you know when we get there."

"How?"

"I will send a telegram and let y'all know that we're there and doing fine. Houston has a house there, and some of his kin folks live in Minden. I think we'll do just fine."

"You know if things don't go well with you and Jonas, you have a home here."

"I know that Mama. Thank you." Ollie took Jonas by the hand, and they left.

Houston was already home and packing his things. "How did you get home so soon? She asked Houston when she walked in.

"We didn't have to wait in line, so we bought the tickets and left. Did you talk to Ruby?'

"Yes, and I gave her a set of keys to our house, so she can come in when we leave. She will take care of things and send things to us as needed."

"I think everything is going to be alright. How did your mama take it?"

"I didn't tell her that we were going to stay. She might have an idea, but she didn't say anything. When we get there and settled in, I will let her know."

"She will also have a place to visit sometimes. I believe she likes to travel. Most Grandmas do. She will be so welcome."

"What kind of work will you be doing there?"

"I will work in the shipyard. When the logs are brought into us, we shave the barks off, smooth them and prepare them for building houses, furniture and office buildings. We can go too far without using lumber. We walk across the floor made of lumber, and our furniture is made of lumber, so I think I have a very important job."

Ollie hugged Houston. "I think you have an important job, too. I will be the best wife of a lumberman. Is your boss nice?"

"Yes, he is. He's a tall elderly man with white flowing hair. I don't think he was ever a slave holder. You will like him right away."

Houston walked to the back door. I just had a hunch that someone was coming."

"Who is it?" Ollie asked.

"It's your sister, Ruby."

Ollie rushed to the door to greet her. I hope she is still going to help us."

Ollie opened the door and held it open until Ruby for Ruby to enter. "Come on in. Is everything alright?"

"Yes, Ollie, I think so. But Mama knew something was up, so I had to tell her."

"Come on in and sit at the table. "What did she want to know?"

"Everything." Ruby sat down at the table.

"What did you tell her. I told her everything that you told me, but she wasn't satisfied. She thinks you're going away to stay. I had to tell her that you might stay."

"What did she say?" Houston asked.

"She said she had a feeling that you were up to something. It might be the right thing for her." She said.

Ollie jumped for joy. "I'm so glad she feels that way. I didn't want to slip away. Now, I will have to talk to her about our plans."

"We're leaving in the morning at eight o'clock, Hon. How and when can you talk to your Mama?"

"I'll work out something. Can you help me, Ruby?"

"Y'all just go on, and I will tell her everything. You will have time to make contact with her in a week or two when you reach your destination."

Ollie hugged Ruby, and then Houston took a turn and hugged Ruby, too. "We're so glad you're doing this for us, Ruby. When we get settled in our home, we want you and your Mama to come and visit as long as you want to. Minden is a friendly little town, and you will like the people."

"I know I will like Minden, but most of all, I don't have to live a lie with Mama. She will know the truth today. I love you Sis." Ollie and Ruby hugged each other again, and Ollie rushed out of the door.

Since Ollie and her family were well known in the community, she felt like it was her duty to go around the neighborhood, and say her good-by Jonas hugged everybody, too. Many of the arms had held him since he was a baby. "We're going to miss y'all. I don't want y'all to stay away 'till Jonas gets t be a grown man." One of their neighbors said.

"Y'all, we will be back often. Remember, my Mama and sister are still here, and I will be back as often as I can."

"I know, and I will like the house, and so will Jonas."

Houston adjusted Jonas in his arms and across his shoulders. Jonas continues sleeping while they boarded the train. They sat comfortably on the seats in a double row. There were just a few people traveling that time of evening, so they were comfortable.

The train had traveled many miles from the station when Jonas woke. "We're moving?" He said. "Are we moving, Mama?"

"Yes, Jonas. We are going to another town, and the train is taking us there. You can go back to sleep. When you are ready to wake for the day, you will be in a new place."

"Okay, mama."

"I miss my mama and sister already," Ollie said. "I can hardly wait for them to come to visit us."

"They're welcome." Houston said.

"I believe we'll get there before midnight," Houston said. "We can finish our night sleep and be ready for the next day. I'm anxious to get to the new job, so I can see what it's like. I know I'll like it. It's better than traveling with loggers to cut down trees. That's fine work, but it's really hard work."

"I bet you'll miss some of your old friends," Ollie said.

"I know, but I'll get used to it. I thought Henry was leaving today, too." Ollie said.

"He'll come on later. Perhaps they couldn't get on this scheduled."

"But there are only a few people riding this morning." Ollie said.

"That's true, but they have a lot of stops to make. By one o'clock, the train will probably be packed." Houston said.

"It probably will. Jonas is certainly getting his rest." Ollie said.

"Yes, he is." Houston adjusted Jonas on his lap.

"Houston, I believe you're right. I see the sign out the window that says, Minden, Louisiana. It isn't quite mid night." She noticed the clock inside the train by the door. It was eleven thirty.

"I have made this trip a few times in my life, so I have an idea about the time." Houston said. "I know you will like this little town."

"I can hardly wait to see our home. I'm going to dress it up and make it beautiful."

"We have some furniture in all rooms, but we don't have curtains for the windows." Houston said.

"I can and will take care of that. Don't worry. While you're at work, I will keep busy making things work at home. I like doing things for the home."

Houston hugged Ollie. "I know you're tired of riding." The train pulled into the station, and they got off. "I'll will get our bags and get a ride home. There is always somebody around the station trying to make money, so we won't have a problem getting home."

As soon Ollie, Houston and Jonas walked out the depot, a wagon was waiting for the next passengers. A tall, slim Indian man got out of the wagon. "Do y'all need a ride, Sir?

"Yes, we do, sir, and thank you/" Houston said.

"Y'all follow me." He led them to the rear of the train station. "This is my wagon." He pointed to a well-groomed wagon, pulled by two gray mules. "This is it. My mules are calm and won't hurt you, so take your time getting in."

"Thank you, Sir." Houston said. He helped Ollie inside the wagon and then lifted Jonas up to her and got in himself.'

"We're ready."

"The owner got in and pulled the mules away from the hitching post. "Which way are you going?"

"Straight ahead.' Houston said.

"Hee Haw," the driver yelled to the mules.

"You may pull to the right." Houston said.

"Hee." The driver yelled to his mules.

"See that big house on the corner?" Houston asked.

"Yes, I do. Is that your house?"

"Yes, sir. It is. You can let us out near the front porch."

"Yes, sir. You have a mighty fine house."

"Thank you." Houston responded, and he helped Ollie and Houston down from the wagon. Houston paid the fee, while Ollie and Jonas rushed to open the door. Houston joined them at the door and opened the door with a key hanging on a string. He watched the man steer his mules back to the depot.

Houston opened the door and Ollie rushed in with Jonas. "I could hardly wait to see your home. It's wonderful. When did you get all these things together."

"Most of them were here when I bought it. The owners were leaving town, and they couldn't take them, so I paid for the things they left behind. It was better than going out and buying more."

"You did a good job. I won't need Ruby to send much. Otherwise, we won't have a place to put anything else."

Jonas pulled his hand away from Ollie and ran to the back rooms. He ran into the room to the right and yelled and screamed happy yells and screams. Ollie went to him to see what he was yelling about. Things couldn't be any better than what she was seeing. She went into the room and saw a room loaded with toys. "Oh". She yelled.

"Houston, how did you do this?"

"I have the most wonderful neighbors in the world. I sent them some money and asked them to supply the room with toys for a two-year-old."

"They didn't miss a thing." Ollie said. "I would like to meet them and thank them."

"You will. They will go to the courthouse with us tomorrow to get our licenses. They have the transportation, remember?"

"We can marry in our new home. We won't have to pack and load thing to take away to another home. And our neighbors are next door, and that is convenient for them." Ollie said.

"Hon, I didn't tell you, but I think they want us to marry in their home. They will contact their pastor, Rev. Booker. He's known to keep ceremonies short." Houston said.

"Sounds like you've been working on this case. I will make some refreshments."

"No, Hon. That's taken care of, too."

Ollie stamped her feet. "Well, what do I do?"

"Nothing. Just stand by me and be pretty as ever."

"After the ceremony is over, everyone can come to our home for punch and cake. I will work on the refreshments today. I will do something.".

"I will sample them for you, Hon." Houston said and laughed. "I'm a good taster." "I know you are, and I will let you do the tasting. I will work on Jonas and let him know that you are going to be his dad. I will hold his hand during the ceremony. I will also talk to him about behaving. He has pretty good manners, though, but I want to remind him of them."

"Y'all come on in. The madam wants to meet y'all anyway before the wedding."

Just as he mentions his wife, she came from the kitchen to the living room to meet their new neighbors. She reached her hand out. "I'm Thelma, and I guess you have already met Zack."

"Ollie reached for her hand. "I'm glad to meet you, and y'all have already met Houston. This is Jonas." She patted him on the head.

247

Thelma reached down to Jonas and grabbed his hand. "I'm glad to meet you, Jonas. You can call me Aunt Thelma if you like."

"Thank you." Jonas said softly.

"Now that we're all acquainted, we'd better get back to our house, and see y'all on the 24th at 10:00 o'clock at your house."

"Houston, that will be fine." Zack said. "We're only next door."

Houston lifted Jonas up, and grasped Ollie by the hand, and they went out the door. "See y'all in the morning." Ollie called to them

43

On December 24, 1902, Ollie ease up from the bed. She didn't want to wake Houston. She planned to have breakfast ready by 7:30 for her and Houston. Jonas liked to eat, but he was never in a hurry to get up early in the morning to eat anything. Houston had put his clothes and Jonas's clothes on two chairs in a back room. He bathed Jonas before going to bed, so his job was going to be easy. Ollie pink dress and black knitted shawl was hanging in the bathroom on a nail. Ollie had perfectly planned routine for the morning. With a little cooperation from Houston and Jonas, everything will go as planned.

Ollie began waking Houston and Jonas at 7 o'clock. Jonas whimpered a little. "I don't want to get up now, Mommy."

"Don't you want to eat breakfast and go next door to the neighbors' house?"

"Naw, I don't, Mama."

"Mommy and Houston are getting married. Do you know what that means?"

"Naw. I want to go back to bed."

"You can go back to bed and sleep as long as you wish, when we come back from our neighbors' house. A preacher will be there, and he will marry us. I will be Houston's wife, and you will be his little son. You can come home and sleep as long as you want."

"Oh, alright. You promise?" He asked.

"I promise." She said. "We will leave after breakfast, and when we get there, you might meet some new people. The man is a preacher, and he will have us to stand while he begins to make me and Houston man and wife. You will stand beside me. I will hold your hand."

"Okay, Mama."

Ollie prepared breakfast and had it ready to serve by 8:30. "Y'all can come on in and sit down and eat breakfast. We might be a little early, but I would rather be early than late."

Handsome little Jonas is ready. Now, that he has eaten, I will wash him up again, put him on the potty to be y."safe, and then we will be ready."

"Sounds good to me. I'm just about ready. I have this long house coat over my dress. It won't take me long to tidy up again."

Houston washed Jonas's face again, parted his wavy hair to the side and brushed it. Jonas was almost fully dressed, but Houston had to put his blue jacket on him, get his jacket from a nail in the bathroom, and put it on. "No, Jonas, I believe we're ready for the wedding. Mommy and I are going to get married today. Let's go and see if she's read.

Jonas and Houston walked toward the kitchen. "Oh, my two good looking men. You both look great."

Jonas turned around and around so she could get a good look. "See, Mommy?"

"Yes, he sees, and so do I." He hugged her and had her to model for him.

Ollie wore a deep pink dress with a black knitted shawl around her shoulders. She turned around and around for Houston and Jonas to get a good look. "Let's go, now. I don't want to be late for my own wedding." She said.

They left about 9:35. 'It only takes a few minutes to get to Zack's and Thelma's house."

When they stepped on the porch, they were met at the door by Thelma and Zack. Thelma opened the screen door wider. "Y'all come on in.

"Thank you," Ollie said. "Is your pastor in yet?" Ollie asked.

"Not yet, but he and his wife are on the way. They're seldom late." Zack said.

Ollie walked over to a chair by the side window. "I believe I see them. She stood to get a good look. "They're blond. Do they know we're colored?"

"No, they don't." Zack said. "But they don't care, either."

When the pastor and his wife reached the front door, everyone stood as they entered the door. "Y'all come on in, Rev. Booker. Our couple lives next door, so they're a little early." Zach said.

Rev. Booker shook hands with Houston, Ollie and Jonas. He introduces his wife as just Mrs. Booker. She gave a friendly smile and shook their hands, too. "We're so glad y'all like our little community. We want y'all to come to church with Zack and Thelma. We will give y'all a good welcoming." Mrs. Booker said.

"Thank you, Mrs. Booker. We will do that."

"I think we'd better get them married first, so if you don't mind, we can do the ceremony here in the living room." Rev. Booker said. "Y'all can stand with your backs to the door and facing me. Zack, why don't you stand by Houston, and Thelma you can stand by the bride."

They took their place as designated, but Ollie grabbed Jonas's hand. Jonas stood between Ollie and Thelma. The only guest was Mr. Booker.

After a brief prayer, the ceremony began. After Houston and Ollie said "I do". They socialized for thirty or forty minutes, and the celebration was over, and they all went home. Ollie and Houston went home as Mr. and Mrs. Frazier.

"Hon," Houston said. "We will have to change Jonas's name, too. Right now, he is Jonas Jefferson, but we will need to go to the courthouse and change his name to Jonas Frazier."

"I agree. We can do that shortly after Christmas." Ollie said.

When they reached home and opened the door, Houston embraced Ollie warmly, "my wife, we're home."

"Yes Dear. We are. This is the best Christmas gift that one could have. I will get the message to Ruth and Mama soon."

"When we get dressed comfortably, we can go to the train station and wire the messages to your family. I bet they will be surprised."

"I believe they will be, too. If we, do it today, they will have a merry Christmas tomorrow. I know my mama. She will shout all over the church during Christmas services."

"I hate to ask Zack to take us to the courthouse in his wagon, but Hon, that's the only way we're going to get there. I'll rush over there and see." When Houston reached the neighbors, their pastor and his wife were still there.

"That was a quick trip home, Houston." Zack said.

"We want to change Jonas's last name to mine, but we need a way to get to the courthouse. I hate to ask you for another favor, but we don't have a way to get there."

"Brother Houston, my wife and I can take y'all. If you wait here for a few minutes while I get our wagon, we'll get you there in no time."

"Should I go home and get my wife and son and bring them over here?"

"No, we'll stop by and get them. It will be my pleasure."

"Rev. Booker, I sure appreciate this."

Rev. Booker and Houston walked to the corner of the block to get his wagon. Houston got in and sat on the back row.

"Are you comfortable back there, Houston?"

"Yes, sir. I see my wife and son standing near our house, waiting on us."

"I'll stop and let them in, and then we're on our way."

"Thank you so much, Rev. Booker. When Ollie sees us, she will bring Jonas out and get in, too."

"I see them standing by the side of the road." Mrs. Booker said.

"You're right, Mrs. Booker. that's my wife and son. "Houston said proudly. They're ready."

Rev. Booker steered the wagon to Ollie and Jonas. Houston got out and helped them into the car.'

'Is this everybody?" Rev. Booker asked teasing them.

"Yes, Sir. We're ready.

"Now, we're on our way to the courthouse."

"How long do you think it will be, Rev. Booker?" Ollie asked.

252

"Not long as you're wedding. Y'all will have to signs some papers to change the name. If no one object to the change, it will take only a few minutes."

"I don't have to worry about anyone objecting." Ollie said.

"We're here. Let's get it done." Mrs. Booker said.

"I can sign a few more papers." Ollie said. "I wonder if we can send a telegram to Mama and Ruth, and tell them the good news? I believe the train depot is near."

"Y'all take care of everything you need while we're out."

"Thank you so much, Rev. Booker.

"I hope y'all get some good rest tonight and come to our Christmas service and program tomorrow morning." Mrs. Booker said.

"We have that as number one on our plans for tomorrow." Houston said. "Why don't you go and send the wire to your folks, while we're Hon?"

"That's a good idea, and they will pass the word on to your folks, too." She rushed to the clerk to send the wire.

"Rev. Booker, I am buying a wagon and two mules. They should be ready to pick up in a matter of days. I have already paid for them. Our barn is well equipped and ready for them, too."

"Houston, you're doing a good job as a family man, and y'all are some good neighbors, too. Here comes your wife. That was a quick message."

"I made sent the wire." Ollie said. I know that will have a happy Christmas at the Christmas services."

Houston took Jonas by the hand. I think we'd better get to the wagon, and not hold up Rev. and Mrs. Booker any longer. I promised them that we'd attend Christmas program in the morning, so we can get on our way, and not hold them up any longer."

"Rev. Booker, we certainly appreciate everything that y'all have done for us. We will certainly attend Christmas services in the morning, and we appreciate the invitation." Ollie said.

"Y'all are welcome. I'll have y'all home in a few minutes."

When they reached their home, Rev. Booker got out and offered assistant to Houston, but he declined. "I can do this, Rev. Booker. Y'all have done enough." He helped Ollie and Jonas down from the wagon. "We'll see y'all in the morning, Rev. Booker."

"We will be looking for y'all. If y'all need any help, let us know."

"Yes, Sir."

"Hon, I forgot to tell you, but we're getting a wagon."

"What?" She yelled.

"Shh. Don't be so loud. Do you remember that covered wagon you saw near the train station?"

"Yes, I do, but we can't afford something like that."

"I wanted to surprise you. I have already paid for it. I'm having a few touch ups on the wagon. The mules are well trained. They won't run away with us." He laughed.

When they reached home, Houston opened with his key. "We're back." He said.

"I hope you know what you're doing. We don't have that kind of money." Ollie said as she entered the door.

"I saved up some money for our needs. I will go back to work after New Year and begin to save and put the money back in our savings. This is the last vacation I'll have for a long time. We can't depend on neighbor and friends to take me to work every morning or take us to church every Sunday."

"How will you get to work after New Year, if some work is being done on the wagon?"

"I will go in our wagon. It will be ready by that time. We will go to church in the morning with Zack and his wife. He promised that he would pick us up at 10:15. Instead of two wagons leaving for the same job every morning, we will take turns. I will drive Zack one week, and he will drive me in his wagon another week. That will help us both."

"Seems like y'all got everything worked out. What time is the program tomorrow morning?" Ollie asked.

"Eleven o'clock." Houston said. He released Jonas's hand. "Jonas, Can you say Dada"

"Yeah. Da Da."

367

STATE OF LOUISIANA—PARISH OF WEBSTER.

CLERK'S OFFICE—DISTRICT COURT.

TO *Rev David Brooks* _____ OR ANY MINISTER OF THE GOSPEL, JUDGE, OR JUSTICE OF THE PEACE, AUTHORIZED BY LAW TO CELEBRATE MARRIAGE—GREETING:

In the name of the State of Louisiana, and by authority of the same, you are hereby authorized and empowered to celebrate marriage between Mr. *Houston Frazier* .

and M *Ollie Jefferson* _____ and to join them together in Holy Wedlock, and return this license in thirty days, as the law directs.

Given under my hand and seal of office, at Minden, La., on this *24* day

of *Dec* _____ A. D. 1*901*

J A Colbert

Dy _____ Clerk District Court.

STATE OF LOUISIANA—PARISH OF WEBSTER.

BE IT REMEMBERED, That by virtue of the above marriage license I have celebrated marriage between Mr. *Houston Frazier* and *Ollie Jefferson*

according to law, and have caused them to sign this certificate in token of their consent, in presence of the subscribing witnesses, on this *24* day of *Dec* _____ A. D. 18*00*

WITNESSES:

Pedro Leopold

Lynch Brantly

Percy Harden

Officiating Officer: *J D Booker*

PARTIES:

Houston X Frazier
    his mark

Ollie Jefferson
    her mark

A true record of the original, made on this *26* day of *Dch* _____ A. D. 18*901*

J A Colbert

Dy _____ Clerk District Court.

255

44

At seven o'clock on Christmas morning, Ollie was up and, in the kitchen, and had put breakfast on the table. Houston and Jonas were still asleep.

"Christmas programs are always crowdy, because Grandmas, grandpas, and other kin folks are visiting, and want to hear their grandchildren say their speeches," Ollie remembered Thelma telling her. She peeped in on Houston and Jonas again.

"Houston?" She called.

Houston didn't answer. She called again, and then he mumbled, "Okay."

It's time to get up. I know we have three hours to get to the program, but we want to be ready when Zack and Thelma get here."

Houston turned over and yawned. "And what time is that?"

"They will be here at 10:30. The program starts at 11:00 o'clock, Thelma said that the program was always crowdy, so we don't want to be late."

"It only takes about ten minutes to get to the church."

"True, but I told her we won't make them late, and I want to keep my word."

"Hon, you don't have to worry. I will see that you keep your word, but we'll have plenty of time."

"That's true, Houston. But they will have to find a place for the mules and wagon. There will be plenty of those out there, trying to find a place to leave their wagon. I also need you to get Jonas ready. After we eat, we'll dress and by that time, Zack and Thelma will be on their way."

Houston went to Jonas's bedroom and called him. Jonas didn't want to be bothered, so he turned over, pulled the cover up around his neck, and closed his eyes again.

"Jonas, it's time to get up, eat and dress so we can go to see a Christmas program. We the program is over, and we come home, you will have more Christmas gifts to open, so let's get up and, eat and get ready."

"Okay.' Jonas said softly.

The morning went at Ollie had planned. At exactly 10:30, Zack and Thelma pulled their wagon to the back of Houston's and Ollie's house.

"Hon, they're on time>"

"And so are we."

Houston picked up Jonas and followed Ollie out the front door.

"Good morning," Houston said.

"Good morning, and it is a good morning," Mrs. Booker said. "We look forward to this event every year. The little children practice their speeches for months, now, the next program for them is Easter. They will probably get their speeches in February. This is special for them, because they will have on their Easter dresses for the girls and suits for the little boys."

"I can hardly wait for Jonas to reach the age when he can say speeches. He will be three in two more months." Ollie said.

"Some of the children that you will hear today are five and six. You won't have to wait too long."

Rev. Booker saw a comfortable place to hitch his wagon. "We can get out here and walk around to the front door. I see people are here already."

Houston got out and helped Ollie and Jonas out, too. "This is comfortable. You were fortunate to get this place, Rev. Booker." Houston said.

"If I had waited a little longer, this place would be almost full." He waved his arms around. "See those wagons coming down that road?

Pretty soon both roads will be packed with wagons, and it will be the same on Easter morning. You see. We support our children."

"I agree." Ollie said. "I want to take part in these celebrations."

"All you need to do, Mrs. Frazier, is join our church, and the women will get you acquainted with our programs."

"I can do that, Mrs. Booker."

Rev. Booker led them around to the front door. The usher met them at the door and took the needed information for introduction. After everyone was seated, Rev. Booker stood silently, and looked over the audience. The regular attendance is usually sixty-five, but with a few guests, the pews were almost filled with seventy-five worshipers. HE smiled pleasantly. He looked back at the choir stand and saw a dozen or more little boys and girls, dressed in black bottoms, such as pants and skirts and white shirts and blouses. He nodded toward the deacons to begin service with a hymn. Everyone stood and sang SILENT NIGHT.

After the pastor's preliminaries, such as prayer service and introductions. The program began. Proud parents and grandparents beamed as Rev. Booker looked at the children. There were thirteen little boys and girl around the ages from five to thirteen. Every child had a speech to deliver. The younger children only had five- or six-line speeches and the older children had longer lines. There was a Christmas Carol after every five or six speeches.

The program ended with everyone singing Joy to the World.

Rev. Booker complimented the children for doing a great job. When all of the service, Rev. Booker stood at the front door and gave out a bag of hard candy to everyone. "Merry Christmas and a Happy New Year" he said to everyone.

Houston picked Jonas up and said, "One day you will be up there saying a speech. Would you like that?"

"I like that," Jonas said.

They gathered at the wagon behind the church. "Where is Zack?" Houston asked.

"Zack knows everybody," Thelma said. "And he is speaking to everybody. We can get inside the wagon and wait on him. It won't be long."

We're in no hurry." Ollie said.

Thelma saw Zack coming toward the wagon. "Here he comes." Thelma said. "Did y'all enjoy the program?'

"Yes, Thelma. We did. I can hardly wait for Jonas to get old enough to say speeches."

Zack got out of the wagon to assist others in. "Did you hear that, Zack?"

"Hear what, Thelma?"

"It sounds like Ollie and Houston are going to join our church."

"They're welcome. We can use their gifts and talents. Someday, Jonas will be able to be in the children's choir and sing for Christmas and Easter. Sometimes, we have Children's Day, and the children perform during our services with their music."

When Jack's passengers were loaded, we steered the mules toward home. "What are y'all 's plans for the day?" Thelma asked.

"We will have a house load by 1 o'clock. All of our folks and children will be over." Thelma said. "What about y'all?"

"We will call our folks after supper this evening and see how they're doing. After that, we'll help Jonas's play with his toys."

Hee Haw, Jack yelled to the mules. We have to hurry, 'cause we don't want Jonas to miss that occasion." The mules turned the wagon around and proceeded toward their homes.

When they reached home, Thelma got out and helped Ollie down from the wagon. "This wagon was built for tall people, Ollie. You're a little short." They all laughed, because Ollie was barely five feet and two inches tall.

"I can make it, Thelma, but thanks anyway."

They parted by saying, "Merry Christmas and a Happy New Year."

"This is not a Merry Christmas for me," Ollie said.

"Why, Hon? You sound sad."

"I miss my family. I know by now, they're gathered at mama's house with pots and pots of food, laughing and joking around. I miss that."

"Do you want to go to be with them?"

"No. I'll get used to it."

"Next year, they might want to come to see us. We know how things are there, but they don't know about things here in Minden."

"We will open our gifts when we get home. Jonas has a few more. You will like your gifts, Hon."

"You will like yours, too." Ollie said.

Olllie and Houston enjoyed many years of happiness. Jonas grew up and became a member of the children's church choir. He looked forward to singing for Christmas and Easter. Ollie and Houston found church groups to join. It didn't take long for Jonas to find boys his age at church, where he could join in their activities for the church. Things were going well for the Frazier family.

On July 24, 1906, Ollie and Houston had their first child, a daughter. They named her Clemmie. On October 10, 1910, they had another girl, and she was named, Quincy. Jonas loved his little sisters, and they loved him. When they began to walk, they followed Jonas wherever they could.

One day in June in 1914, Jonas walked away. After looking for him for hours, Houston promised Ollie that Jonas would be home for supper. Houston didn't come home, and no one saw him leave their little community. Ollie cried daily. "I don't know why he left."

"Jonas knows where we are. We don't know where he is. When he gets ready to come home, he will. We will continue to look for him. Somebody had to see him leave." Houston said. "He is fifteen years old, and he thinks he's a man. No one knows where he is. If they do, they won't say. Why would he want to leave anyway? What happened to make him want to leave his family?" Ollie cried.

"He didn't have to have a reason, Hon. He just wants to get out on his own. He knows how to get back, and he will when he is ready."

"He seemed to have been happy here with his family; especially with his little sisters." Ollie said.

His little sisters grew up and left home, too, but they never cease looking for Jonas. After so many years, they soon decided that he might have died, and the family wasn't notified.

Ollie died in August of 1920 at age 43.

One day in June of 1988, I received a call from my mother, Clemmie. I could hear from her voice that she had been crying. "Mama, what's wrong?"

"We found him. We found him." She cried.

"We found who?" I asked.

"We found Jonas."

"How did we find Jonas?"

Quincy and I received letters today. Each letter had a one-hundred-dollar bill in it. He's in Redding, California. He must have been there a long time, because his house is on Frazier Road."

"He's not too far from me, Mama. Give me his address, and I will write him. We can have a reunion here at my home this month."

"He has a wife. Her name is Minnie, and she's blind."

"We can take care of her; I want to see the uncle that I've heard about so long but haven't seen."

"He sent us his telephone number, too. Here it is." Lillian.

"Wait," I said. I need to get a pencil and some paper. After missing for seventy-three years from his family, I wonder what he's going to say? I haven't missed him at all, and I was tired of hearing about him, but I will be polite."

"You shouldn't feel like that. He's your uncle."

"He knew he had a family, too." I said.

"I hope you will be nice to him."

"I will. I have a pencil and paper, Let me have the number so I can call him. I'll call you right back, and let you know when we can have the reunion. I hope it can be this June."

I made the call to Jonas. He answered with a deep baritone voice. "This is AJ Frazier speaking."

I was startled because I thought I was calling Jonas. "Pardon me," I said. I thought I was calling my uncle, named Jonas Frazier."

"You re, and who are you?" He asked sternly.

I thought to myself, I'm not going to like this. "I am your niece, Lillian. I' am Clemmie's daughter. She and her sister, Quincy have been looking for you for years. I live in Portland, Oregon, which is near

261

Redding, California. We would like to have a reunion at my hoe this summer. Do you think that will be a good idea?"

"Of course. I have a wife, too. Her name is Minnie, and she's blind. She has sickle cell Anemia, and it caused her to be blind."

"Bring her, too. We can take care of her."

"Give me your number, and I can get back to you about possible dates and times that might be suitable for all of us.'"

I assumed he had pencil and paper handy, so I gave him my telephone number. "I will call Mama and let her know that we have met and are making plans. I hope it can be this month."

"This is the first week in June. We can get ready by the third week. It only takes a little while to pack a few things for two or three days. I will call Quincy and let you know about dates and time. We will arrange any time that will suit Jonas and his wife."

"Let me know for sure. My family and I can prepare for everyone."

"i will call Jonas and see if this date fits him and his wife. I'll get back to you."

45

I went to the bus station at 3:00 o'clock to get Jonas and his wife, Minnie, who were arriving at 3:33 PM. I didn't have to wait too long, before a tall dark tan gentleman stepped on the bus, holding his hand out for his wife to hold onto, while she descended the bus. Minnie was an attractive woman. She didn't give the impression that she was blind and needed help. "Don't you think you need to help her down the steps from the bus?" I asked.

"She'd rather do it herself." He said in a deep baritone voice." Jonas shook her hand and lead Minnie to do the same.

"Everyone is here at my house waiting on you and Minnie. I know this is going to be a great reunion. Follow me to my car. I'm parked across the street over there." I pointed to the car. They followed me to the car and Minnie sat in front with me and Jonas sat in the back. "They haven't stopped talking about the old days when y'all were little and the followed you around."

"I had two little sisters, and I was so proud of them. My friends didn't have little sisters. Some didn't have sisters at all." He said as I drove towards home. When I drove in front of the house, I said, "this is it. We can go to the front door or to the back."

"The front is closer, and I can hear them already. I believe they can see me and Minnie."

"The door is open. Let's go in." I lead Jonas and Minnie in through the front door. Clemmie and Quincy screamed and hollered. That's our brother." They screamed again and hugged him.

He returned their hugs and turned to Minnie. "This is Minnie, my wife."

"They hugged her and she responded in kind.

"Y'all come on in and make yourselves at home. We have food and cold water on the table."

"I can take both." Jonas said.

The entire day was spent on talking about the past. Your mother and our mother, Ollie, died 1920.

We didn't know how to find you to let you know." Quincy said to Jonas.

"I heard about it, Quincy." He said.

"Papa died in 1928, so this is most of your family from the past."

"I missed everyone a lot." Jonas said. "What happened to The Kid, Bossy and Charlie?"

"Bossy and The Kid were loved by all of the farmers, and the pets picked their own owners by staying with them. Charlie was an invited guest, because he could never get the farmer up on time. He would go Mitch's house and stand on the corner near the front door and crow at five o'clock every morning. The farmers would hit the floor every morning at 5 o'clock, before they found out that Charlie got his time off and they were getting up an hour earlier ever since." Quincy said.

"I bet they didn't like that." Minnie said and laughed.

They all joined Minnie and laughed. "No, they didn't like that at all." Quincy said.

There were two more days of fun and laughter, when Jonas reminds everyone that it was time to begin packing to leave for the next reunion.

"Where will the reunion be next year?" Clemmie asked.

"Minnie and I can take it next year. Is that alright with you, Minnie?'

"I will be glad to have y'all next year." She said. "We'll find a date in 1989 that will suit everyone." Clemmie and Quincy went back to their homes in Lawton, Oklahoma so thrilled that they would meet with

Jonas and Minnie again. I drove Minnie and Uncle Jonas to the bus station, and remained with them until they left for Redding, California.

I realized that I saw an uncle that I had heard about all of my life. I will make it my duty to see him often, since he is so close to Oregon.

One day in June 1989, Clemmie received a letter from Minnie about the reunion. Everyone was invited to come to Redding, California to another type of reunion. It would be Jonas's funeral. He died on the eighteen of June. The 1989 happy occasion wasn't happy as the 1988. "Well, at least, we got to see Jonas again. It was our last time seeing him. Instead of attending a second reunion, it was Jonas's funeral. He was eight-nine.

No one never asked Jonas why did he walked away from Minden in 1915, and he never did tell.

My mama, Clemmie died five months after taping the Forward in February 1996. Quincy lived until 2008. She died here in Portland, Oregon at age 98. Her pet calf, Bossy and Dee's pet goat were welcomed to graze with another farmer. Quincy's pet Rooster, Charlie made a home with one farmer. His favorite place was the corner of Mitch's house. He would crow every morning at 5 o'clock, and the farmers would "hit the floor" without thinking about the time.

After several months crowing from the corner of Mitch's house, Charlie decided to go to the corn field, where he could nibble on the tender corn.

One morning the farmers "**Hit the floor**". Then, they remember that they didn't hear from Charlie, but it was five o'clock. Why didn't Charlie crow? Mitch put on his robe and house slippers and went outside. He looked toward the corner of his house, once a favorite place for Charlie, but Charlie wasn't there. He ran across the road to the corn fields looked down several rows of corn, before he saw a reddish bundle on the ground. He rushed to the bundle and bent down and picked it up. "Oh, Charlie." He cried. He cradled Charlie to his chest and walked slowly toward home. Three farmers walked toward Mitch's home, too. One farmer had a rake. When he got to the corner of Mitch's house, he began digging a hole. Mitch took his time getting to the hole. He wanted to hold Charlie a little longer. Finally, he placed Charlie in the deep hole, folded his wings over his chest tenderly and walked away. The farmer with the rake covered the hole and patted it down as smoothly as he could. Each farmer went out into the field, and each picked up a rock by the size of their fist. They came back to the small mound where Charlie was buried and placed the rocks on his grave.

After a few moments of silence, they walked away. The farmers continued to **"hit the floor at five o'clock."**

John became famous with his pottery. His shop, John Milligan Frazier Pottery produced beautiful pottery, and he became famous for his bowls, jars and other objects. Most of all, he continued to take care of Grandma Elena.

Elena and the family decided to give the church offering to Anna and Mac for the baby and assisting them on their journey to freedom.

Benjamin and his family remained in Anna's and Mac's home with his mother, Beulah Branch, children, and Uncle Jim.

Ollie died 1920 AT THE AGE OF 43.

Houston died February 20, 1928, at age 54.